The Metaverse

The Metaverse: Hype or Hoax? offers a rigorous, balanced, and evidence-based examination of one of the most contested technology narratives of the twenty-first century. Set against the backdrop of accelerated digital transformation, this book situates the metaverse within the longer history of technological disruption, platform evolution, and socio-economic change. Rather than accepting optimistic forecasts or dismissing the metaverse as speculative hype, this book critically evaluates its foundations, ambitions, and constraints.

Drawing on industry research, academic literature, and real-world case analysis, this book explores how immersive technologies, cloud platforms, artificial intelligence, blockchain, and spatial computing converge to shape emerging virtual ecosystems. It examines where genuine transformation is taking place; where value remains unproven; and how organisations, regulators, and societies can navigate this uncertain terrain with strategic clarity.

Key features include:

- A clear conceptual framework distinguishing metaverse reality from hype cycles
- A layered architectural view of metaverse ecosystems and enabling technologies
- A critical assessment of business, economic, social, and governance implications
- Practical guidance for enterprises, policymakers, and technologists

Written for technology leaders, policymakers, researchers, and postgraduate students, this book provides a grounded reference for understanding whether immersive digital worlds represent a substantive evolution of the internet or a rebranding of existing technologies amplified by market enthusiasm.

The Metaverse
Hype or Hoax?

Kapil Sharma

CRC Press is an imprint of the
Taylor & Francis Group, an **informa** business

Designed cover image: Shutterstock ID: 2123964845

First edition published 2027
by CRC Press
2385 NW Executive Center Drive, Suite 320, Boca Raton FL 33431

and by CRC Press
4 Park Square, Milton Park, Abingdon, Oxon, OX14 4RN

CRC Press is an imprint of Taylor & Francis Group, LLC

ISBN: 978-1-032-52182-4 (hbk)
ISBN: 978-1-032-52183-1 (pbk)
ISBN: 978-1-003-40556-6 (ebk)

DOI: 10.1201/9781003405566

Typeset in Sabon
by Apex CoVantage, LLC

Contents

Preface

The reason for writing this book came from a growing gap between how the metaverse is described and how technology actually develops and succeeds in practice. Over recent years, the metaverse has been promoted as the next version of the internet, a new economic system, and a major social shift. These claims are often presented with certainty and urgency. Yet when examined closely, real-world adoption has been limited, fragmented, and, in many cases, difficult to justify.

After more than two decades working on large technology transformation programmes, particularly in regulated and risk-sensitive environments, I have seen this pattern many times. Technologies rarely fail because they are imaginary or dishonest. They fail because expectations move faster than capability, governance is weak or missing, and systems are deployed before the basics are properly in place. For this reason, asking whether the metaverse is a hype or a hoax often misses the real issue.

This book does not argue that the metaverse is either inevitable or meaningless. Instead, it looks at the conditions under which immersive technologies can deliver value, and why so many initiatives have struggled to do so. The focus is practical and structural. Rather than starting with visions of the future, the chapters examine infrastructure, platforms, data, identity, interoperability, security, governance, and operational resilience. These are the factors that ultimately determine whether any complex digital system can work at scale.

Throughout this book, the metaverse is treated not as a single destination or platform but as a collection of technologies and design choices, each with different levels of maturity and risk. Where relevant, failed initiatives and limitations are discussed alongside more focused and realistic use cases. The aim is not to discourage innovation but to encourage better judgement and more disciplined decision-making.

This book is written for technology leaders, architects, policymakers, and practitioners who are required to make decisions under uncertainty. It is intended for those who must assess emerging technologies based on feasibility, control, and long-term sustainability, rather than promise alone. If the metaverse does become a lasting part of the digital landscape, it will be because these fundamentals are addressed with care and realism. This book examines whether that is happening today.

Acknowledgements

This book was written alongside professional responsibilities and would not have been possible without the support of my family. I am grateful to my wife, Usha Sharma, for her patience and encouragement throughout the writing process and to my children, Dhruv Sharma and Karina Sharma, whose curiosity and perspective continue to remind me that technology should serve people, not abstract ideas.

I would also like to thank my close friends and colleagues for their support, discussions, and honest challenges. Those conversations helped refine the thinking in this book and reinforced the importance of questioning narratives rather than accepting them without scrutiny.

I thank my late father, Girdhari Lal Sharma, whose memory continues to inspire me. I also dedicate this book to my mother, Bimla Devi Sharma, with love, gratitude, and respect.

About the Author

Kapil Sharma is a technology strategist, author, and consultant with over two decades of experience across digital transformation, cloud computing, cybersecurity, data platforms, and emerging technologies. He has led and advised large-scale transformation programmes for global financial institutions, public-sector organisations, and multinational enterprises operating in highly regulated environments.

Kapil is the founder of a UK-based consulting and education firm specialising in cybersecurity, blockchain, artificial intelligence, and digital transformation. He is an established technical author, having authored a number of books and professional publications on enterprise technology, operating systems, and distributed platforms. His work is recognised for combining deep technical understanding with strategic and regulatory insight.

Based in London, Kapil focuses on helping organisations navigate technological disruption without succumbing to hype-driven decision-making. His research interests include immersive technologies, platform economics, operational resilience, and the governance of complex digital ecosystems.

Chapter 1

Introduction to the Metaverse

1.1 TECHNOLOGY DISRUPTION AND THE POST-PANDEMIC DIGITAL SHIFT

Over the course of the last decade, technology has undergone repeated waves of disruption that have fundamentally reshaped how organisations operate, compete, and create value. What was once regarded primarily as an operational support function has progressively evolved into a central driver of strategy, innovation, and long-term resilience. Technology is no longer confined to improving efficiency or reducing costs; instead, it increasingly defines business models, market positioning, and competitive advantage. Figure 1.1 illustrates the broader pattern of technology disruption and the post-pandemic digital shift that frames the current metaverse discussion.

Historically, organisations adopted technology in relatively discrete phases. Early enterprise systems focused on automation and record-keeping, followed by the rise of personal computing, networked systems, and the commercialisation of the internet. Each wave not only introduced new efficiencies but also demanded organisational change. The emergence of mobile computing, cloud platforms, and data-driven decision-making further accelerated this transformation, enabling businesses to scale rapidly, reach global markets, and operate with unprecedented agility.

In recent years, digital transformation has moved beyond incremental improvement towards structural reinvention. Cloud-native architectures, platform-based business models, artificial intelligence, and advanced analytics have enabled organisations to rethink how products are designed, services are delivered, and customers are engaged. Digital capability has become inseparable from organisational performance, influencing everything from supply chain resilience to customer experience and workforce productivity.

The global business environment continues to reflect the long-term effects of the COVID-19 pandemic. The pandemic represented an unprecedented disruption, forcing governments, businesses, and institutions to rethink long-established assumptions about physical presence, work, education, and social interaction. Lockdowns and travel restrictions rapidly dismantled traditional operating models, accelerating the adoption of digital alternatives.

DOI: 10.1201/9781003405566-1

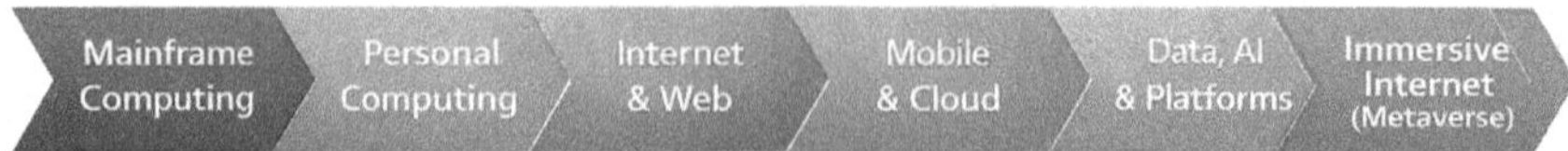

Figure 1.1 Technology disruption and the post-pandemic digital shift.

Remote working, which had previously been adopted selectively, became the default mode of operation for large segments of the global workforce. Educational institutions transitioned to online delivery at scale, often with limited preparation. Retailers and service providers accelerated their shift towards e-commerce and digital engagement. In many cases, these changes were implemented out of necessity rather than strategy, exposing both the strengths and weaknesses of existing digital infrastructures.

The pandemic highlighted a stark contrast between organisations with mature digital capabilities and those reliant on legacy systems and physical processes. Businesses that had already invested in cloud platforms, digital collaboration tools, automation, and online channels were better positioned to adapt. Many were able to maintain continuity, protect revenue streams, and even expand their market presence during periods of disruption. Conversely, organisations with limited digital readiness faced operational paralysis, supply chain breakdowns, and an inability to respond effectively to rapidly changing customer behaviour.

As a result, technology has become a defining factor in organisational resilience. Digital transformation is no longer viewed as a discretionary initiative or a future aspiration. It is increasingly recognised as a prerequisite for survival in an environment characterised by volatility, uncertainty, and rapid change. The pandemic acted as a catalyst, accelerating trends that were already underway and reinforcing the strategic importance of digital capability across all sectors.

It is within this broader context of accelerated digital transformation that the concept of the metaverse has gained prominence. The metaverse is frequently positioned as the next major phase in the evolution of digital interaction, promising immersive environments that blur the boundaries between the physical and virtual worlds. Proponents argue that it represents a natural progression from today's internet, enabling richer forms of collaboration, engagement, and economic activity.

However, the emergence of the metaverse has also been accompanied by significant hype. Media narratives, corporate announcements, and investment activity have often portrayed the metaverse as an inevitable future, while critics have questioned its maturity, practicality, and real-world value. This divergence of perspectives reflects a broader pattern observed in previous waves of technological innovation, where genuine breakthroughs coexist with exaggerated expectations.

The purpose of this book is not to advocate uncritically for the metaverse nor to dismiss it prematurely. Instead, it seeks to examine the metaverse within the broader trajectory of technological disruption and digital transformation. By situating the metaverse alongside earlier waves of innovation, this book aims to assess whether it represents a substantive shift in how digital systems are designed and experienced, or whether it is primarily a repackaging of existing technologies under a compelling new label.

This chapter establishes the foundation for that analysis. It introduces the origins of the metaverse concept; explores what the metaverse is and how it differs from existing digital platforms; and outlines its objectives, components, and enabling technologies. It also addresses the benefits and limitations associated with metaverse adoption, providing a balanced framework through which its potential impact can be evaluated.

By the end of this chapter, the reader will have a clear understanding of the metaverse as a technological and socio-economic phenomenon, as well as the context required to assess whether it constitutes a meaningful transformation or a hype-driven response to a period of rapid digital change.

1.2 METAVERSE INVENTION, CONCEPTUAL ORIGINS, AND EARLY VIRTUAL WORLDS

The conceptual evolution of the metaverse is summarised in Figure 1.2.

The concept of the metaverse did not emerge suddenly with the arrival of modern virtual reality (VR) headsets or recent corporate investment announcements. Instead, it has evolved gradually through a combination of speculative fiction, early digital experimentation, and successive waves of technological innovation. Understanding these origins is essential, as the

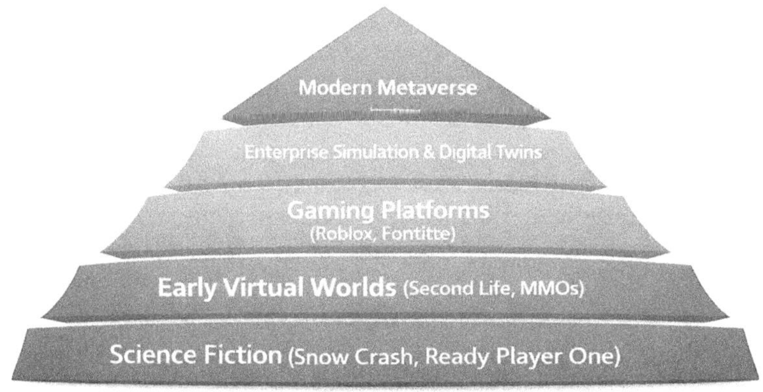

Figure 1.2 Conceptual origins and early virtual worlds.

narratives that surround new technologies often shape both expectations and adoption patterns.

The term "metaverse" was first introduced in 1992 by the American science-fiction author Neal Stephenson in his novel *Snow Crash* (Stephenson, 1992). In the book, Stephenson described a vast, shared virtual environment in which users interacted through digital avatars. Within this environment, individuals could socialise, conduct business, own digital property, and construct alternative identities. Although fictional, the metaverse in *Snow Crash* exhibited characteristics that closely resemble those attributed to modern metaverse platforms, including persistence, shared space, real-time interaction, and digital economies.

Stephenson's vision is notable not because it predicted specific technologies but because it articulated a coherent model of how virtual worlds could function as extensions of social and economic life. The novel explored themes of identity, control, corporate power, and digital inequality, many of which remain central to contemporary debates about immersive technologies. As such, *Snow Crash* provided a conceptual blueprint rather than a technical roadmap, influencing how technologists and entrepreneurs later framed immersive digital environments.

The idea of immersive virtual worlds gained further prominence through popular culture in the decades that followed. In 2011, Ernest Cline published *Ready Player One* (Cline, 2011), a science-fiction novel depicting a future in which much of humanity retreats into a fully immersive virtual universe known as OASIS. This digital world served not only as a form of entertainment but also as a primary venue for education, employment, commerce, and social interaction. The subsequent film adaptation, released in 2018 and directed by Steven Spielberg, brought this vision to a global audience.

The significance of *Ready Player One* lies in its portrayal of the metaverse as a comprehensive alternative reality rather than a niche technology. The story highlighted both the appeal and the risks of such environments, including economic opportunity, escapism, and the concentration of power within platform owners. These themes resonate strongly with present-day discussions about the metaverse, particularly concerns around monopolisation, governance, and the social consequences of immersive digital life.

While fictional narratives played an important role in shaping public imagination, early real-world implementations of virtual worlds began to emerge long before the term "metaverse" entered mainstream business discourse. One of the most notable examples is *Second Life*, launched in 2003. Unlike traditional online games, *Second Life* offered an open-ended virtual environment where users could create content, build structures, trade virtual goods, and establish digital communities. It also introduced an early form of virtual economy, allowing users to exchange virtual currency for real-world money.

Despite initial media attention and corporate experimentation, *Second Life* did not achieve mass adoption on the scale anticipated at the time. However, it demonstrated several key principles that continue to underpin metaverse platforms today, including user-generated content, digital ownership, and persistent virtual identity. Importantly, it also exposed limitations around usability, scalability, and sustained engagement, offering valuable lessons for later platforms.

The gaming industry has played a particularly significant role in advancing the practical foundations of the metaverse. Massively multiplayer online (MMO) games, such as *World of Warcraft*, introduced persistent shared worlds capable of supporting millions of users simultaneously. These environments enabled social interaction, collaboration, competition, and economic exchange within structured virtual spaces. Although primarily designed for entertainment, MMOs demonstrated the technical feasibility of large-scale virtual interaction.

More recently, platforms such as *Roblox*, *Minecraft*, and *Fortnite* have blurred the distinction between games and social platforms. These environments allow users not only to play but also to create, monetise, and share content. In doing so, they have laid the groundwork for creator economies that are central to many contemporary etaverse narratives. These platforms are particularly notable for their appeal to younger demographics, suggesting that future adoption of immersive digital environments may be driven by generational change.

From a technological perspective, the evolution of the metaverse has been closely linked to advances in computing power, graphics processing, and network infrastructure. Improvements in three-dimensional rendering, real-time physics simulation, and cloud computing have enabled increasingly sophisticated virtual environments. At the same time, the proliferation of high-speed internet and mobile devices has expanded access to digital platforms globally.

VR and augmented reality (AR) technologies have also progressed significantly over the past two decades. Early VR systems were often expensive, cumbersome, and limited in functionality. Advances in hardware design, display resolution, motion tracking, and ergonomics have gradually improved the user experience, although widespread adoption remains constrained by cost and usability challenges. AR, delivered through smartphones and wearable devices, has offered a more accessible entry point, integrating digital content into physical environments.

A defining moment in the modern commercialisation of the metaverse occurred when Facebook announced its rebranding as Meta (Meta Platforms 2023). This decision represented a strategic repositioning of one of the world's largest technology companies towards immersive digital platforms. Mark Zuckerberg articulated a long-term vision in which social interaction, work, and commerce would increasingly take place within virtual environments. While the rebrand generated significant media attention, it also intensified scrutiny around the feasibility, timeline, and economic viability of the metaverse.

The scale of investment that followed signalled that the metaverse had moved beyond speculative discussion. Major technology firms, gaming companies, and venture capital investors began allocating substantial resources towards immersive technologies, virtual platforms, and supporting infrastructure (McKinsey & Company 2022; Gartner 2022). At the same time, scepticism persisted, with critics questioning whether existing use cases justified the level of hype and expenditure.

From an analytical perspective, it is important to recognise that the metaverse is not a single invention or platform. Rather, it represents the convergence of multiple technological, cultural, and economic trends that have been developing over several decades. Fictional narratives provided early conceptual frameworks, gaming platforms demonstrated practical feasibility, and recent advances in computing and connectivity have enabled more ambitious experimentation.

Understanding these origins allows for a more nuanced assessment of the metaverse. It highlights that while the concept is grounded in longstanding ideas and technologies, its future impact remains uncertain. The gap between vision and implementation, as evidenced by earlier virtual worlds, serves as a reminder that technological possibility does not automatically translate into widespread adoption or sustainable value.

1.3 WHAT IS THE METAVERSE? DEFINITIONS, CORE CHARACTERISTICS, AND WHAT IT IS NOT

Figure 1.3 outlines the defining characteristics of the metaverse.

The term "metaverse" is widely used across media, technology marketing, and investment discourse, yet it is often applied inconsistently. One of the challenges in assessing whether the metaverse represents a genuine technological transformation or a hype-driven phenomenon lies in the absence of a universally accepted definition. Different stakeholders, technology companies, academics, investors, and users, frequently describe the metaverse in ways that reflect their own priorities and commercial interests.

At a high level, the metaverse can be described as a persistent, immersive, and interactive digital environment that enables users to experience a sense of presence within a shared virtual space. Unlike traditional digital platforms, which rely primarily on two-dimensional interfaces, the metaverse emphasises three-dimensional interaction, real-time engagement, and continuity across experiences. Users are represented through digital identities, often in the form of avatars, which persist across sessions and, in some cases, across platforms.

From a functional perspective, the metaverse extends the internet from a network of connected information pages into a network of connected

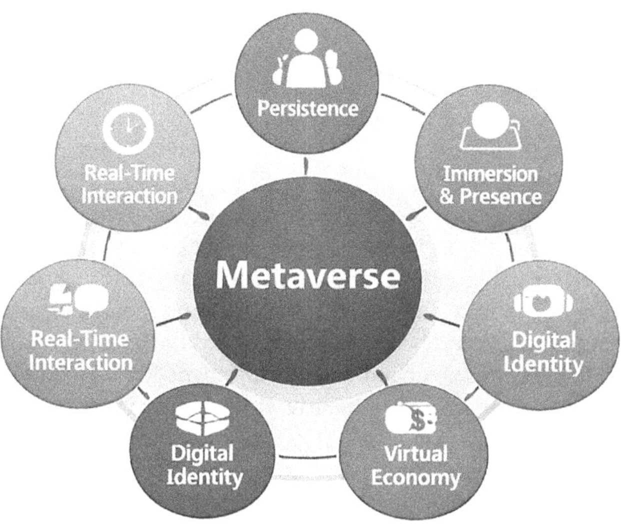

Figure 1.3 Core characteristics of the Metaverse.

experiences. In the same way that the early internet transformed access to information and communication, proponents argue that the metaverse has the potential to transform how people work, learn, socialise, and conduct economic activity in digital environments.

1.3.1 Core Characteristics of the Metaverse

While definitions vary, most interpretations of the metaverse share a common set of characteristics that distinguish it from existing digital platforms.

Persistence is a foundational characteristic. A metaverse environment continues to exist regardless of whether individual users are logged in. Changes made within the environment, such as the construction of virtual buildings, the creation of digital assets, or the outcome of events, remain over time. This differentiates the metaverse from session-based experiences such as video calls or single-player games, which reset when the session ends.

Real-time interaction is another defining feature. Users interact with each other and with digital objects simultaneously, experiencing events as they unfold. This real-time nature supports social interaction, collaboration, and shared experiences that more closely resemble physical-world interaction.

Immersion and presence distinguish the metaverse from conventional digital platforms. Through technologies such as VR, AR, and spatial audio, users experience a sense of "being there" rather than simply observing content on a screen. Even when accessed through traditional devices such as laptops or smartphones, metaverse platforms aim to simulate spatial interaction and embodied presence.

Digital identity and representation are central to metaverse participation. Users typically engage through avatars that represent their identity within the virtual environment. These avatars may be customised and, in some cases, persist across multiple platforms. Digital identity extends beyond visual representation to include reputation, social connections, and ownership of digital assets.

Economic systems are also a key component of many metaverse platforms. Virtual economies enable users to create, buy, sell, and trade digital goods and services. These economies may be supported by traditional payment systems or by blockchain-based mechanisms such as cryptocurrencies and non-fungible tokens. The existence of economic incentives differentiates the metaverse from purely social or entertainment-focused digital spaces.

Interoperability, although frequently cited, remains largely aspirational. In theory, interoperability would allow users to move seamlessly between different metaverse platforms while retaining their identity, assets, and social connections. In practice, most current implementations operate as closed ecosystems. The extent to which true interoperability will be achieved remains a critical question in determining the long-term viability of the metaverse.

1.3.2 What the Metaverse Is not

Clarifying what the metaverse is not is just as important as defining what it is. Much of the hype surrounding the metaverse stems from conflating it with existing technologies or overstating its current capabilities.

The metaverse is *not simply virtual reality*. While VR plays an important role in enabling immersive experiences, the metaverse can also be accessed through non-immersive devices such as smartphones, tablets, and computers. Reducing the metaverse to VR hardware overlooks the broader ecosystem of platforms, services, and economic systems involved.

Similarly, the metaverse is *not just online gaming*. Although gaming platforms have pioneered many of the technical and social elements associated with the metaverse, the concept extends beyond entertainment. The inclusion of work, education, commerce, and social infrastructure differentiates the metaverse from traditional games, which are typically goal-oriented and constrained by pre-defined rules.

The metaverse is also not a single platform or product. There is no single metaverse owned or controlled by one organisation. Instead, the metaverse is better understood as an emerging ecosystem of platforms, technologies, and experiences. While some companies may attempt to position themselves as central players, the long-term structure of the metaverse remains contested.

Finally, the metaverse is not a guaranteed or inevitable future. Although investment levels and corporate interest are significant, history demonstrates that not all technological visions achieve widespread adoption. Many promising technologies fail to reach maturity due to cost, usability, regulatory barriers, or lack of compelling use cases. Treating the metaverse as inevitable risks overlooking these constraints and repeating the mistakes of earlier technology hype cycles.

1.3.3 The Metaverse in the Context of Technological Hype Cycles

The enthusiasm surrounding the metaverse closely resembles patterns observed in previous waves of technological innovation. Emerging technologies are often accompanied by inflated expectations, followed by periods of disillusionment as practical challenges become apparent. Over time, a subset of applications may stabilise and deliver value, while others fade away.

Understanding the metaverse through this lens provides a more balanced framework for evaluation. Rather than asking whether the metaverse will succeed or fail as a single entity, it is more useful to consider which components, use cases, and sectors are most likely to benefit from immersive digital environments. This approach aligns with the central theme of this book, which seeks to distinguish genuine transformation from hype-driven narratives.

1.4 OBJECTIVES OF THE METAVERSE: BUSINESS, SOCIAL, ECONOMIC, AND TECHNOLOGICAL PERSPECTIVES

The objectives of the metaverse are often presented in broad, aspirational terms, ranging from global connectivity to immersive digital lifestyles. However, to assess whether the metaverse represents a meaningful transformation rather than a speculative vision, it is necessary to examine its objectives in more concrete terms. These objectives can be broadly categorised into business, social, economic, and technological dimensions, each of which carries distinct implications and challenges.

1.4.1 Business Objectives

From a business perspective, the metaverse is positioned as a platform for enhancing productivity, collaboration, and customer engagement. One of its primary objectives is to reduce the limitations imposed by physical distance, enabling organisations to operate more effectively across global teams and markets. By creating immersive virtual environments, businesses aim to replicate aspects of physical presence that are often lost in traditional digital communication tools.

Virtual offices, meeting spaces, and collaborative environments are frequently cited as examples of how the metaverse could transform the workplace. Unlike conventional videoconferencing, these environments allow participants

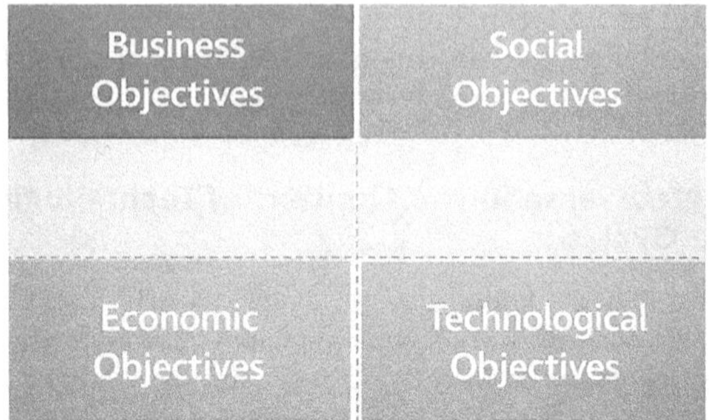

Figure 1.4 Strategic objectives underpinning Metaverse development.

to interact spatially, move within shared spaces, and engage with digital artefacts collectively. Proponents argue that this can improve collaboration, creativity, and employee engagement, particularly in distributed or hybrid work models. Figure 1.4 summarises the strategic objectives underpinning metaverse development across business, social, economic, and technological dimensions.

Another business objective is the creation of new revenue streams. The metaverse enables organisations to develop virtual products, services, and experiences that complement or extend physical offerings. Examples include virtual retail spaces, digital fashion, branded events, and immersive marketing campaigns. For some organisations, particularly in creative and consumer-facing industries, the metaverse represents an opportunity to experiment with new business models that are not constrained by physical infrastructure.

At a strategic level, participation in the metaverse is also driven by competitive positioning. As with earlier waves of digital innovation, organisations may feel pressure to establish a presence in emerging platforms to avoid being perceived as technologically lagging. This dynamic can accelerate adoption, even in the absence of clear short-term returns, contributing to both innovation and hype.

1.4.2 Social Objectives

The social objectives of the metaverse centre on enhancing human interaction and connectivity. By enabling immersive digital experiences, the metaverse seeks to create environments in which people can socialise, collaborate, and express themselves in ways that more closely resemble physical interaction.

During the COVID-19 pandemic, the limitations of existing digital social platforms became increasingly apparent. While social media and videoconferencing enabled communication, they often lacked depth, spontaneity, and emotional richness. The metaverse aims to address these shortcomings by supporting shared spaces where individuals can interact more naturally through avatars, gestures, and spatial audio.

The metaverse also aspires to foster inclusivity by enabling participation regardless of geographic location. In theory, immersive virtual environments could allow individuals from different regions, cultures, and socio-economic backgrounds to interact on equal footing. Virtual events, communities, and social spaces may reduce barriers associated with travel, physical disability, or access to traditional venues.

However, these social objectives are accompanied by significant challenges. Issues of digital exclusion, harassment, identity representation, and psychological well-being raise questions about whether the metaverse can deliver meaningful social benefits at scale. As such, social objectives must be evaluated alongside governance, moderation, and ethical considerations.

1.4.3 Economic Objectives

Economically, the metaverse is often framed as the foundation for a new digital economy. Virtual environments enable the creation, exchange, and monetisation of digital assets, services, and experiences. These economic activities are supported by virtual currencies, digital marketplaces, and, increasingly, blockchain-based systems.

One of the key economic objectives of the metaverse is to enable digital ownership. Through mechanisms such as non-fungible tokens, users can own unique digital assets, including virtual land, art, and in-game items. Proponents argue that this creates new forms of economic participation and value creation, particularly for creators and independent developers.

The metaverse also aims to support decentralised economic models. Decentralised autonomous organisations and blockchain-based governance structures are frequently cited as mechanisms for distributing control and value more equitably among participants. In this context, the metaverse is positioned not only as a technological platform but also as an experiment in alternative economic systems.

At the same time, economic objectives are a major source of scepticism. Questions remain regarding the sustainability of virtual economies, the speculative nature of digital assets, and the concentration of value within platform owners. Distinguishing between genuine economic innovation and speculative excess is therefore central to evaluating the metaverse's long-term viability.

1.4.4 Technological Objectives

From a technological standpoint, the metaverse serves as a unifying vision for the convergence of multiple advanced technologies. Its objectives include pushing the boundaries of what is possible in real-time computing, immersive interaction, and large-scale digital infrastructure.

The metaverse drives demand for advances in areas such as graphics processing, network latency, spatial computing, and human–computer interaction. Achieving seamless, immersive experiences requires significant improvements in hardware, software, and connectivity. As such, the metaverse acts as a catalyst for innovation across the broader technology ecosystem.

Another technological objective is interoperability. In theory, the metaverse aspires to enable seamless movement between different virtual environments, platforms, and services. While current implementations remain fragmented, the pursuit of interoperability influences standards development, platform design, and regulatory discussions.

Finally, the metaverse represents an attempt to reimagine the user interface of the internet itself. Moving beyond keyboards and touchscreens, immersive technologies explore new modes of interaction, including voice, gesture, and haptic feedback. Whether these technologies achieve widespread adoption will depend on usability, accessibility, and user acceptance.

1.4.5 Objectives versus Reality

While the objectives of the metaverse are ambitious, there is often a gap between stated goals and practical implementation. Many of the benefits described remain aspirational, dependent on technological maturity, cost reduction, regulatory clarity, and social acceptance. Recognising this gap is essential to maintaining a critical perspective.

In evaluating the metaverse, it is therefore important to distinguish between long-term objectives and near-term realities. Doing so allows organisations and policymakers to make informed decisions, balancing experimentation with caution and avoiding overcommitment based on unproven assumptions.

1.5 BENEFITS OF THE METAVERSE: OPPORTUNITIES ACROSS SECTORS

Figure 1.5 presents a balanced view of benefits and limitations.

The potential benefits of the metaverse are often presented in sweeping terms, promising transformation across nearly every aspect of digital interaction. While such claims should be approached with caution, it is nevertheless clear that immersive digital environments introduce capabilities that extend beyond those offered by existing platforms. These benefits are most clearly understood when examined across specific domains, including work, education, commerce, technology adoption, and the structure of virtual environments themselves.

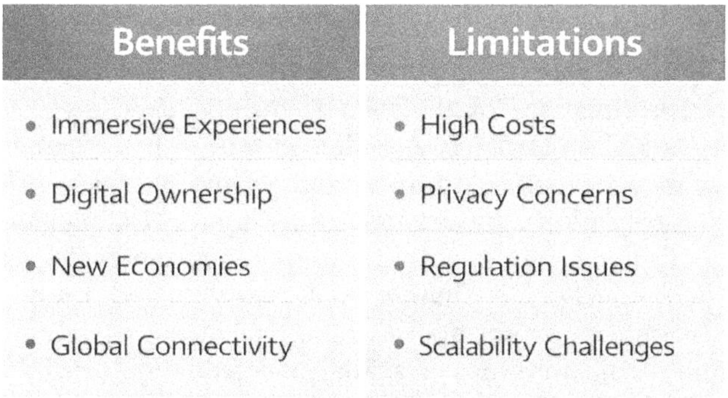

Benefits	Limitations
• Immersive Experiences	• High Costs
• Digital Ownership	• Privacy Concerns
• New Economies	• Regulation Issues
• Global Connectivity	• Scalability Challenges

Figure 1.5 Benefits and limitations of the Metaverse.

1.5.1 Enhanced Remote and Hybrid Working

Remote working has evolved from a niche employment benefit into a mainstream operating model for many organisations. Prior to the COVID-19 pandemic, remote work was largely limited to specific roles, sectors, or progressive employers. The pandemic forced a sudden and large-scale transition, demonstrating that many forms of work could be performed effectively without physical co-location.

Despite these successes, remote working has also exposed limitations in existing digital collaboration tools. Videoconferencing platforms, while effective for meetings, often struggle to replicate informal interaction, spontaneous collaboration, and the sense of shared presence that emerges naturally in physical workplaces. Over time, these limitations can contribute to reduced engagement, weaker team cohesion, and challenges in onboarding new employees.

The metaverse is frequently positioned as a solution to these challenges. Immersive virtual offices allow employees to interact spatially within shared environments, moving between virtual meeting rooms, informal social spaces, and collaborative work areas. Through avatars and real-time interaction, participants can experience a greater sense of presence than is possible through conventional video calls.

From a business perspective, these environments have the potential to support more effective hybrid working models. Organisations may reduce reliance on physical office space while preserving aspects of in-person collaboration. For global teams, the metaverse offers the possibility of creating a shared digital headquarters that is accessible regardless of geographic location. However, the extent to which these benefits outweigh costs and complexity remains an open question and will vary significantly by industry and organisational culture.

1.5.2 Transformation of Digital and Hybrid Education

Education represents one of the most frequently cited use cases for the metaverse. Over the past decade, online education has expanded rapidly, with universities, professional bodies, and private providers offering digital degrees, certifications, and training programmes. The pandemic further accelerated this trend, forcing institutions to adopt remote delivery at scale.

While online education has improved accessibility and flexibility, it often lacks immersion and experiential learning. Subjects that rely on practical demonstration, collaboration, or spatial understanding can be difficult to teach effectively through static content or video lectures alone. Student engagement and retention are also persistent challenges in fully remote learning environments.

The metaverse introduces new possibilities for immersive education. Virtual classrooms, laboratories, and simulation environments allow learners to interact with content in three dimensions. For example, medical students could practise procedures in virtual operating theatres, engineering students could explore complex machinery, and history students could experience reconstructed historical environments.

These capabilities have the potential to enhance learning outcomes by combining theoretical instruction with experiential learning. They also enable collaboration between learners from different locations, creating global classrooms that transcend physical boundaries. However, the effectiveness of such approaches depends on pedagogy, accessibility, and cost and should not be assumed to be universally superior to traditional methods.

1.5.3 Expansion of Blockchain and Digital Asset Ecosystems

Blockchain technology plays a central role in many metaverse narratives, particularly in relation to digital ownership and virtual economies. While blockchain adoption predates the metaverse, immersive virtual environments provide a context in which blockchain-based applications can become more visible and widely used.

Non-fungible tokens enable the representation of unique digital assets, including virtual land, artwork, and in-game items. Cryptocurrencies and decentralised finance platforms facilitate economic exchange within virtual worlds, allowing users to buy, sell, and trade digital goods. Decentralised autonomous organisations introduce new models of governance, enabling communities to participate directly in decision-making processes.

In this context, the metaverse can be seen as an accelerator for blockchain adoption, embedding decentralised technologies into everyday digital experiences. For creators, this may offer new opportunities for monetisation and ownership. For users, it introduces new forms of participation in digital economies.

At the same time, these developments raise important questions about regulation, speculation, and sustainability. The volatility of digital asset markets and the concentration of value within certain platforms highlight the need for critical evaluation rather than uncritical enthusiasm.

1.5.4 New Models for Brand Engagement and Marketing

The metaverse offers organisations new ways to engage with customers beyond traditional advertising and e-commerce. Brands can create immersive experiences that allow users to interact with products, participate in events, and express identity through digital goods.

Virtual retail spaces, branded environments, and digital fashion are among the most prominent examples. Rather than simply viewing products on a website, customers can explore virtual stores, attend product launches, or customise digital representations of physical goods. For some brands, particularly those targeting younger demographics, such experiences align with existing patterns of digital engagement.

Global reach is another key benefit. Metaverse platforms are not constrained by physical location, enabling brands to engage with audiences worldwide simultaneously. This can reduce barriers to market entry and support global marketing strategies.

However, the effectiveness of metaverse-based marketing depends on user adoption and engagement. Without a sufficiently large and active user base, branded experiences risk becoming costly experiments with limited return on investment.

1.5.5 Integration and Unification of Virtual Worlds

Virtual environments have existed for many years in the form of online games, social platforms, and virtual meeting tools. However, these environments are typically fragmented, with limited interoperability and continuity. Users often maintain separate identities, assets, and social networks across platforms.

One of the longer-term benefits associated with the metaverse is the potential to unify these experiences into a more cohesive ecosystem. In theory, users could move between different virtual environments while retaining aspects of their identity, digital assets, and social connections. This continuity could enhance user experience and reduce friction between platforms.

In practice, achieving such integration presents significant technical, commercial, and regulatory challenges. Platform owners may have limited incentives to support interoperability, and standards remain underdeveloped. Nevertheless, the aspiration to unify virtual worlds represents a key differentiator between the metaverse vision and existing digital platforms.

1.5.6 Broader Societal and Economic Implications

Beyond specific sectors, the metaverse is often associated with broader societal and economic implications. Proponents argue that immersive digital environments could enable new forms of work, reduce geographic inequality, and support more flexible lifestyles. For individuals in remote or underserved regions, virtual participation may offer access to opportunities that are otherwise unavailable.

At the same time, these benefits are unevenly distributed and contingent on access to technology, connectivity, and digital literacy. Without careful design and governance, the metaverse risks reinforcing existing inequalities rather than alleviating them.

1.6 LIMITATIONS, RISKS, AND STRUCTURAL CONSTRAINTS OF THE METAVERSE

While the metaverse is often presented as a transformative technological frontier, it is accompanied by a substantial set of limitations and risks that must be examined critically. These constraints are not merely short-term implementation challenges but structural issues that may shape the trajectory, adoption, and ultimate impact of immersive digital environments. A balanced assessment of the metaverse requires careful consideration of these factors, particularly in light of historical precedents where technological optimism outpaced practical reality.

1.6.1 Infrastructure and Connectivity Constraints

One of the most fundamental limitations of the metaverse is its dependence on robust digital infrastructure. Immersive experiences require high-bandwidth, low-latency connectivity to support real-time rendering, spatial audio, and synchronous interaction among large numbers of users. In many regions, such infrastructure is either unavailable or prohibitively expensive.

Although advances in fibre networks, 5G, and edge computing promise improvements in performance, global connectivity remains uneven. This digital divide presents a significant barrier to widespread adoption. Without reliable infrastructure, the metaverse risks becoming accessible primarily to users in technologically advanced and economically developed regions, reinforcing existing inequalities in digital participation.

Even in well-connected environments, network congestion, latency variability, and reliability issues can undermine user experience. Immersive platforms are far less tolerant of performance degradation than traditional web applications, meaning that infrastructure limitations are likely to remain a persistent constraint.

1.6.2 Cost and Accessibility of Hardware

Another major barrier to metaverse adoption is the cost and accessibility of hardware. While immersive environments can be accessed through conventional devices such as laptops and smartphones, many of the most compelling experiences rely on VR headsets, AR devices, and high-performance computing hardware.

These technologies remain expensive relative to mass-market consumer devices. Although prices are expected to decline over time, cost remains a significant deterrent, particularly for users in lower-income regions and for organisations considering large-scale deployment. In enterprise contexts, the cost of procuring, maintaining, and supporting immersive hardware must be justified by clear productivity or revenue gains, which are not yet consistently demonstrated.

In addition to cost, usability presents another challenge. VR headsets can be uncomfortable for prolonged use, and issues such as motion sickness, visual fatigue, and physical discomfort limit the duration and frequency of engagement. These factors constrain the practical use of immersive technologies in everyday work and learning environments.

1.6.3 Privacy, Security, and Data Protection Risks

The metaverse introduces new and complex privacy and security challenges. Immersive platforms collect vast quantities of data, including behavioural patterns, biometric information, spatial movements, and social interactions. This level of data collection exceeds that of traditional digital platforms and raises significant concerns about surveillance, misuse, and data exploitation.

Security risks are also heightened in virtual environments. Digital assets, virtual currencies, and identity systems create new attack surfaces for cybercriminals. High-profile breaches in cryptocurrency exchanges and blockchain platforms illustrate the vulnerabilities inherent in decentralised systems. As metaverse platforms grow in scale and economic significance, they are likely to attract increased attention from malicious actors.

Regulatory frameworks for data protection and cybersecurity are still evolving and may struggle to keep pace with the complexity of immersive environments. Ensuring user trust will require robust governance models, transparent data practices, and effective enforcement mechanisms.

1.6.4 Governance, Regulation, and Platform Control

Governance represents one of the most contentious issues surrounding the metaverse. Questions about who controls virtual environments, how rules are enforced, and how disputes are resolved remain largely unanswered. In centralised platforms, governance is typically dictated by platform owners, raising concerns about monopolistic behaviour and lack of accountability.

Decentralised governance models, often associated with blockchain-based metaverse platforms, promise greater transparency and user participation. However, these models introduce their own challenges, including complexity, scalability, and the risk of governance capture by influential stakeholders. In practice, decentralised governance often falls short of its egalitarian aspirations.

Regulatory uncertainty further complicates governance. Existing legal frameworks are not well suited to addressing issues such as virtual property rights, cross-border jurisdiction, digital identity, and economic activity within immersive environments. Policymakers face the challenge of balancing innovation with consumer protection, a task made more difficult by the rapid pace of technological change.

1.6.5 Social, Psychological, and Health Implications

The immersive nature of the metaverse raises important questions about its impact on human behaviour, mental health, and social relationships. Prolonged engagement in virtual environments may contribute to social isolation, addiction, or detachment from physical reality. These concerns echo earlier debates around social media and online gaming but are potentially amplified by the depth of immersion offered by the metaverse.

Issues of identity and representation also warrant attention. Avatars allow users to experiment with identity in ways that may be empowering for some but disorienting or harmful for others. The psychological effects of inhabiting alternative digital personas over extended periods remain poorly understood.

Physical health considerations, including eye strain, posture-related injuries, and reduced physical activity, further complicate the picture. These factors limit the extent to which immersive technologies can be integrated into daily routines without adverse effects.

1.6.6 Economic Sustainability and Speculative Risk

Economic sustainability represents a significant uncertainty for the metaverse. Many current platforms rely heavily on speculative investment, particularly in virtual real estate and digital assets. Rapid price appreciation in these markets has attracted attention, but such activity is often driven by short-term speculation rather than underlying utility.

History suggests that speculative bubbles are common in emerging technology markets. While some innovations survive and mature, others collapse once expectations exceed practical value. Distinguishing between sustainable economic activity and speculative excess is therefore critical in evaluating the metaverse's long-term prospects.

For organisations considering investment in the metaverse, this uncertainty complicates strategic decision-making. The risk of overinvestment in unproven platforms must be weighed against the potential opportunity cost of inaction.

1.6.7 Limitations in Use Case Maturity

Finally, many proposed metaverse use cases remain immature or poorly defined. While demonstrations and pilot projects illustrate technical possibilities, they often lack clear pathways to scalable, repeatable value. In some cases, metaverse implementations replicate existing digital experiences with added complexity rather than delivering fundamentally new capabilities.

This gap between vision and execution is not unusual in early-stage technologies, but it underscores the need for cautious evaluation. Without compelling, widely applicable use cases, the metaverse risks remaining a niche phenomenon rather than achieving mainstream adoption.

1.7 CORE COMPONENTS OF THE METAVERSE: A LAYERED ARCHITECTURAL VIEW

The metaverse is best understood not as a single technology or platform but as a complex, multi-layered ecosystem composed of interdependent components. Each component performs a distinct function, yet none can operate effectively in isolation. Together, these layers enable immersive digital experiences, economic activity, and large-scale interaction. Analysing the metaverse through a layered architectural lens allows for a clearer understanding of both its potential and its limitations. Figure 1.6 presents a layered architectural model of the metaverse, showing how infrastructure, human interface, decentralisation and ownership, spatial computing, creator economy, discovery, and experience layers work together to support immersive digital ecosystems.

Figure 1.6 Layered architectural model of the Metaverse.

1.7.1 Experience Layer

The experience layer represents the most visible and user-facing component of the metaverse. It encompasses the environments and activities through which users interact with virtual worlds. These experiences include gaming, social interaction, business meetings, virtual events, education, training simulations, entertainment, and digital commerce.

Unlike traditional digital platforms, metaverse experiences are designed to be immersive and spatial. Users are not merely consumers of content but active participants within shared environments. The quality of these experiences depends heavily on realism, responsiveness, and intuitive interaction. Poorly designed experiences risk undermining user engagement, regardless of underlying technological sophistication.

From a business perspective, the experience layer is also where value is most immediately perceived. Virtual offices, branded environments, and interactive simulations are often the first points of experimentation for organisations exploring metaverse adoption. However, sustaining meaningful engagement over time remains a challenge, particularly outside entertainment-focused use cases.

1.7.2 Discovery Layer

The discovery layer determines how users find, access, and navigate metaverse experiences. In traditional digital ecosystems, discovery is facilitated through search engines, social media, app stores, and advertising platforms. In the metaverse, discovery mechanisms must adapt to immersive environments and spatial navigation.

This layer includes inbound discovery, such as recommendations, virtual signage, and curated environments, as well as outbound discovery, including advertising, promotional events, and influencer-driven engagement. Effective discovery is critical to user retention and platform growth, yet it also raises concerns around manipulation, surveillance, and commercialisation of user attention. As metaverse platforms mature, the discovery layer is likely to become a significant battleground for competition, with implications for content visibility, creator revenue, and platform governance.

1.7.3 Creator Economy Layer

The creator economy is central to the scalability and sustainability of the metaverse. Rather than relying solely on centrally produced content, metaverse platforms depend heavily on user-generated content to populate virtual environments. This includes digital assets, environments, experiences, and interactive objects.

Creator tools enable users to design, build, and monetise content within the metaverse. These tools range from simple visual editors to sophisticated development environments that require programming and design expertise. Marketplaces facilitate the exchange of digital goods, allowing creators to generate income and users to personalise their experiences.

The success of the creator economy depends on fair monetisation models, accessible tools, and clear ownership rights. Tensions often arise between platform owners and creators, particularly regarding revenue sharing, intellectual property, and control over distribution. These dynamics mirror earlier conflicts observed in social media and app ecosystems.

1.7.4 Spatial Computing Layer

Spatial computing underpins the immersive nature of the metaverse. This layer enables digital objects and environments to exist and behave in three-dimensional space, responding to user movement and interaction in real time. Technologies such as 3D engines, real-time rendering, physics simulation, and spatial mapping are central to this component.

Spatial computing also encompasses AR, which overlays digital information onto physical environments. In this context, the metaverse extends beyond fully virtual worlds to include hybrid experiences that blend physical and digital elements. These capabilities have applications across sectors, including retail, manufacturing, healthcare, and urban planning.

However, spatial computing is computationally intensive and demands significant processing power. Balancing realism with performance remains a key technical challenge, particularly for platforms targeting mass-market adoption.

1.7.5 Decentralisation and Ownership Layer

Decentralisation is frequently highlighted as a defining feature of the metaverse, particularly in Web3-based narratives. This layer encompasses blockchain technologies that enable decentralised ownership, governance, and economic exchange. Digital assets, smart contracts, and decentralised identity systems are key components.

In theory, decentralisation reduces reliance on central authorities and empowers users by granting ownership over digital assets and participation in governance. In practice, decentralised systems often face challenges related to scalability, usability, and governance complexity. Power can still concentrate among early adopters or influential stakeholders.

The role of decentralisation within the metaverse remains contested. While some platforms embrace fully decentralised models, others adopt hybrid approaches that combine centralised control with selective decentralised features.

1.7.6 Human Interface Layer

The human interface layer defines how users interact with the metaverse. This includes input and output devices such as VR headsets, AR glasses, mobile devices, keyboards, controllers, voice interfaces, gesture recognition systems, and haptic feedback technologies.

User experience is heavily influenced by the quality, comfort, and accessibility of these interfaces. While immersive devices offer greater presence, they also introduce barriers related to cost, usability, and physical comfort. As a result, many metaverse platforms support multiple modes of access to accommodate different user preferences and constraints.

Advances in human–computer interaction will play a critical role in determining the metaverse's long-term adoption. Interfaces that are intuitive, inclusive, and minimally intrusive are more likely to gain widespread acceptance.

1.7.7 Infrastructure Layer

The infrastructure layer provides the foundational computing resources required to support metaverse platforms. This includes cloud computing, edge computing, graphics processing units, networking infrastructure, and data storage systems. High-performance infrastructure is essential to deliver real-time, immersive experiences at scale.

The infrastructure demands of the metaverse are significantly higher than those of traditional digital platforms (NVIDIA 2022). Supporting millions of concurrent users in persistent virtual environments requires substantial investment in computing and networking resources. Energy consumption and environmental impact are also emerging concerns associated with large-scale infrastructure deployment. The scalability and sustainability of the metaverse will depend heavily on continued advances in infrastructure efficiency, cost reduction, and network performance.

1.8 ENABLING TECHNOLOGIES OF THE METAVERSE

Figure 1.7 provides an expanded view of the enabling technologies associated with the metaverse, while Figure 1.8 consolidates the core technologies into a simplified, integrated model.

The metaverse is not enabled by a single breakthrough technology but by the convergence of multiple technological domains that have matured over time. Each of these technologies contributes a specific capability, and the metaverse emerges only when they operate together as an integrated system. Understanding these enabling technologies is essential to assessing both the feasibility and limitations of metaverse platforms.

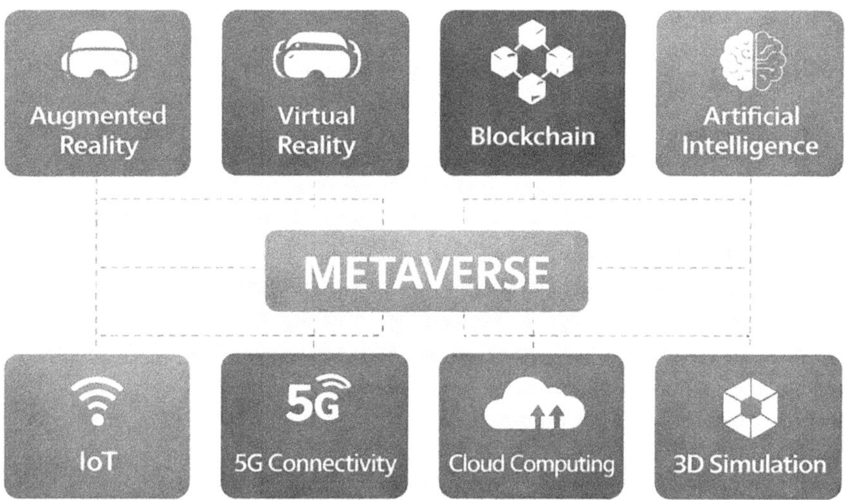

Figure 1.7 Expanded view of enabling technologies of the Metaverse.

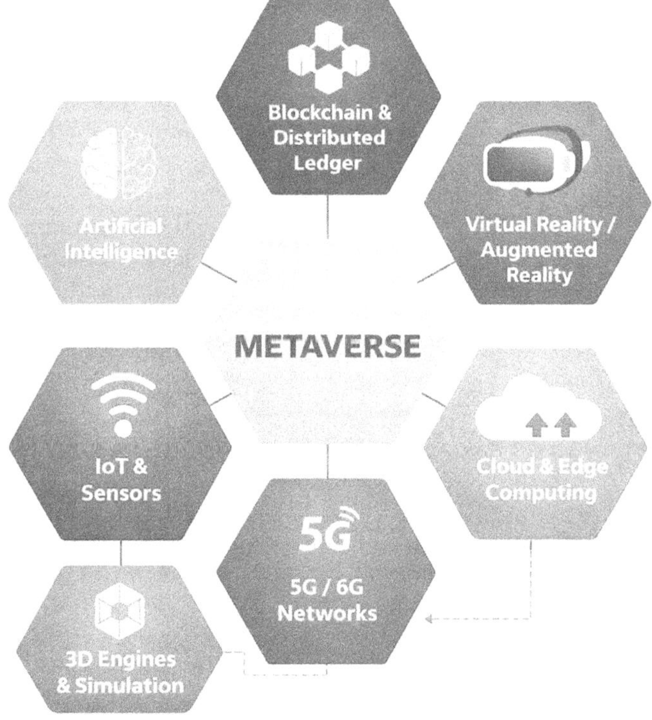

Figure 1.8 Consolidated view of the core enabling technologies of the Metaverse.

1.8.1 Artificial Intelligence

Artificial intelligence plays a foundational role in enabling scalable, responsive, and adaptive metaverse environments. AI systems support a wide range of functions, including real-time rendering optimisation, natural language interaction, intelligent non-player characters, content moderation, and personalised user experiences.

In immersive environments, AI-driven agents can populate virtual worlds, creating dynamic and responsive ecosystems. These agents may act as guides, assistants, or autonomous participants, contributing to the sense of realism and continuity. AI is also essential for managing the complexity of large-scale virtual environments, enabling systems to adapt dynamically to user behaviour and system load.

However, reliance on AI introduces challenges around bias, transparency, and accountability. As AI systems increasingly influence user experience and economic activity within the metaverse, governance mechanisms must ensure that these systems operate fairly and ethically.

1.8.2 Internet of Things and Sensor Technologies

The Internet of Things extends the metaverse beyond purely digital environments by linking physical objects and spaces to virtual representations. Sensors embedded in physical devices collect data that can be visualised or acted upon within immersive environments. This capability enables applications such as digital twins, where physical assets are mirrored in real time within virtual spaces.

In industrial contexts, digital twins allow organisations to simulate operations, monitor performance, and test scenarios without disrupting physical systems. In urban planning, IoT-enabled metaverse environments can support the modelling of traffic flows, energy consumption, and infrastructure resilience.

The integration of IoT data into immersive platforms increases realism and utility, but it also raises concerns about data security, privacy, and system complexity. Ensuring reliable and secure data flows between physical and virtual systems is a significant technical challenge.

1.8.3 Blockchain and Distributed Ledger Technologies

Blockchain technologies underpin many of the economic and governance models associated with the metaverse. Distributed ledgers enable the creation of decentralised systems for identity, ownership, and transaction processing. Within virtual environments, blockchain can support digital asset ownership, secure transactions, and transparent governance mechanisms.

Non-fungible tokens are commonly used to represent unique digital assets, including virtual land, digital art, and in-game items. Smart contracts automate transactions and enforce rules within decentralised systems. Decentralised identity solutions offer the potential for user-controlled identity management across platforms.

Despite these capabilities, blockchain technologies face limitations related to scalability, energy consumption, and user experience. Transaction throughput and latency remain constraints for real-time applications, and the complexity of blockchain interfaces can deter mainstream adoption.

1.8.4 Virtual Reality and Augmented Reality

VR and AR technologies provide the most direct pathway to immersive metaverse experiences. VR enables fully immersive environments by replacing the user's visual and auditory perception with digital content. AR overlays digital information onto the physical world, creating hybrid experiences that blend real and virtual elements.

Advances in display resolution, motion tracking, and spatial audio have significantly improved the quality of immersive experiences. However, hardware constraints, including cost, comfort, and battery life, continue to limit adoption. AR technologies, delivered through smartphones and wearable devices, offer a more accessible entry point but provide a different level of immersion. The balance between VR and AR adoption will influence how the metaverse evolves, particularly in enterprise and consumer contexts.

1.8.5 Three-Dimensional Modelling and Simulation

Three-dimensional modelling and simulation technologies form the visual and structural foundation of the metaverse. These tools enable the creation of realistic environments, objects, and avatars. Advances in real-time rendering, physics simulation, and lighting have significantly improved visual fidelity.

Simulation capabilities extend beyond visual realism to include physical behaviour, environmental dynamics, and system interactions. In professional contexts, simulation-based metaverse applications support training, design, and scenario analysis.

The creation of high-quality 3D content remains resource-intensive, requiring specialised skills and tools. Democratizing content creation is therefore essential to scaling metaverse adoption.

1.8.6 Cloud and Edge Computing

Cloud computing provides the scalable infrastructure required to support metaverse platforms. Centralised cloud resources enable storage, computation, and coordination across distributed users. Edge computing complements cloud infrastructure by processing data closer to the user, reducing latency and improving performance.

The combination of cloud and edge computing is particularly important for immersive applications, which are sensitive to delays and performance fluctuations. Efficient orchestration between cloud and edge resources is a key determinant of user experience.

Infrastructure cost and energy consumption remain significant concerns. As metaverse platforms scale, the sustainability of large-scale computing infrastructure will become increasingly important.

1.8.7 Networking Technologies

High-performance networking is essential to the metaverse. Technologies such as 5G, future 6G networks, and advanced fibre infrastructure enable the low-latency communication required for real-time interaction. Network reliability and consistency are particularly important in immersive environments, where disruptions can significantly degrade user experience.

Despite ongoing advances, networking limitations remain a barrier to universal access. Variability in network quality across regions reinforces the digital divide and constrains adoption in less-developed areas.

1.9 HOW THE METAVERSE WORKS: ECOSYSTEMS, PLATFORMS, AND INTERACTION MODELS

The operating model is illustrated in Figure 1.9.

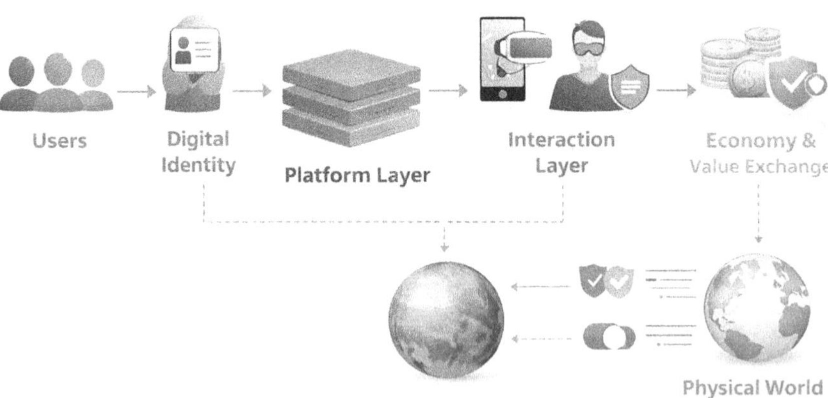

Figure 1.9 Metaverse operating model: ecosystems and interaction.

To understand the metaverse beyond abstract vision, it is necessary to examine how it functions in practical terms. The metaverse operates as an ecosystem composed of users, platforms, technologies, and economic systems that interact continuously. Rather than a single system, it is better understood as a layered network of platforms and services that collectively enable immersive digital interaction.

At its core, the metaverse functions through the orchestration of identity, environment, interaction, and value exchange. Each of these elements must operate reliably and at scale for immersive experiences to be meaningful and sustainable.

1.9.1 Users, Avatars, and Digital Identity

The primary participants in the metaverse are users, represented through digital identities that persist within virtual environments. These identities are most commonly expressed through avatars, which serve as the user's embodiment in the virtual world. Avatars enable spatial interaction, social presence, and personal expression.

Digital identity in the metaverse extends beyond visual representation. It includes user credentials, reputation, social connections, and ownership of digital assets. In some implementations, identity is platform-specific and centrally managed, while in others it is decentralised and user-controlled through blockchain-based identity systems.

The management of digital identity has significant implications for privacy, security, and interoperability. Persistent identities enable continuity across experiences, but they also raise concerns around surveillance, profiling, and misuse of personal data. Balancing continuity with user control is a central challenge in metaverse design.

1.9.2 Platforms and Virtual Environments

Metaverse platforms provide the environments in which interaction occurs. These platforms host virtual spaces, manage user access, coordinate interaction, and integrate enabling technologies, such as rendering engines, networking, and AI systems.

Virtual environments may range from open-ended worlds to purpose-built spaces designed for specific activities, such as meetings, education, or entertainment. Some platforms emphasise realism and simulation, while others adopt stylised or abstract designs. The choice of design influences user experience, accessibility, and system performance.

From a structural perspective, most current platforms operate as closed ecosystems. Users, assets, and content are typically confined to a single platform, limiting interoperability. While this approach simplifies governance and monetisation, it constrains the broader metaverse vision of seamless movement between environments.

1.9.3 Interaction Models and Social Dynamics

Interaction within the metaverse occurs through a combination of spatial movement, communication tools, and object manipulation. Users navigate environments, interact with digital objects, and communicate with others through voice, text, gestures, and, in some cases, haptic feedback.

These interaction models aim to replicate aspects of physical-world behaviour while introducing new forms of engagement unique to digital environments. For example, users may teleport between locations, manipulate objects at scale, or interact with AI-driven entities. Social dynamics within the metaverse are shaped by platform design, community norms, and governance mechanisms.

The richness of interaction contributes to immersion, but it also introduces complexity. Designing intuitive and inclusive interaction models that accommodate diverse users remains a significant challenge.

1.9.4 Content Creation and World Building

Content creation is central to the functioning of the metaverse. Virtual environments are populated with digital assets, structures, and experiences created by platform developers, professional creators, and users themselves. World-building tools enable participants to design spaces, objects, and interactions within the metaverse.

These tools vary widely in sophistication, from visual editors accessible to non-technical users to advanced development environments requiring specialised skills. The availability and usability of creation tools influence the diversity and quality of content within the metaverse.

Effective content governance is essential to maintaining quality, safety, and legal compliance. Platforms must balance creative freedom with moderation, intellectual property protection, and user safety.

1.9.5 Economic Systems and Value Exchange

Economic activity is a defining feature of many metaverse platforms. Virtual economies enable the exchange of digital goods, services, and experiences. These economies may be supported by platform-specific currencies, traditional payment systems, or blockchain-based mechanisms.

Value exchange occurs through marketplaces, auctions, subscriptions, and direct transactions. Digital assets may include virtual land, clothing, tools, access rights, and experiences. For creators, these systems offer opportunities to monetise content and participate in digital economies.

However, virtual economies are vulnerable to speculation, fraud, and imbalance. Platform design choices, such as transaction fees and asset scarcity, significantly influence economic dynamics. Sustainable economic models require careful calibration to avoid excessive volatility or exploitation.

1.9.6 Governance and Moderation Mechanisms

Governance mechanisms determine how rules are established, enforced, and evolved within metaverse platforms. These mechanisms include content moderation policies, dispute resolution processes, and decision-making structures.

Centralised platforms typically enforce governance through terms of service and administrative control. Decentralised platforms may rely on community voting and smart contracts. Each approach presents trade-offs between efficiency, transparency, and inclusivity.

Effective governance is critical to maintaining trust and safety within immersive environments. As the metaverse scales, governance challenges are likely to intensify, particularly in relation to harmful behaviour, misinformation, and economic exploitation.

1.9.7 Integration with the Physical World

The metaverse does not exist in isolation from the physical world. Many applications involve integration with physical systems, including work processes, education, commerce, and infrastructure. Digital twins, remote collaboration tools, and hybrid events exemplify this integration.

This interplay between physical and virtual systems not only increases the practical relevance of the metaverse but also introduces complexity. Aligning digital representations with physical reality requires accurate data, reliable sensors, and effective coordination.

Although the metaverse is often discussed as a single concept, in practice it encompasses a range of architectural and governance models. These models differ in how control, ownership, and decision-making are distributed between platform providers and users. Understanding these distinctions is critical for assessing the strategic, economic, and ethical implications of metaverse adoption.

Broadly, metaverse platforms can be categorised into centralised, hybrid, and decentralised models. Each approach reflects different priorities and trade-offs, particularly in relation to scalability, governance, interoperability, and user empowerment. A comparative overview is provided in Figure 1.10.

1.9.8 Centralised Metaverse Platforms

Centralised metaverse platforms are operated and controlled by a single organisation or corporate entity. In this model, the platform owner is responsible for infrastructure, content moderation, governance, monetisation, and user management. Examples include metaverse initiatives developed by large technology companies and gaming platforms that operate as closed ecosystems.

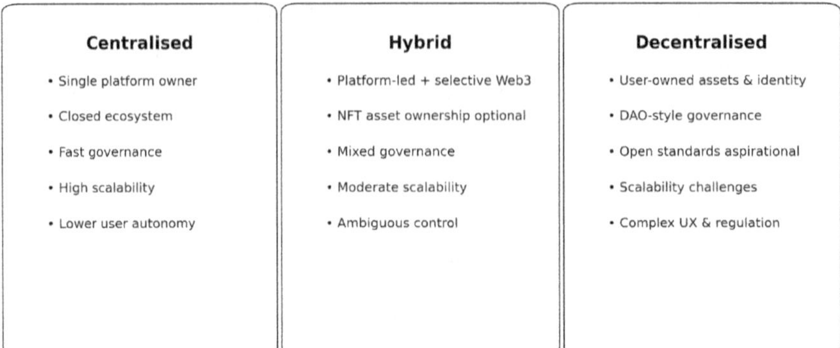

Figure 1.10 Types of Metaverse: control and ownership models.

Note: This figure presents a comparative overview of centralised, hybrid, and decentralized models.

From a technical and operational perspective, centralisation offers several advantages. Platform owners can optimise performance, enforce consistent standards, and deliver a cohesive user experience. Centralised control also simplifies governance, enabling rapid decision-making and enforcement of rules. These characteristics are particularly important for platforms targeting mass-market adoption.

Economically, centralised platforms often benefit from strong monetisation mechanisms, including advertising, subscriptions, and transaction fees. Control over the platform ecosystem allows providers to capture a significant share of the value generated by user activity.

However, centralisation raises concerns around monopolisation, data ownership, and user autonomy. Users typically have limited control over platform rules, content moderation decisions, and economic structures. Digital assets and identities may be locked into proprietary ecosystems, limiting interoperability and long-term ownership. These concerns mirror debates surrounding existing social media and app platforms.

1.9.9 Hybrid Metaverse Models

Hybrid metaverse models combine elements of centralised control with selective decentralisation. In this approach, core infrastructure and governance remain under the control of a platform provider, while certain functions, such as asset ownership or identity management, are decentralised through blockchain technologies.

Hybrid models aim to balance the efficiency and scalability of centralised platforms with the empowerment and transparency associated with decentralised systems. For example, a platform may allow users to own digital assets through non-fungible tokens while retaining centralised control over environment design and content moderation.

This approach is attractive to organisations seeking to experiment with Web3 concepts without relinquishing full control over their platforms. It also reflects practical constraints, as fully decentralised systems often struggle with scalability and usability.

However, hybrid models can introduce complexity and ambiguity. Users may assume a level of decentralisation that is not fully realised in practice, leading to mismatched expectations. Transparency around governance and ownership structures is therefore essential to maintaining trust.

1.9.10 Decentralised Metaverse Platforms

Decentralised metaverse platforms are built on blockchain and distributed ledger technologies, with the aim of minimising central authority. In this model, ownership of digital assets, identity, and governance mechanisms is distributed among users rather than controlled by a single organisation.

Decentralised autonomous organisations are often proposed as governance mechanisms for such platforms, enabling participants to vote on rules, upgrades, and economic policies. Smart contracts automate transactions and enforce rules without the need for intermediaries.

Advocates argue that decentralisation promotes user empowerment, transparency, and resilience. By reducing reliance on central authorities, decentralised platforms aim to prevent monopolistic control and align incentives between platform providers and users.

In practice, decentralised metaverse platforms face significant challenges. Governance processes can be slow and complex, and decision-making may be dominated by a small number of influential stakeholders. Technical limitations, such as transaction throughput and latency, constrain real-time interaction. User experience is often less polished than that of centralised platforms.

1.9.11 Comparative Analysis and Trade-Offs

Each metaverse model presents distinct trade-offs. Centralised platforms prioritise scalability, usability, and commercial viability but often at the expense of user autonomy and interoperability. Decentralised platforms emphasise ownership and governance but struggle with performance and mainstream adoption. Hybrid models attempt to balance these considerations, though they may compromise on both fronts.

From a strategic perspective, organisations must align their choice of metaverse model with their objectives, risk tolerance, and regulatory environment. For users, understanding these models is essential to making informed decisions about participation, investment, and digital identity.

The coexistence of multiple metaverse models suggests that the future metaverse is unlikely to be uniform. Instead, it may consist of a diverse ecosystem of platforms serving different needs and preferences.

1.10 EVOLUTION OF THE METAVERSE: HISTORICAL MILESTONES AND TECHNOLOGICAL PROGRESSION

The metaverse did not emerge as a sudden or isolated innovation. Rather, it represents the cumulative outcome of decades of technological development, conceptual experimentation, and cultural change. Tracing the historical evolution of the metaverse provides important context for understanding both its current form and its future potential. It also reinforces the central theme of this book: that the metaverse is best assessed as part of a broader technological continuum rather than as a standalone revolution.

1.10.1 Early Conceptual Foundations

The conceptual roots of the metaverse can be traced back well before the advent of modern computing. Early experiments with stereoscopic vision in the nineteenth century demonstrated that human perception could be manipulated to create the illusion of depth. These experiments laid the psychological groundwork for later immersive technologies by revealing how visual cues influence perception and presence.

In the twentieth century, advances in computer graphics, simulation, and human–computer interaction further developed these ideas. Flight simulators, used extensively in military and aviation training, represented some of the earliest practical applications of immersive simulation. Although limited by the technology of the time, these systems demonstrated the value of simulated environments for training and decision-making.

Science fiction played a particularly influential role during this period. Writers and futurists explored the social, economic, and ethical implications of immersive digital worlds long before they were technically feasible. These narratives shaped expectations and inspired generations of technologists, contributing to a shared vision of what immersive digital environments might become.

1.10.2 The Rise of Personal Computing and Networked Worlds

The widespread adoption of personal computers in the late twentieth century marked a significant step towards immersive digital environments. As computing power became more accessible, developers began experimenting with three-dimensional graphics and networked interaction. Early virtual worlds and online communities emerged, allowing users to interact through text-based or rudimentary graphical interfaces.

The expansion of the internet in the 1990s enabled these environments to scale beyond isolated systems. Online multiplayer games and virtual chat spaces introduced persistent identities and shared digital spaces, foreshadowing key elements of the metaverse. While these early platforms were limited in scope and fidelity, they established foundational concepts such as avatars, virtual economies, and online communities.

1.10.3 Advances in Graphics, Gaming, and Simulation

The gaming industry has been a primary driver of technological progress relevant to the metaverse. Improvements in graphics processing units, rendering techniques, and game engines enabled increasingly realistic and complex virtual environments. Real-time physics simulation, advanced lighting, and detailed character animation contributed to more immersive experiences.

MMO games demonstrated the feasibility of hosting large numbers of users in shared virtual worlds. These platforms supported persistent environments, social interaction, and economic activity at scale. Although primarily entertainment-focused, they provided valuable insights into user behaviour, community dynamics, and system scalability.

Game engines developed for entertainment purposes have since been repurposed for a wide range of professional applications, including architecture, engineering, training, and simulation. This convergence highlights how technological innovation in one domain can influence broader applications relevant to the metaverse.

1.10.4 Emergence of Virtual and Augmented Reality

VR and AR technologies represent a critical milestone in the evolution of the metaverse. Early VR systems were often prohibitively expensive and limited in performance, restricting their use to specialised research and industrial contexts. However, continued advances in hardware design, display technology, and motion tracking gradually improved accessibility and user experience.

The introduction of consumer-grade VR headsets renewed interest in immersive environments, bringing them closer to mainstream adoption. AR, delivered through smartphones and wearable devices, expanded the scope of immersive experiences by integrating digital content into physical spaces.

Despite these advances, adoption has remained uneven. Hardware constraints, usability challenges, and limited compelling use cases have slowed widespread uptake. These limitations underscore the gap between technological capability and practical application.

1.10.5 Platformisation and Commercial Expansion

In recent years, the metaverse has entered a phase of intensified commercial interest and platform development. Large technology companies, gaming studios, and startups have invested heavily in immersive platforms, infrastructure, and content. This period has been characterised by ambitious visions, substantial capital investment, and heightened media attention.

The rebranding of major technology firms around metaverse initiatives marked a symbolic turning point, signalling that immersive environments had become a strategic priority rather than a niche experiment. At the same time, this surge in interest amplified hype and raised expectations regarding the pace and scale of adoption.

This phase mirrors earlier moments in technological history, such as the early days of the internet and social media, where rapid expansion was accompanied by both innovation and overstatement. Understanding this pattern provides a useful lens for evaluating current metaverse narratives.

1.10.6 Continuity Rather Than Disruption

Viewed historically, the metaverse appears less as a sudden disruption and more as a continuation of existing trends. It builds on established technologies, such as networking, graphics, cloud computing, and digital platforms, extending them into more immersive forms. This perspective challenges claims that the metaverse represents a radical break from the past.

Recognising continuity does not diminish the potential significance of the metaverse. Instead, it provides a more realistic framework for assessing its development. Technological transformations often unfold gradually, with incremental advances accumulating over time. The metaverse, like previous digital innovations, is likely to follow a similar trajectory.

1.11 GLOBAL FOOTPRINT, ADOPTION TRENDS, AND INDUSTRY PARTICIPATION

The global footprint of the metaverse has expanded rapidly in recent years, driven by a combination of technological advancement, corporate investment, and shifting user behaviour. While adoption remains uneven across regions and sectors, the scale and diversity of participation provide valuable insight into how the metaverse is being positioned and tested in practice.

1.11.1 Geographic Distribution and Regional Adoption

Metaverse adoption exhibits significant regional variation, reflecting differences in infrastructure, economic conditions, and cultural attitudes towards digital technology. North America and parts of East Asia have emerged as early centres of metaverse experimentation, supported by advanced digital infrastructure, strong gaming cultures, and substantial venture capital investment.

In regions with high levels of broadband penetration and mobile connectivity, immersive platforms have found receptive audiences, particularly among younger demographics. By contrast, adoption in developing regions has been constrained by limited infrastructure, high hardware costs, and competing economic priorities. This uneven distribution reinforces concerns that the metaverse may initially deepen global digital inequalities.

Nevertheless, emerging markets also present long-term opportunities. As connectivity improves and hardware costs decline, immersive platforms may offer alternative pathways to education, employment, and entrepreneurship. The extent to which these opportunities materialise will depend on inclusive design and equitable access.

1.11.2 Industry Participation and Corporate Strategy

Industry participation in the metaverse spans a wide range of sectors, including technology, gaming, retail, finance, education, healthcare, and entertainment. Large technology firms have invested heavily in immersive platforms, infrastructure, and research, often positioning the metaverse as a long-term strategic priority rather than a near-term revenue driver.

Consumer-facing brands have also established a presence within metaverse platforms, experimenting with virtual stores, branded experiences, and digital goods. These initiatives are frequently positioned as marketing experiments aimed at engaging younger audiences and exploring new forms of brand expression. While some campaigns have generated significant attention, others have struggled to deliver measurable returns.

In enterprise contexts, metaverse adoption has focused on training, simulation, and collaboration. Industries such as manufacturing, aviation, and healthcare have explored immersive environments for skills development and operational planning. These use cases are often more narrowly defined and outcomes-driven than consumer applications, reflecting a pragmatic approach to adoption.

1.11.3 Investment Trends and Market Dynamics

Investment activity provides another indicator of metaverse momentum. Venture capital funding, corporate acquisitions, and strategic partnerships have increased significantly, particularly during periods of heightened market enthusiasm. This influx of capital has not only accelerated platform development and experimentation, but it has also contributed to speculative behaviour. Figure 1.11 summarises the global metaverse footprint by linking the wider global context, industry participation, and the platform and technology base that supports current adoption patterns.

Figure 1.11 Global Metaverse footprint and industry participation.

Market volatility has underscored the risks associated with hype-driven investment. Fluctuations in digital asset values and shifting corporate priorities have led some organisations to scale back or reassess metaverse initiatives. These dynamics highlight the importance of distinguishing between long-term value creation and short-term speculative trends.

1.11.4 User Adoption and Engagement Patterns

User adoption of metaverse platforms remains concentrated within specific demographics, particularly younger users familiar with gaming and digital creation. Engagement levels vary widely depending on platform design, content availability, and social dynamics. Sustaining long-term engagement has proven challenging, particularly outside entertainment-focused environments.

These patterns suggest that while interest in immersive experiences is significant, mainstream adoption is not guaranteed. The success of the metaverse will depend on its ability to deliver compelling, repeatable value across a broad range of use cases (Deloitte 2022; OECD 2021; McKinsey & Company 2022).

1.12 CHAPTER SUMMARY AND FORWARD OUTLOOK

This chapter has established the foundational context required to evaluate the metaverse critically. Rather than treating the metaverse as a singular or inevitable technological revolution, it has been presented as an evolving ecosystem shaped by historical precedent, technological convergence, and socio-economic forces.

The analysis has demonstrated that the metaverse draws on long-standing ideas and technologies, including immersive simulation, virtual worlds, and digital economies. Its objectives span business, social, economic, and technological domains, reflecting both genuine opportunities and aspirational narratives. At the same time, significant limitations and risks remain, including infrastructure constraints, governance challenges, privacy concerns, and uncertain economic sustainability.

By examining the components, enabling technologies, operational models, and adoption trends associated with the metaverse, this chapter has provided a balanced framework for assessing its potential impact. This framework is essential for distinguishing between transformative innovation and hype-driven speculation.

The chapters that follow will build on this foundation by examining specific metaverse platforms, business models, governance structures, and use cases in greater detail. Through this analysis, this book seeks to answer the central question posed by its title: whether the metaverse represents a substantive evolution of the digital landscape or a rebranding of existing technologies amplified by market enthusiasm.

REFERENCES

Ball, M. (2022). *The Metaverse: And How It Will Revolutionize Everything.* New York: Liveright Publishing.

Cline, E. (2011). *Ready Player One.* New York: Crown Publishing Group.

Deloitte. (2022). *Technology Trends 2022.* London: Deloitte Insights.

Gartner. (2022). *Emerging Technologies and the Metaverse: Market Analysis and Forecasts.* Stamford, CT: Gartner Research.

McKinsey & Company. (2022). *Value Creation in the Metaverse: How Businesses Can Capture Opportunity.* New York: McKinsey Global Institute.

NVIDIA. (2022). *The Omniverse and the Industrial Metaverse: Enabling Real-Time Digital Twins.* Santa Clara, CA: NVIDIA Corporation.

OECD. (2021). *Virtual Worlds and the Metaverse: Policy, Governance, and Economic Implications.* Paris: Organisation for Economic Co-operation and Development.

Stephenson, N. (1992). *Snow Crash.* New York: Bantam Books.

Chapter 2

Metaverse Platforms

2.1 INTRODUCTION TO METAVERSE PLATFORMS

The evolution of the metaverse from a speculative concept to a set of deployable platforms marks a significant shift in how immersive digital environments are understood and implemented. Early discussions of the metaverse were dominated by futuristic narratives and science fiction analogies. In contrast, contemporary metaverse development is grounded in concrete platforms that integrate immersive interfaces, digital identity systems, content creation tools, and economic mechanisms into operational ecosystems.

Metaverse platforms function as *multi-sided digital infrastructures*. On one side, they provide end users with immersive environments for social interaction, entertainment, work, and learning. On another, they offer creators and developers the tools required to build experiences, assets, and services. On a third, they enable economic activity through marketplaces, virtual currencies, and monetisation frameworks. This platform-based structure aligns the metaverse more closely with established digital platform models than with monolithic virtual worlds.

A defining characteristic of metaverse platforms is *persistence*. Unlike traditional online applications that reset between sessions, metaverse environments continue to exist and evolve even when individual users are offline. This persistence not only underpins long-term value creation but also introduces new technical, governance, and regulatory challenges.

From a technological standpoint, metaverse platforms are not built on a single innovation. Instead, they combine advances in cloud computing, real-time rendering engines, spatial computing, networking, and, in some cases, blockchain-based systems. The convergence of these technologies enables scalable, shared environments that can support thousands or millions of concurrent users.

From a business perspective, the metaverse should be understood less as a destination and more as an *operating model*. Organisations do not invest in "the metaverse" as an abstract construct; they invest in specific platforms that offer defined capabilities, user bases, and commercial opportunities. As

 DOI: 10.1201/9781003405566-2

a result, platform choice becomes a strategic decision with implications for governance, data ownership, interoperability, and risk exposure.

This chapter therefore adopts a *platform-first lens*. Rather than attempting to define what the metaverse *should* be, it examines what metaverse platforms *actually are today*, how they function, and how they are being used in practice. By grounding the discussion in existing platforms, this chapter provides readers with a practical foundation for evaluating metaverse initiatives in real-world contexts.

2.2 CLASSIFICATION OF METAVERSE PLATFORMS

Metaverse platforms exhibit substantial variation in architecture, governance, and intended use cases. Without a clear classification framework, discussions of the metaverse risk becoming imprecise and overly generalised. To enable systematic analysis, metaverse platforms can be categorised according to their dominant structural and functional characteristics.

2.2.1 Governance-Based Classification

One of the most significant differentiators between metaverse platforms is their governance model. Governance determines who controls platform rules, how decisions are made, and how disputes are resolved.

Decentralised platforms distribute governance across blockchain-based mechanisms, typically using decentralised autonomous organisations. These platforms emphasise user ownership of digital assets and collective decision-making. However, decentralisation often introduces coordination challenges and uneven participation.

Centralised platforms, by contrast, concentrate governance authority within a corporate entity. This allows for rapid decision-making, consistent enforcement, and scalability, but it also places significant power over users and creators in the hands of platform operators.

2.2.2 Use Case–Based Classification

A second axis of classification relates to primary use cases.

Consumer-focused platforms prioritise entertainment, social interaction, and user-generated content. Their success is typically measured in user engagement and cultural relevance.

Enterprise-focused platforms emphasise productivity, simulation, collaboration, and training. Adoption in this category is driven less by user numbers and more by integration into existing organisational workflows.

2.2.3 Hybrid and Emerging Platforms

Some platforms occupy hybrid positions, blending consumer and enterprise features or experimenting with new governance approaches. These platforms often reflect strategic exploration rather than fully articulated long-term visions. Figure 2.1 visually summarises this classification by mapping platforms across governance and use case dimensions, providing a consistent reference point for the remainder of this chapter.

2.3 DECENTRALISED METAVERSE PLATFORMS

Figure 2.2 illustrates the layered architecture of a metaverse platform, highlighting the relationships between user interfaces, platform services, economies, governance, and infrastructure.

Decentralised metaverse platforms represent one of the most distinctive and debated approaches to building immersive virtual environments. These platforms are characterised by their reliance on blockchain technology to support digital ownership, peer-to-peer transactions, and distributed governance. Unlike centralised platforms, decentralised metaverse environments aim to reduce reliance on a single controlling authority and instead distribute power among users, creators, and token holders.

At a conceptual level, decentralised metaverse platforms are motivated by dissatisfaction with existing platform economics. Traditional digital

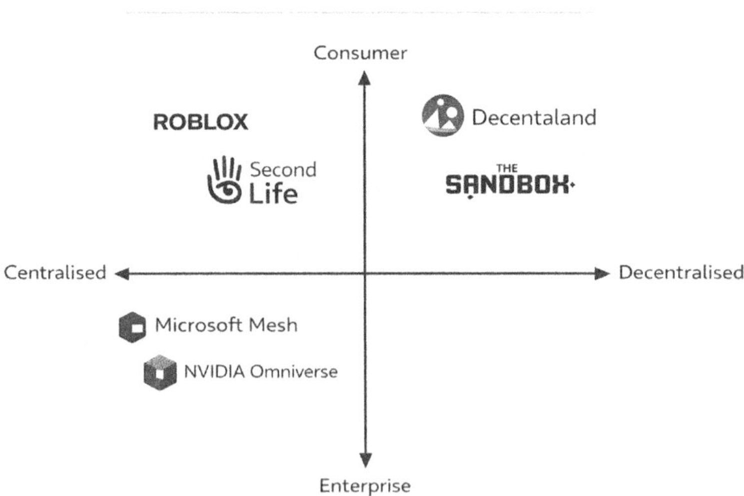

Figure 2.1 Classification of Metaverse platforms based on governance model and primary use case.

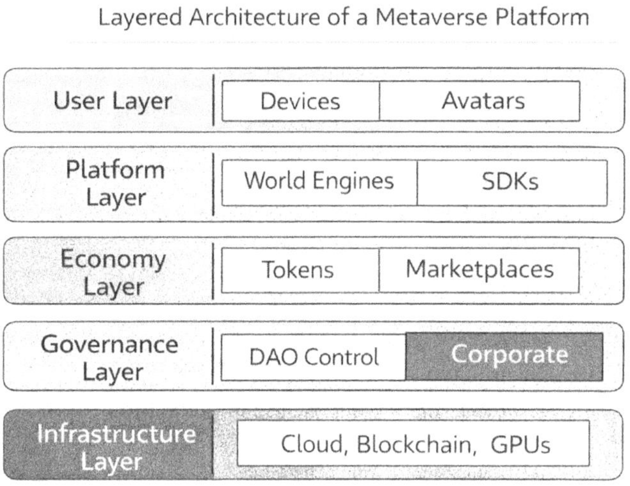

Figure 2.2 Layered architecture of a Metaverse platform, showing user interfaces, platform services, economies, governance, and infrastructure.

platforms typically retain ownership of user-generated content, control monetisation mechanisms, and dictate governance policies. Decentralised platforms seek to invert this model by granting users ownership of digital assets and a formal role in decision-making processes.

In practice, decentralised metaverse platforms operate as *crypto-economic systems* layered on top of immersive virtual worlds. They combine real-time rendering engines and cloud infrastructure with blockchain-based asset registries, smart contracts, and decentralised governance mechanisms. This hybrid architecture introduces both novel opportunities and significant complexity.

Two platforms dominate discussions of decentralised metaverse development: *Decentraland* and *The Sandbox*. While they share common principles, their design choices, tooling, and ecosystem dynamics differ in important ways.

2.3.1 Decentraland

Decentraland is widely regarded as the earliest large-scale implementation of a decentralised metaverse platform. Built on the Ethereum blockchain, it provides a persistent, browser-based three-dimensional virtual world in which users can own, develop, and monetise digital land and assets.

The foundational unit of the Decentraland ecosystem is *LAND*, a non-fungible token representing a specific parcel of virtual space defined by Cartesian coordinates. The total supply of LAND is finite, introducing artificial scarcity into the platform's spatial design. Ownership of LAND grants users the ability to deploy content, host experiences, and construct interactive environments.

This land-based model has significant implications. From an economic perspective, it creates a real estate market within the virtual world, complete with speculation, leasing, and development strategies. From a governance perspective, it ties influence and visibility within the platform to asset ownership, raising questions about inequality and access.

2.3.1.1 Platform Architecture and Tooling

Decentraland's architecture combines a decentralised asset layer with a more conventional application layer. Blockchain technology is used to record ownership of LAND and assets, while content delivery and rendering rely on off-chain infrastructure. This design reflects current technological constraints, particularly the limited throughput and latency characteristics of public blockchains.

Content creation within Decentraland is supported by multiple tools. A graphical builder allows non-technical users to assemble scenes and environments using pre-defined components. For more advanced use cases, a software development kit enables developers to write custom logic and interactions using standard web technologies.

This dual tooling approach lowers the barrier to entry while still supporting sophisticated experiences. However, it also creates disparities in capability between casual creators and technically skilled developers.

2.3.1.2 Governance and the Decentraland DAO

Governance in Decentraland is managed through a decentralised autonomous organisation. The DAO controls critical smart contracts and platform parameters, including marketplace policies, content moderation frameworks, and resource allocation.

Token holders can submit proposals and vote on governance decisions. In theory, this creates a transparent and participatory governance model. In practice, participation is uneven, with voting power often concentrated among large token holders. This dynamic introduces governance challenges similar to those observed in traditional shareholder models. Despite these limitations, the DAO structure represents a meaningful experiment in decentralised platform governance and has influenced the design of subsequent metaverse initiatives.

2.3.1.3 Economic Activity and Marketplaces

Economic activity within Decentraland is facilitated through its native cryptocurrency, which serves as the medium of exchange for asset purchases, land transactions, and marketplace activity. Users can buy and sell avatar wearables, digital art, event tickets, and other virtual goods.

The marketplace enables creators to monetise their work directly, without relying on platform-controlled revenue sharing models. However, transaction costs associated with blockchain usage and exposure to cryptocurrency price volatility introduce friction and risk for participants.

2.3.1.4 Adoption and Practical Limitations

While Decentraland has achieved significant visibility, user adoption remains modest relative to mainstream gaming platforms. Monthly active user numbers are low when compared to platforms such as Roblox or Fortnite. This gap highlights a recurring challenge for decentralised metaverse platforms: aligning ideological appeal with mass-market usability.

Onboarding complexity, wallet management, and performance limitations remain barriers for non-technical users. As a result, Decentraland's user base tends to skew towards early adopters, developers, and cryptocurrency enthusiasts.

2.3.2 The Sandbox

The Sandbox represents a complementary but distinct approach to decentralised metaverse development. Like Decentraland, it is built on the Ethereum blockchain and emphasises digital ownership and creator-driven economies. However, The Sandbox places greater emphasis on gaming mechanics and user-generated experiences.

The platform uses voxel-based graphics and a modular world design, which simplifies asset creation and encourages experimentation. Virtual land is represented as non-fungible tokens, and ownership enables users to deploy games and interactive environments.

2.3.2.1 Creator Tools and Ecosystem Design

The Sandbox ecosystem is structured around a set of integrated creator tools. Asset creation is supported through a dedicated editor that allows users to design and animate voxel-based objects. These assets can be minted as non-fungible tokens and traded within the platform's marketplace.

Game creation is supported through a visual development environment that enables users to define gameplay logic without writing code. This approach significantly lowers the barrier to entry for creators and aligns the platform more closely with gaming communities.

By prioritising ease of creation, The Sandbox has attracted a broad base of creators and brand partners. This strategy contrasts with Decentraland's more developer-oriented tooling.

2.3.2.2 *Governance and Token Economics*

Governance within The Sandbox is mediated through a decentralised autonomous organisation, with token holders participating in decision-making processes. The platform's native token is used for transactions, governance voting, and incentives.

As with other blockchain-based platforms, governance participation tends to be uneven, and economic activity is influenced by broader cryptocurrency market dynamics. These factors introduce volatility and uncertainty into the platform's long-term trajectory.

2.3.2.3 *Adoption Patterns and Sustainability*

The Sandbox has benefited from high-profile partnerships and marketing initiatives, which have driven awareness and initial adoption. However, sustained user engagement remains a challenge. As with Decentraland, long-term success depends on the platform's ability to transition from speculative interest to enduring communities and meaningful experiences. An overview of leading metaverse platforms and their governance models is provided in Table 2.1.

2.4 CENTRALISED AND GAMING-LED METAVERSE PLATFORMS

Centralised and gaming-led metaverse platforms represent the most mature and widely adopted segment of the metaverse landscape. Unlike decentralised platforms, these environments are operated by single corporate entities

Table 2.1 Metaverse Platform Overview

Platform	*Platform Type*	*Governance Model*	*Asset Ownership*	*Primary Focus*
Decentraland	Decentralised	DAO	NFT-based	Social virtual world
The Sandbox	Decentralised	DAO	NFT-based	Gaming and creation
Roblox	Centralised	Corporate	Licensed assets	Gaming platform
Second Life	Centralised	Corporate	Licensed assets	Virtual world
Microsoft Mesh	Centralised	Corporate	No ownership	Enterprise collaboration
NVIDIA Omniverse	Centralised	Corporate	No ownership	Simulation and digital twins
Meta Horizon Worlds	Centralised	Corporate	Licensed assets	Social virtual world

that retain control over infrastructure, governance, content moderation, and monetisation. While this model limits user ownership of digital assets, it has proven highly effective in achieving scale, usability, and sustained engagement.

From a historical perspective, many of the defining characteristics of the metaverse – persistent identities, shared virtual spaces, user-generated content, and virtual economies – were first realised in centralised platforms. As a result, these platforms provide valuable empirical insight into what works, what scales, and where governance trade-offs emerge in practice. Two platforms are particularly instructive in this category: *Second Life*, which represents an early virtual world model, and *Roblox*, which exemplifies a modern, platform-driven creator economy at scale.

2.4.1 Second Life

Second Life is one of the earliest large-scale virtual worlds and remains a foundational reference point for metaverse development. Launched in the early 2000s, it introduced many concepts that are now central to contemporary metaverse discourse, including avatar-based interaction, virtual land ownership, user-generated environments, and a functioning virtual economy.

Second Life operates under a fully centralised governance model, with Linden Lab maintaining authority over platform rules, technical infrastructure, and economic mechanisms. Users can purchase virtual land, build structures, create digital goods, and offer services to other users. These activities are facilitated through the platform's internal currency, which can be exchanged for real-world money.

2.4.1.1 Virtual Economy and Monetisation

One of Second Life's most notable achievements is the longevity of its virtual economy. Over time, a diverse ecosystem of creators, designers, educators, and entrepreneurs has emerged, generating real-world income through virtual goods and services. This includes digital fashion, architectural design, event hosting, and consultancy services.

The existence of a stable currency exchange mechanism has been critical to this success. By enabling conversion between virtual and real-world currencies, Second Life blurred the boundary between virtual labour and real economic activity long before similar discussions emerged around blockchain-based platforms.

2.4.1.2 Education and Institutional Use

Second Life has also been adopted extensively for educational and institutional purposes. Universities, training providers, and non-profit organisations have used the platform to host virtual classrooms, simulations, and collaborative learning environments. These applications demonstrate the potential of immersive environments to support experiential learning and remote collaboration. However, adoption in these contexts has often been constrained by usability challenges, technical requirements, and the learning curve associated with navigating complex virtual environments.

2.4.1.3 Governance Trade-Offs and Limitations

The centralised governance model of Second Life enables consistent rule enforcement and platform stability, but it also places significant power in the hands of the platform operator. Content moderation policies, economic rules, and technical changes are determined unilaterally, limiting user influence over platform evolution.

Over time, Second Life has faced challenges related to graphical fidelity, user interface complexity, and declining mainstream visibility. Nevertheless, its continued operation demonstrates that virtual worlds can sustain long-term communities even without decentralised ownership models.

2.4.2 Roblox

Roblox represents one of the most successful implementations of a gaming-led metaverse platform. Unlike Second Life, which emerged before the rise of modern platform economics, Roblox was designed explicitly as a *platform for creators*. Its architecture, tooling, and monetisation systems are optimised to support large-scale user-generated content and sustained engagement.

Roblox provides a persistent virtual environment in which users interact through avatars and access a vast library of user-created experiences. These experiences range from simple games to complex social environments, simulations, and educational tools.

2.4.2.1 Creator Economy and Platform Tooling

At the core of Roblox's success is *Roblox Studio*, an integrated development environment that enables users to design and publish interactive experiences. The platform provides extensive documentation, templates, and tutorials, allowing creators with varying levels of technical expertise to participate.

Monetisation within Roblox is facilitated through the platform's virtual currency. Creators can generate revenue through in-experience purchases, subscriptions, and premium access. Roblox retains a share of this revenue, reflecting a traditional platform revenue-sharing model.

This creator-centric approach has resulted in a highly active developer ecosystem, with some creators generating substantial income. The platform's scale and accessibility have also made it an entry point for learning programming, game design, and digital entrepreneurship.

2.4.2.2 *Education and Youth Engagement*

Roblox has achieved particularly strong adoption among younger demographics. Its emphasis on creativity and social interaction has positioned it as both an entertainment platform and an informal learning environment. Educational institutions and non-profit organisations have leveraged Roblox to deliver interactive lessons and workshops.

However, the platform's popularity among younger users also raises governance and safety concerns. Content moderation, age-appropriate experiences, and data protection are ongoing challenges that require continuous platform oversight.

2.4.2.3 *Governance and Control*

Roblox operates under a centralised governance model, with strict control over platform policies, content standards, and economic rules. While this enables rapid response to safety issues and scalability, it also creates dependency for creators, who are subject to policy changes and revenue-sharing terms determined by the platform.

The Roblox case illustrates a central tension in metaverse development: the trade-off between creator empowerment and platform control. While creators benefit from access to infrastructure and audiences, they remain reliant on the platform's governance framework.

2.4.3 Comparative Insights from Centralised Platforms

Taken together, Second Life and Roblox demonstrate that centralised platforms can successfully support metaverse-like environments at scale. They also reveal recurring challenges related to governance concentration, user dependency, and long-term sustainability.

These platforms highlight that decentralisation is not a prerequisite for immersive virtual worlds. However, they also underscore why debates around ownership, governance, and control have become increasingly prominent as metaverse platforms grow in economic and cultural significance. The comparative use case strengths of major metaverse platforms are summarised in Table 2.2.

2.5 ENTERPRISE AND INFRASTRUCTURE METAVERSE PLATFORMS

While consumer-facing metaverse platforms have attracted the majority of public attention, some of the most substantive and commercially viable metaverse activity is occurring within enterprise and industrial contexts.

Table 2.2 Platform Use Case Matrix

Platform	*Social Interaction*	*Gaming*	*Education*	*Enterprise*	*Creator Economy*	*Virtual Economy*
Decentraland	High	High	Medium	Low	High	High
The Sandbox	High	High	Medium	Low	High	High
Roblox	Medium	High	High	Medium	High	High
Second Life	High	Medium	Medium	Low	High	Medium
Microsoft Mesh	Low	Low	Medium	High	Medium	Low
NVIDIA Omniverse	Low	Low	Medium	High	Low	Low
Meta Horizon Worlds	High	Medium	Low	Low	Medium	Medium

Enterprise and infrastructure metaverse platforms differ fundamentally from consumer platforms in both intent and design. Rather than prioritising entertainment or social interaction, they focus on productivity, simulation, collaboration, and operational optimisation.

Enterprise metaverse platforms are best understood as *enabling infrastructures* rather than destinations. They provide organisations with tools to model physical systems, support immersive collaboration, and integrate digital twins into business processes. Adoption in this category is driven by measurable outcomes such as efficiency gains, risk reduction, and improved decision-making rather than user engagement metrics. Three platforms are particularly influential in shaping this segment: *Microsoft Mesh*, *NVIDIA Omniverse*, and related enterprise virtualisation initiatives.

2.5.1 Microsoft Mesh

Microsoft Mesh is positioned as an enterprise-grade mixed reality platform designed to support shared virtual experiences across devices. Rather than presenting itself as a standalone metaverse, Mesh integrates closely with Microsoft's existing ecosystem of productivity tools, cloud services, and identity management systems.

The platform enables users to collaborate in immersive environments using virtual or AR devices, desktop systems, and mobile interfaces. This device-agnostic approach reflects Microsoft's emphasis on accessibility and incremental adoption rather than full immersion.

2.5.1.1 Integration with Enterprise Workflows

A defining feature of Microsoft Mesh is its integration with established enterprise tools such as collaboration software, cloud services, and directory-based identity systems. By leveraging existing authentication and access control mechanisms, Mesh reduces friction for organisational deployment and aligns with enterprise security requirements.

This integration enables use cases such as virtual meetings, design reviews, training simulations, and collaborative problem-solving. In these scenarios, immersive environments are used selectively to enhance understanding and engagement rather than replace traditional workflows entirely.

2.5.1.2 Governance, Security, and Compliance

Governance within Microsoft Mesh is centralised and aligned with enterprise IT governance frameworks. Organisations retain control over user access, data handling, and compliance policies. This model contrasts sharply with decentralised platforms and reflects enterprise priorities around risk management and regulatory adherence.

From a security perspective, Mesh benefits from Microsoft's investment in cloud security, identity management, and compliance certifications. However, this centralisation also reinforces dependency on a single vendor ecosystem.

2.5.2 NVIDIA Omniverse

NVIDIA Omniverse occupies a distinct position within the metaverse landscape as an infrastructure platform rather than a social or collaborative virtual world. It is designed to enable the creation, simulation, and operation of complex virtual environments, particularly in industrial and engineering contexts.

Omniverse leverages NVIDIA's expertise in graphics processing, artificial intelligence, and simulation technologies. It provides a shared virtual environment in which multiple users and systems can interact with digital representations of physical assets in real time.

2.5.2.1 Digital Twins and Industrial Simulation

One of the most significant applications of NVIDIA Omniverse is the creation of *digital twins*. Digital twins are virtual representations of physical systems that can be used to simulate behaviour, test scenarios, and optimise performance.

In manufacturing, architecture, and infrastructure planning, digital twins enable organisations to model environments before they are built or modified. This capability supports predictive maintenance, risk analysis, and design optimisation, reducing costs and improving outcomes.

2.5.2.2 Interoperability and Ecosystem Integration

Omniverse is designed to integrate with a wide range of existing tools and data sources. Rather than replacing established workflows, it acts as a connective layer that synchronises data across design, simulation, and operational systems.

This interoperability positions Omniverse as a foundational component of the enterprise metaverse stack. It also illustrates a broader trend in enterprise metaverse development: the emphasis on augmentation rather than replacement.

2.5.2.3 Governance and Control

Like Microsoft Mesh, NVIDIA Omniverse operates under a centralised governance model. Control over data, access, and usage is retained by organisations deploying the platform. This approach aligns with enterprise expectations but limits opportunities for user-driven governance experimentation.

2.5.3 Meta Horizon Worlds

Meta Horizon Worlds is a social VR platform developed by Meta (formerly Facebook). It enables users to create and explore virtual worlds, attend events, and interact socially within immersive environments.

Horizon Worlds operates under a centralised governance model and is tightly integrated with Meta's broader ecosystem, including its hardware devices and social media platforms. The platform emphasises social interaction and user-created content, with tools designed to lower the barrier to world creation.

Despite significant investment, Horizon Worlds has faced challenges related to user retention, content moderation, and public perception. These challenges highlight the difficulty of scaling social metaverse platforms while maintaining safety, engagement, and economic sustainability.

2.5.4 Apple and Spatial Computing Platforms

Apple does not position its immersive technology strategy under the term "metaverse". Instead, it has explicitly framed its approach around *spatial computing*, emphasising seamless integration of digital content into physical space rather than persistent, standalone virtual worlds.

The launch of Apple Vision Pro marks Apple's first major commercial entry into immersive computing. Rather than functioning as an open social metaverse platform, Vision Pro operates as a *highly controlled spatial operating environment*, extending Apple's existing ecosystem of devices, applications, and services into three-dimensional space.

Apple's approach differs fundamentally from both consumer metaverse platforms and enterprise virtual world systems. Vision Pro prioritises:

- Individual productivity and media consumption
- High-fidelity mixed reality experiences
- Tight hardware–software co-design
- Strong privacy and on-device processing guarantees

There is no native concept of a shared, persistent virtual world governed by user-generated economies or decentralised ownership. Instead, immersive experiences are delivered through applications distributed via Apple's existing app ecosystem, subject to established platform governance and review processes.

From a governance perspective, Apple's model is *fully centralised*. Identity, access control, application distribution, and monetisation are tightly managed through Apple's account infrastructure and commercial policies. This structure provides strong guarantees around security, performance, and privacy but limits experimentation with user-led governance or asset ownership.

Strategically, Apple's entry into immersive computing has important implications for the broader metaverse landscape. By avoiding open-ended virtual worlds and instead focusing on spatial extensions of existing workflows, Apple reinforces an alternative vision of the metaverse as:

- An interface evolution rather than a parallel digital society
- A productivity and media platform rather than a social universe
- A tightly governed ecosystem rather than an open, interoperable network

While Apple's platform does not currently support many of the defining characteristics associated with decentralised or social metaverse environments, its influence on hardware standards, interaction design, and privacy expectations is likely to shape future industry norms. As such, Apple represents a *parallel trajectory* in metaverse development – one that prioritises control, integration, and user experience over openness and collective governance.

2.5.5 Enterprise Adoption Patterns

Enterprise metaverse adoption differs significantly from consumer adoption. Rather than pursuing large-scale user engagement, organisations typically adopt immersive technologies in targeted contexts where they deliver clear value.

Common enterprise use cases include:

- Training and skills development through immersive simulations
- Remote collaboration for design and engineering teams
- Operational planning using digital twins
- Safety and risk modelling in hazardous environments

These use cases demonstrate that the metaverse, in enterprise contexts, is less about persistent virtual worlds and more about *contextual immersion* applied to specific problems.

2.5.6 Strategic Implications for Organisations

The rise of enterprise metaverse platforms has important strategic implications. Organisations must evaluate not only technological capabilities but also vendor lock-in, data governance, and long-term interoperability.

Enterprise platforms highlight a divergence within the metaverse ecosystem. While consumer platforms experiment with new forms of social interaction and ownership, enterprise platforms focus on reliability, integration, and measurable outcomes. This divergence suggests that the metaverse will evolve along multiple trajectories rather than converging into a single unified environment.

2.6 ADOPTION FOOTPRINT AND MARKET SIGNALS

Understanding the adoption footprint of metaverse platforms requires moving beyond headline narratives and examining how platforms are actually being used across sectors. Public discourse often conflates speculative investment activity with genuine user engagement, obscuring the distinction between short-term interest and long-term adoption.

Metaverse adoption is uneven across platform types. Consumer-focused gaming platforms exhibit high levels of engagement and sustained usage, while decentralised platforms often display lower user numbers but higher levels of asset-based economic activity. Enterprise platforms, meanwhile, show slower but more deliberate uptake driven by targeted use cases rather than mass participation.

2.6.1 Consumer Adoption Patterns

Consumer adoption of metaverse platforms has been strongest in gaming-led environments. Platforms such as Roblox demonstrate that persistent virtual environments can attract tens of millions of daily users when they are accessible, socially engaging, and supported by robust creator ecosystems.

These platforms benefit from network effects: as more users and creators participate, the value of the platform increases. This dynamic reinforces engagement and encourages continued content creation. However, it also creates concentration risk, with a small number of platforms capturing a disproportionate share of user attention.

Decentralised consumer platforms exhibit a different adoption profile. User numbers tend to be significantly lower, but economic activity per user can be comparatively high due to asset trading and speculative investment. This pattern suggests that decentralised platforms currently function more as experimental ecosystems than as mass-market social environments.

2.6.2 Enterprise Adoption Patterns

Enterprise adoption of metaverse platforms follows a fundamentally different trajectory. Rather than pursuing broad deployment, organisations typically adopt immersive technologies in specific domains where they address identifiable problems.

Training and simulation are among the most common enterprise use cases. Immersive environments enable experiential learning in contexts where real-world training is costly, dangerous, or impractical. Similarly, digital twins are increasingly used for operational planning, allowing organisations to model complex systems and test scenarios before implementation.

Enterprise adoption is often incremental, beginning with pilot projects and expanding as value is demonstrated. This cautious approach reflects the need to integrate immersive technologies into existing systems, governance frameworks, and regulatory environments.

2.6.3 Investment Trends and Capital Allocation

Investment activity provides additional insight into metaverse adoption. Venture capital and corporate investment have flowed disproportionately towards enabling technologies rather than fully realised virtual worlds. These include investments in graphics processing, cloud infrastructure, development tools, and spatial computing.

This pattern suggests that investors view the metaverse as a long-term infrastructural shift rather than an immediately monetisable product category. Funding has also become more selective over time, with greater scrutiny of user engagement metrics and revenue models.

2.6.4 Sector-Specific Signals

Different sectors exhibit varying levels of metaverse engagement. Gaming and entertainment remain the most active sectors, followed by education, architecture, and industrial simulation. Retail and marketing initiatives have generated visibility but often struggle to demonstrate sustained value.

Public-sector adoption remains limited but includes exploratory initiatives in urban planning, training, and public engagement. These projects highlight potential societal applications while also underscoring governance and accessibility challenges.

2.6.5 Interpreting Adoption Signals

Taken together, these adoption patterns suggest that the metaverse is not experiencing uniform growth. Instead, it is evolving unevenly across sectors and platform types. Platforms that align closely with existing user behaviours and organisational needs are more likely to achieve sustained adoption. This nuanced adoption landscape challenges simplistic narratives of rapid metaverse convergence and reinforces the importance of platform-specific analysis.

2.7 SECURITY, PRIVACY, AND GOVERNANCE CHALLENGES

As metaverse platforms mature and attract broader participation, issues of security, privacy, and governance move from peripheral concerns to central determinants of platform viability. The immersive and persistent nature of metaverse environments amplifies risks that are already present in conventional digital platforms while also introducing new forms of exposure linked to embodiment, identity, and economic activity.

A key challenge in analysing metaverse risk lies in avoiding generalisation. Security and governance risks are not uniform across platforms; rather, they are shaped by architectural design choices, governance models, and economic structures. Figure 2.3 illustrates how value is created within metaverse platforms through the interaction between users, creators, platform operators and marketplaces, while also showing why governance, trust and economic control become central to platform viability. As illustrated in Figure 2.4, risk is redistributed rather than

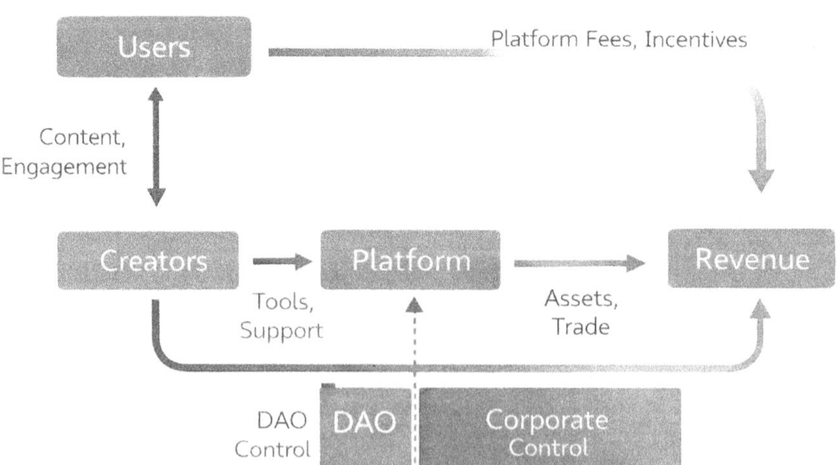

Figure 2.3 Value creation model within metaverse platforms illustrating interactions between users, creators, platforms, and marketplaces.

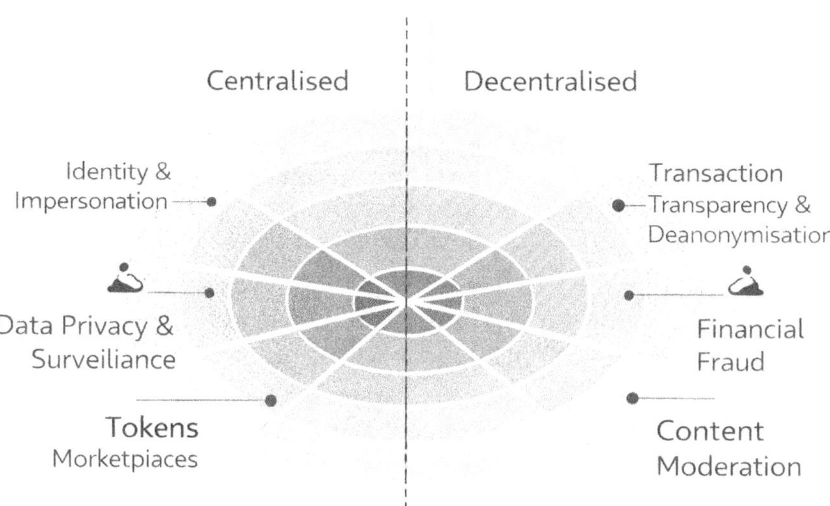

Figure 2.4 Security and governance risk surface across centralised and decentralised Metaverse platforms, highlighting differing privacy, moderation, and financial risk profiles.

eliminated as platforms move along the spectrum from centralised to decentralised governance.

2.7.1 Identity and Authentication Risks

Metaverse platforms rely on persistent digital identities, often represented through avatars. These identities are not merely cosmetic; they mediate access to assets, spaces, and social relationships. As a result, identity compromise can have far-reaching consequences.

In centralised platforms, identity systems are typically account-based and managed by the platform operator. While this enables recovery mechanisms and moderation, it also creates single points of failure. Large-scale data breaches or credential theft can expose millions of users simultaneously.

In decentralised platforms, identity is often tied to cryptographic wallets. While this reduces reliance on central authorities, it shifts responsibility to users. Loss of private keys can result in irreversible loss of assets and identity, with no institutional recourse.

2.7.2 Data privacy and Surveillance

Privacy risks differ substantially between governance models. Centralised platforms collect extensive data on user behaviour, interactions, and sometimes biometric signals. These data sets may be used for analytics, monetisation, or algorithmic optimisation, raising concerns around consent, transparency, and regulatory compliance.

Decentralised platforms, by contrast, reduce central data aggregation but introduce *transaction transparency risks*. Blockchain-based systems record transactions on public ledgers that are persistent and globally accessible. Although identities are pseudonymous, transaction patterns can often be linked to real-world individuals through correlation and off-chain data. This trade-off illustrates a core tension in metaverse privacy: reducing corporate surveillance may increase exposure to long-term, publicly visible data trails.

2.7.3 Content Moderation and Behavioural Governance

Immersive environments intensify the impact of harmful behaviour. Harassment, impersonation, and abuse can feel more immediate and distressing in embodied virtual spaces than in text-based platforms.

Centralised platforms typically implement top-down moderation frameworks, supported by automated tools and human oversight. While this enables consistent enforcement, it also raises concerns around opacity and bias.

Decentralised platforms experiment with community-driven moderation and decentralised autonomous organisations. These approaches align with principles of openness but often struggle with enforcement speed and accountability.

2.7.4 Financial and Economic Risks

The integration of virtual economies introduces financial risk into metaverse environments. In decentralised platforms, exposure to scams, fraudulent tokens, and exploitative smart contracts is significant. Users may lack the expertise required to assess risk, and governance mechanisms for redress are limited.

Even in centralised platforms, economic exploitation can occur through misleading monetisation practices or opaque revenue-sharing arrangements. As virtual economies grow, regulatory scrutiny is likely to increase.

2.7.5 Regulatory and Legal Uncertainty

Metaverse platforms operate across jurisdictions, complicating regulatory compliance. Issues related to data protection, financial regulation, consumer protection, and labour law intersect in novel ways within immersive environments.

Enterprise platforms tend to align more closely with existing regulatory frameworks, while consumer platforms often operate in regulatory grey areas. Over time, regulatory intervention is likely to shape platform design and governance more explicitly.

2.8 PLATFORM COMPARISON AND USE CASE MATRICES

Governance and control mechanisms across platforms are compared in Table 2.3

Comparative analysis provides a structured way to evaluate metaverse platforms beyond individual case studies. Tables and matrices presented earlier summarise key differences across governance, use cases, and adoption patterns. However, these comparisons require interpretation to be meaningful.

2.8.1 Interpreting Governance Differences

Governance models influence not only who controls a platform but also how value is distributed and how risk is managed. Centralised platforms prioritise stability, scalability, and enforceability, making them attractive for enterprise and mass-market use. Decentralised platforms prioritise autonomy and ownership, appealing to users who value control over assets and participation in governance. Neither model is inherently superior. Instead, suitability depends on context, risk tolerance, and strategic objectives.

Table 2.3 Platform Governance and Control

Platform	*Control Type*	*Rule Enforcement*	*Economic Control*	*User Autonomy*
Decentraland	Decentralised	DAO voting	Token-based	Medium–High
The Sandbox	Decentralised	DAO voting	Token-based	Medium–High
Roblox	Centralised	Platform policies	Platform-controlled	Low–Medium
Second Life	Centralised	Platform policies	Platform-controlled	Medium
Microsoft Mesh	Centralised	Enterprise governance	No economy	Low
NVIDIA Omniverse	Centralised	Enterprise governance	No economy	Low

2.8.2 Use Case Alignment

Platforms differ in their alignment with specific use cases. Gaming-led platforms excel at engagement and creativity, enterprise platforms at simulation and collaboration, and decentralised platforms at experimentation with ownership and governance. Attempts to force platforms into unsuitable use cases often result in poor outcomes. For organisations, platform selection should be driven by clearly defined objectives rather than hype-driven expectations.

2.8.3 Interoperability and Fragmentation

A recurring theme in platform comparison is fragmentation. Metaverse platforms are largely siloed, with limited interoperability between assets, identities, and environments. While interoperability is frequently cited as a long-term goal, technical, commercial, and governance barriers remain significant. This fragmentation reinforces the importance of platform-specific strategies and cautions against assumptions of a unified metaverse in the near term. Adoption signals across major metaverse platforms are summarised in Table 2.4.

2.9 SUMMARY AND TRANSITION

This chapter has examined the metaverse through the lens of platforms, grounding the discussion in real systems rather than abstract narratives. By analysing decentralised, centralised, and enterprise platforms, it has highlighted the diversity of approaches currently shaping the metaverse landscape.

The analysis demonstrates that the metaverse is not a single destination but a collection of evolving ecosystems, each reflecting different priorities, trade-offs, and assumptions. While some platforms emphasise ownership and decentralisation, others prioritise scalability, usability, or enterprise integration.

Table 2.4 Adoption Footprint Indicators

Platform	*Adoption Indicator*	*Approximate Scale*
Roblox	Daily Active Users	Tens of millions
Decentraland	Monthly Active Users	Tens of thousands
The Sandbox	Registered Wallets	Hundreds of thousands
Second Life	Active Residents	Stable niche
Microsoft Mesh	Enterprise Pilots	Growing
NVIDIA Omniverse	Industry Adoption	Engineering and simulation

Adoption patterns suggest that meaningful value creation is occurring in targeted contexts rather than through universal virtual worlds. At the same time, unresolved challenges around governance, privacy, and regulation raise questions about long-term sustainability.

These observations set the stage for the next chapter, which moves beyond platform analysis to critically examine the broader metaverse narrative. The following chapter asks whether the metaverse represents a durable transformation of digital interaction or a cyclical wave of technological hype.

BIBLIOGRAPHY

Ball, M. (2022). *The Metaverse: And How It Will Revolutionize Everything*. New York: Liveright Publishing.

Dionisio, J. D. N., Burns, W. G., & Gilbert, R. (2013). 3D virtual worlds and the metaverse: Current status and future possibilities. *ACM Computing Surveys*, 45(3), 1–38.

Dwivedi, Y. K., et al. (2022). Metaverse beyond the hype: Multidisciplinary perspectives on emerging challenges, opportunities, and agenda for research, practice, and policy. *International Journal of Information Management*, 66, 102542.

Lee, L.-H., et al. (2021). All one needs to know about metaverse: A complete survey on technological singularity, virtual ecosystem, and research agenda. *Journal of Latex Class Files*, 14(8).

Meta Platforms, Inc. (2023). *Building the Metaverse Responsibly*. Meta Whitepaper. Meta Platforms, Inc.

NVIDIA Corporation. (2023). *NVIDIA Omniverse Platform Overview*. NVIDIA Technical Documentation. NVIDIA.

Roblox Corporation. (2023). *Roblox Developer and Economy Overview*. Roblox Investor Relations.

Stephenson, N. (1992). *Snow Crash*. New York: Bantam Books.

Zhao, R., Zhou, A., & Wang, J. (2022). Blockchain-enabled metaverse: Architecture, challenges, and open issues. *IEEE Network*, 36(1), 80–86.

Chapter 3

Metaverse – Is It a Hype?

3.1 INTRODUCTION

The idea of the metaverse has captured attention in a way few technologies have in recent years. It has been described as the next phase of the internet, a new digital economy, and a space where physical and virtual life begin to merge. These claims have come not only from technology vendors and start-ups but also from some of the largest corporations in the world, alongside investors, consultants, and policy commentators.

At the same time, there is a growing sense of confusion and frustration around what the metaverse actually is and what it is realistically capable of delivering. For many people, the metaverse feels abstract, inaccessible, or disconnected from everyday needs. High-profile projects have been announced and quietly scaled back. User numbers on some platforms remain low. Headlines that once promised rapid transformation are increasingly replaced by questions about value, cost, and long-term relevance. This gap between promise and reality is what gives rise to the central question of this chapter: *is the metaverse primarily a case of technological hype, or does it represent a genuine transformation that is simply unfolding more slowly and unevenly than expected?*

This question matters because the consequences of getting it wrong are significant. Organisations are making strategic decisions today based on assumptions about the future role of immersive technologies. These decisions include capital investment, platform selection, skills development, and organisational change. If the metaverse is overestimated, resources may be misallocated and opportunities missed elsewhere. If it is underestimated, organisations risk falling behind competitors who learn how to use these technologies effectively.

The term "hype" is often misunderstood. In this chapter, hype does not imply deception or bad faith. Instead, it refers to a familiar pattern in technology adoption where expectations accelerate faster than practical capability, usability, or organisational readiness. Many transformative

DOI: 10.1201/9781003405566-3

technologies have followed this pattern. The internet itself, cloud computing, and artificial intelligence all went through periods where claims exceeded reality, before settling into more grounded and productive roles.

The metaverse sits squarely within this tradition. It combines several existing technologies – three-dimensional graphics, networking, simulation, identity systems, and digital economies – rather than introducing a single breakthrough. This combination creates both opportunity and complexity. It also makes it harder to assess progress, because success depends on multiple components advancing together.

Another reason the hype question is difficult is that the metaverse does not have a single form. As shown in earlier chapters, it exists across a spectrum of platforms and use cases. A virtual factory simulation, a training environment for surgeons, a multiplayer game world, and a branded virtual shopping experience are all described as "metaverse" initiatives, despite having little in common beyond shared terminology. This diversity makes sweeping judgements misleading.

For this reason, this chapter does not attempt to answer whether the metaverse will succeed or fail in general. Instead, it asks a more practical set of questions. Where is the metaverse already being used in meaningful ways? Which sectors are seeing real benefits? Where does adoption stall, and why? What kinds of value are being created, and for whom?

The focus throughout is on *evidence rather than aspiration*. This includes observable adoption patterns, organisational behaviour, investment trends, and practical outcomes. Marketing narratives and speculative forecasts are treated cautiously not because they are irrelevant but because they often reflect intent rather than reality.

This chapter also deliberately avoids treating the metaverse as an inevitable future. Technology does not succeed simply because it exists or because influential actors promote it. It succeeds when it aligns with human behaviour, organisational incentives, and economic constraints. The metaverse must therefore be assessed in the same way as any other major technology: through what it enables, what it costs, and what it replaces or improves.

By the end of this chapter, the aim is to arrive at a balanced and grounded assessment. In some contexts, the metaverse is already proving its worth. In others, it remains more promise than practice. Recognising this distinction is essential for making sensible decisions about adoption, regulation, and long-term strategy.

Figure 3.1 provides a conceptual reference point for this chapter, illustrating how metaverse expectations accelerated ahead of practical adoption. This framing supports the subsequent sector-level and market analysis.

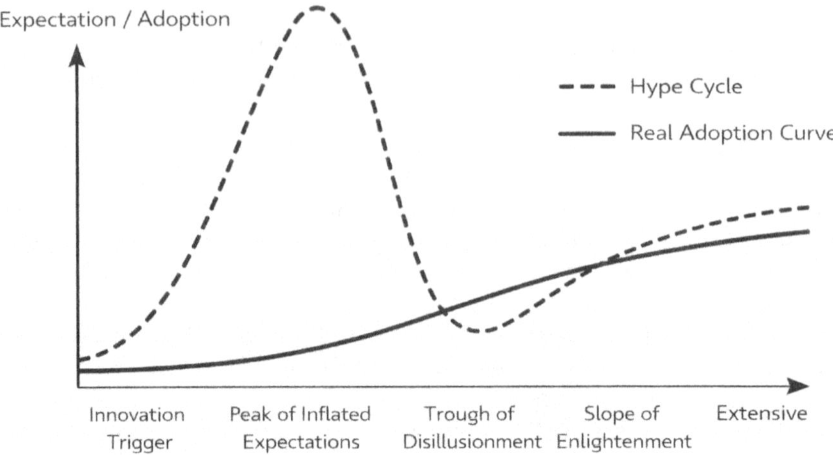

Figure 3.1 Technology hype versus real adoption curve.

Note:Technology hype versus real adoption curve illustrating the divergence between early expectations and sustained organisational use of metaverse technologies.

3.2 METAVERSE FOOTPRINT ACROSS INDUSTRY SECTORS

Assessing whether the metaverse represents hype or transformation requires a grounded examination of how it is being adopted across different industry sectors. Broad claims about disruption obscure the reality that industries differ widely in their structures, incentives, regulatory constraints, and tolerance for experimentation. As a result, the metaverse footprint is neither uniform nor linear.

This section examines sector adoption in depth not by listing examples but by analysing *why adoption occurs*, *where it stabilises*, and *where it fails to progress*. The focus is on real organisational behaviour rather than promotional narratives.

3.2.1 Financial Services

Financial services is often cited as a sector ripe for digital innovation, yet its metaverse footprint remains limited and cautious. This is not due to lack of technological capability but rather due to the nature of financial institutions themselves. Banks, insurers, and asset managers operate in highly regulated environments where trust, data security, and reliability are paramount.

Historically, financial services adopt new technologies selectively and incrementally. Core banking systems, payment infrastructure, and risk platforms evolve slowly because failures carry systemic consequences. This historical pattern strongly shapes how the metaverse is approached.

Most metaverse activity in this sector is internal. Immersive environments are used for staff training, leadership development, and behavioural simulation. These use cases build on existing digital learning platforms, adding realism rather than redefining delivery models. For example, relationship managers may practise complex customer conversations, or compliance teams may rehearse crisis scenarios in controlled virtual environments.

Customer-facing applications have attracted attention but little sustained use. Virtual branches and branded environments generate curiosity, but customers continue to prioritise speed, convenience, and security through established digital channels. In practice, the metaverse does not solve a pressing customer problem in this sector.

The financial services footprint therefore reflects *containment rather than expansion*. Adoption is deliberate, low-risk, and tied to internal efficiency rather than external transformation. This pattern suggests that, for this sector, the metaverse is an enhancement tool rather than a disruptive force.

3.2.2 Manufacturing and Industrial Sectors

Manufacturing and industrial sectors present a very different picture. Here, the metaverse footprint is deeper, more stable, and closely tied to operational value. These industries deal with complex physical systems, long asset lifecycles, and high costs of error. As a result, tools that improve planning, simulation, and coordination have immediate appeal.

The use of digital twins is central to adoption. Virtual replicas of factories, equipment, and supply chains allow organisations to simulate changes before committing resources. Engineers can test layouts, workflows, and maintenance strategies without disrupting live operations.

This approach aligns well with existing industrial practices. Manufacturing has long relied on modelling and simulation; immersive environments simply extend these capabilities. Collaboration is improved when geographically distributed teams can explore the same virtual space and resolve issues visually.

Importantly, adoption in this sector is not driven by the idea of a shared virtual world. It is driven by cost reduction, safety, and productivity. The metaverse here functions as *invisible infrastructure*, embedded into everyday decision-making rather than showcased as innovation. This depth of integration explains why industrial use cases are among the strongest indicators that parts of the metaverse are delivering real value.

3.2.3 Retail and Consumer Industries

Retail and consumer industries have been among the most visible adopters of metaverse concepts, particularly in marketing and brand engagement. Virtual stores, digital fashion, and immersive brand experiences have been widely promoted as evidence of transformation.

However, visibility masks fragility. Retail operates on thin margins, high volume, and convenience. Any new channel must compete with highly optimised e-commerce platforms and physical stores. In this context, immersive experiences struggle to justify their cost unless they clearly improve conversion or customer understanding.

Many metaverse retail initiatives function as campaigns rather than channels. They generate media attention, social engagement, and limited digital sales but rarely integrate into core retail operations. Once novelty fades, sustained customer participation is difficult to maintain.

This does not mean the metaverse has no role in retail. For high-value or complex products, immersive visualisation can improve decision-making. However, these are niche applications rather than mass-market solutions.

The retail footprint therefore illustrates a common pattern: *experimentation without consolidation.* The metaverse is explored but rarely embedded.

3.2.4 Education and Professional Training

Education is frequently cited as a natural application for immersive technologies, and there is substance behind this claim. Learning benefits from experience, repetition, and visualisation, particularly in technical or practical subjects.

Professional training shows the clearest adoption. Industries such as healthcare, engineering, aviation, and energy use immersive simulations to train staff safely and efficiently. These environments reduce reliance on physical equipment and allow consistent training across locations.

Formal education presents a more complex picture. While immersive environments can enrich learning, large-scale adoption faces barriers related to cost, infrastructure, accessibility, and curriculum integration. Schools and universities must balance innovation against inclusivity and resource constraints.

As a result, the metaverse footprint in education is *selective and uneven.* Where it aligns with clear learning objectives and institutional capacity, adoption progresses. Where it does not, initiatives remain isolated.

3.2.5 Healthcare

Healthcare adoption of metaverse-related technologies is pragmatic and evidence-driven. VR has established roles in surgical training, rehabilitation, pain management, and mental health therapy. These applications are evaluated through clinical outcomes rather than novelty.

The broader idea of persistent virtual environments is less relevant in clinical contexts. Healthcare prioritises safety, reliability, and regulatory compliance. Technologies are adopted only when they demonstrate clear benefit and minimal risk.

This cautious but effective adoption pattern reinforces an important point: transformation does not require spectacle. In healthcare, the metaverse footprint is narrow but credible, focused on well-defined problems.

3.2.6 Media, Entertainment, and Cultural Sectors

Media and entertainment are often positioned as the natural home of the metaverse. Virtual concerts, social worlds, and interactive storytelling align well with audience expectations and creative exploration.

Some initiatives have achieved significant scale, particularly when they build on existing fan bases. However, sustaining engagement remains challenging. Users are selective about how much time they spend in immersive environments, and competition for attention is intense.

The entertainment footprint demonstrates both opportunity and limitation. Immersive experiences can be compelling, but they must compete on content quality rather than technological novelty alone.

3.2.7 Public Sector and Government

Public-sector adoption of the metaverse is emerging slowly. Use cases include urban planning visualisation, emergency response training, and stakeholder engagement. These applications benefit from immersive representation of complex systems.

However, public-sector constraints around procurement, governance, and budget limit scale. Adoption tends to remain at pilot level, driven by specific needs rather than broad strategy.

3.2.7.1 Cross-Sector Synthesis

Across all sectors, a consistent pattern emerges. The metaverse gains traction where it addresses *specific, high-value problems* and integrates with existing practices. It stalls where it is introduced as a general-purpose innovation without a clear purpose.

This uneven footprint does not indicate failure. It indicates selectivity. The metaverse is not transforming all sectors equally, nor should it be expected to. Its value is contextual, not universal.

Understanding this distinction is essential for separating hype from substance. Table 3.1 summarises the metaverse footprint across industry sectors, highlighting variations in use cases, adoption levels, realised value, and key constraints.

As illustrated in Figure 3.2, the adoption of metaverse technologies is highly uneven across sectors, with manufacturing and industrial use cases demonstrating deeper integration than consumer-facing domains.

Table 3.1 Metaverse Footprint across Industry Sectors

Sector	*Primary Use Cases*	*Level of Adoption*	*Value Realised*	*Key Constraints*
Financial Services	Training, behavioural simulation	Low to Moderate	Internal efficiency	Regulation, data risk
Manufacturing	Digital twins, simulation, design	High	Cost reduction, productivity	Integration complexity
Retail and Consumer	Brand engagement, visualisation	Low	Marketing visibility	Low repeat engagement
Education and Training	Simulation-based learning	Moderate	Skill retention	Cost, accessibility
Healthcare	Clinical training, therapy	Targeted	Outcome improvement	Regulation, evidence
Media and Entertainment	Events, social worlds	Moderate	Engagement spikes	Sustainability
Public Sector	Planning, emergency training	Low	Scenario understanding	Budget, procurement

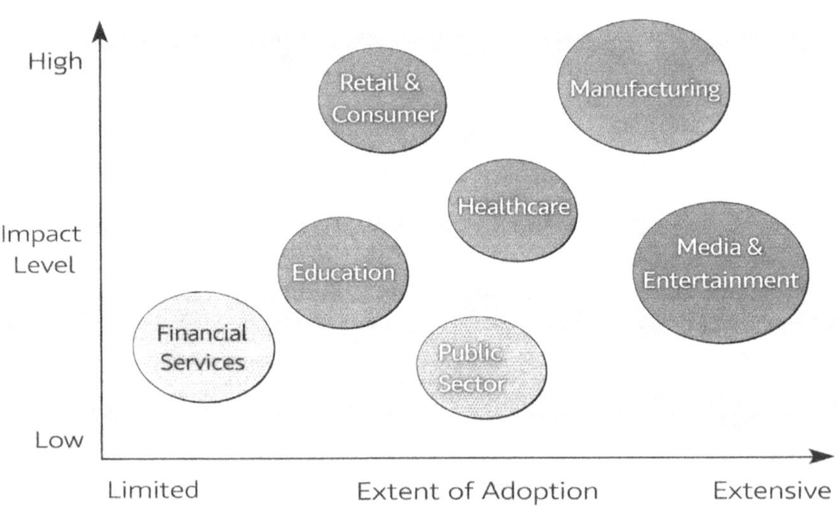

Figure 3.2 Comparative footprint of Metaverse adoption across industry sectors, highlighting variations in maturity, value realisation, and integration depth.

3.3 MARKET VALUE POSITIONING AND ADOPTION SIGNALS

Discussions about the metaverse are frequently framed in terms of market size. Industry reports, consultancy papers, and investment briefings regularly project valuations running into hundreds of billions or even trillions of dollars. These figures are often accompanied by optimistic timelines suggesting rapid adoption across consumer and enterprise domains. While such projections attract attention, they provide limited insight into whether value is actually being created.

Market value is not determined by forecasts or narratives. It is determined by sustained adoption, repeat usage, integration into organisational processes, and the willingness of customers to pay over time. For this reason, evaluating the metaverse requires a shift away from headline numbers and towards *adoption signals* that reflect real behaviour. This section examines how the metaverse is currently positioned in value terms, how adoption signals differ from hype signals, and what these patterns reveal about the likely trajectory of metaverse-related markets.

3.3.1 Market Value versus Market Narrative

Early metaverse narratives positioned the technology as a successor to the internet itself. This framing implied a broad, consumer-led transformation in which social interaction, commerce, entertainment, and work would converge in persistent virtual environments. Market value estimates were therefore constructed on the assumption of mass participation and network effects.

As adoption failed to materialise at the expected pace, this narrative began to fragment. Instead of a single unified market, the metaverse increasingly appears as a collection of overlapping but distinct markets, each with different value drivers. Consumer platforms, enterprise tools, simulation environments, and enabling infrastructure operate under different economic logics.

This fragmentation matters because it undermines the validity of aggregate market size claims. A trillion-dollar figure obscures the fact that value may accrue slowly and unevenly across multiple domains rather than explosively in one.

3.3.2 Investment Behaviour as a Leading Indicator

Investment patterns provide one of the clearest signals of how the metaverse is being re-evaluated. In the initial phase, capital flowed heavily into consumer-facing platforms, virtual land projects, and token-based ecosystems. These investments were often speculative, driven by expectations of rapid user growth and secondary market activity.

Over time, investor behaviour has shifted. Funding has increasingly moved towards enabling technologies such as graphics processing units, simulation software, development frameworks, and enterprise collaboration platforms. These investments are less visible to the public but more closely aligned with long-term value creation.

Corporate investment follows a similar pattern. Organisations are more willing to allocate capital to immersive technologies when they can be linked directly to productivity, risk reduction, or operational improvement. Projects framed primarily as brand experiments or innovation signals struggle to secure ongoing funding.

This shift suggests a recalibration of expectations rather than abandonment. Investors are not rejecting the metaverse outright; they are narrowing their focus to areas where value is more defensible.

3.3.3 Pilot Activity versus Embedded Adoption

One of the most important distinctions in assessing market value is the difference between pilot activity and embedded adoption. Many organisations run metaverse pilots funded by innovation budgets, research teams, or marketing departments. These pilots generate insight and publicity, but they do not necessarily indicate long-term commitment.

Embedded adoption, by contrast, involves structural change. It requires integration with existing systems, modification of workflows, and allocation of operational budgets. It also involves accountability, as outcomes must be measured and justified.

Across sectors, embedded adoption remains limited. Where it occurs, it is usually confined to specific functions, such as training, design, or simulation. This pattern suggests that while the metaverse can deliver value, its scope is narrower than early narratives implied. Table 3.2 contrasts common market value claims about the metaverse with the observed realities of adoption, user behaviour, monetisation, and enterprise demand.

Figure 3.3 further illustrates the gap between headline market value claims and realised value in practice.

Table 3.2 Market Value Claims versus Observed Adoption

Dimension	*Common Market Claims*	*Observed Reality*
Market Size	Trillion-dollar economy	Fragmented sub-markets
Adoption Speed	Rapid mass adoption	Slow, sector-specific
User Behaviour	Persistent daily usage	Episodic, task-driven
Revenue Models	Virtual goods at scale	Inconsistent monetisation
Enterprise Demand	Platform replacement	Tool augmentation

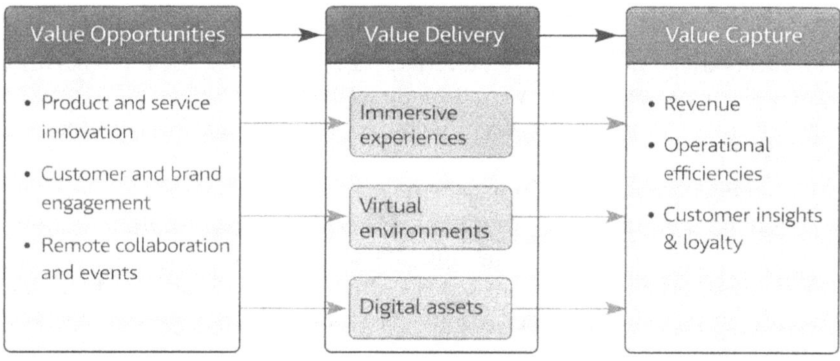

Figure 3.3 Market value claims versus realised value.

Note: This figure reinforces the distinction between headline market forecasts and observable adoption behaviour discussed in this section.

3.3.3.1 Revenue Generation and Monetisation Constraints

Revenue generation remains a significant challenge for many metaverse initiatives. Consumer platforms often rely on virtual goods, subscriptions, or advertising, but user willingness to pay is inconsistent. Revenue spikes driven by novelty or speculation are difficult to sustain.

Enterprise monetisation presents different challenges. While organisations may be willing to pay for immersive tools that deliver clear benefits, procurement cycles are slow and expectations are high. Vendors must demonstrate reliability, security, interoperability, and long-term support.

These constraints explain why revenue growth has lagged behind early projections. They also highlight the difference between *potential value* and *realised value.*

3.3.3.2 Adoption Signals That Matter

To assess whether market value is being created, it is necessary to focus on adoption signals that reflect sustained use rather than initial interest. These include repeat usage, expansion of scope, integration into core processes, and budget continuity.

When evaluated against these criteria, the metaverse shows uneven but genuine progress. In industrial and training contexts, adoption signals are relatively strong. In consumer and social contexts, hype signals often dominate without corresponding behavioural change. This imbalance reinforces the need for sector-specific analysis rather than generalised conclusions.

3.3.3.3 *Repositioning the Metaverse in Value Terms*

The cumulative effect of these patterns is a repositioning of the metaverse in market discourse. Rather than a single transformative wave, it is increasingly understood as a portfolio of technologies with varying maturity and applicability.

This repositioning does not negate the metaverse's potential. It places that potential on a more realistic footing. Value is likely to accrue incrementally, driven by specific use cases rather than broad adoption.

For organisations and policymakers, this implies a need for discipline. Decisions should be grounded in observed behaviour and measurable outcomes, not in speculative projections.

3.3.3.4 *Implications for Long-Term Market Development*

The metaverse's long-term market value will depend on its ability to move from experimentation to integration. This transition requires not only technological improvement but also organisational learning, cultural acceptance, and regulatory clarity.

Markets that succeed in this transition will likely do so quietly, without the dramatic narratives that characterised the early hype phase. In this sense, the future of the metaverse may be less visible but more substantial than its past promotion suggests. Table 3.3 distinguishes pilot activity from embedded adoption across funding, time horizon, integration, and accountability.

3.4 METAVERSE FOR REAL BUSINESS PROBLEMS

One of the most effective ways to move beyond hype is to examine whether the metaverse addresses real business problems that organisations already recognise and are actively trying to solve. Technologies that succeed at scale rarely create new problems to justify themselves. Instead, they reduce friction, cost, or risk in areas where existing approaches are inadequate.

When examined through this lens, the metaverse does not appear as a single solution but as a set of capabilities that can be applied to specific problem classes. Where these problem classes are well defined, immersive

Table 3.3 Pilot Activity versus Embedded Adoption

Dimension	*Pilot Activity*	*Embedded Adoption*
Funding Source	Innovation budgets	Operational budgets
Time Horizon	Short-term	Long-term
Integration	Standalone	System-integrated
Accountability	Experimental	Measured outcomes

technologies can deliver meaningful value. Where they are vague or aspirational, outcomes tend to disappoint. This section analyses the metaverse through the problems it attempts to solve, rather than through the platforms that promote it.

3.4.1 Operational Complexity and Decision-Making

Many organisations operate in environments characterised by high complexity. Physical layouts, interconnected processes, and dynamic constraints make it difficult to understand how changes in one area affect outcomes elsewhere. Traditional tools, such as spreadsheets and two-dimensional diagrams, struggle to represent these relationships effectively.

Immersive environments offer a different approach. By representing systems spatially, they allow decision-makers to see relationships, bottlenecks, and dependencies more clearly. This is particularly valuable in operations such as manufacturing, logistics, healthcare facilities, and transport networks.

In these contexts, the metaverse does not replace existing analytics or planning tools. It complements them by providing a shared visual and experiential layer. Teams can explore scenarios together, discuss trade-offs, and align understanding before changes are implemented. The value lies in better decisions made earlier, rather than in the immersive experience itself. Table 3.4 identifies the main classes of business problems addressed by the metaverse, linking traditional limitations with the specific contributions of immersive and spatial technologies.

Figure 3.4 summarises the problem-led adoption model outlined in this section, demonstrating how value emerges when immersive technologies are applied selectively.

3.4.2 Training, Skills Transfer, and Workforce Readiness

Training remains one of the most consistent and defensible applications of immersive technologies. Many industries face persistent challenges related to skills shortages, ageing workforces, and the cost of hands-on training. In

Table 3.4 Business Problem Classes Addressed by the Metaverse

Business Problem	*Traditional Limitation*	*Metaverse Contribution*
Complex training	Risk, cost	Safe repetition
Design errors	Late discovery	Early visual validation
Operational planning	Abstract models	Spatial simulation
Emergency response	Tabletop limits	Experiential rehearsal
Remote collaboration	Context loss	Shared spatial context

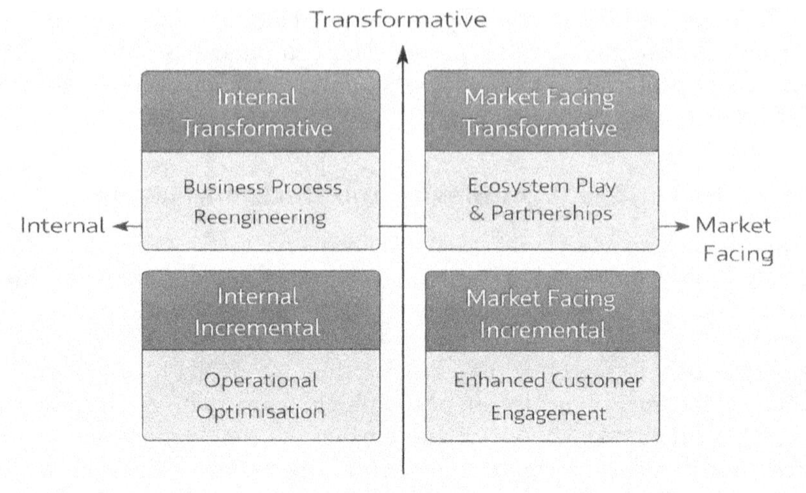

Figure 3.4 Business problem–solution mapping

some cases, training opportunities are limited by safety concerns or availability of equipment.

Virtual training environments allow employees to practise tasks repeatedly without real-world consequences. This is particularly important in safety-critical roles, where mistakes can be costly or dangerous. Learners can experience realistic scenarios, receive feedback, and build confidence before performing tasks in live environments.

From a business perspective, the value of this approach lies in reduced training time, improved retention, and lower incident rates. These outcomes can be measured, making it easier to justify investment. Importantly, successful training applications treat the metaverse as a tool, not as a destination. Learners enter immersive environments for specific purposes and leave when those purposes are fulfilled.

3.4.3 Design, Engineering, and Product Development

Design and engineering problems often involve translating abstract requirements into physical outcomes. Misunderstandings at early stages can lead to costly rework later. Traditional design tools are powerful, but they can obscure spatial relationships and experiential factors.

Immersive environments allow teams to interact with designs at scale. Engineers, designers, and stakeholders can explore products, buildings, or infrastructure in three dimensions, identifying issues that might not be apparent in drawings or models.

This capability is particularly valuable when multiple disciplines must collaborate. Visualising designs together reduces miscommunication and accelerates consensus. The business value lies in fewer late-stage changes, faster decision-making, and improved alignment across teams.

3.4.4 Risk Management and Scenario Planning

Many organisations face risks that are difficult to rehearse in the real world. These include emergency response, system failures, and rare but high-impact events. Traditional tabletop exercises provide limited realism and engagement.

Immersive simulations allow organisations to rehearse scenarios in controlled environments that approximate real conditions. Participants can experience stress, uncertainty, and time pressure, revealing weaknesses in procedures or coordination.

The metaverse's value here lies in preparedness rather than prevention. By exposing vulnerabilities before incidents occur, organisations improve resilience. This application aligns particularly well with sectors such as energy, healthcare, transport, and public safety.

3.4.5 Customer Understanding and Complex Decision Support

In some cases, the metaverse helps customers make complex decisions. This is most relevant for high-value or bespoke products, where understanding spatial or experiential aspects matters. Examples include property, infrastructure, and specialised equipment.

Immersive visualisation allows customers to explore options, compare alternatives, and understand implications more clearly than static representations. Where successful, this reduces uncertainty and increases confidence.

However, this use case has clear limits. For everyday consumer decisions, the additional effort required to engage with immersive environments often outweighs perceived benefits. As a result, customer-facing applications must be targeted carefully.

3.4.6 Collaboration across Distance and Disciplines

Remote collaboration is frequently cited as a justification for the metaverse. While conventional videoconferencing tools are effective for many tasks, they struggle to support collaboration around complex spatial artefacts.

Immersive environments provide a shared sense of presence and spatial reference. Teams can gather around virtual objects, point to features, and manipulate representations together. This is particularly valuable for design reviews, planning sessions, and technical discussions.

The business value here depends on context. For routine meetings, immersive environments add little. For tasks involving spatial reasoning or complex artefacts, they can improve efficiency and understanding.

3.4.7 Where the Metaverse Does not Help

Equally important is recognising where the metaverse does not solve meaningful problems. Many roles do not benefit from immersion, and many tasks are better served by simple, familiar tools. Forcing immersive solutions onto unsuitable problems leads to frustration and disengagement.

Successful organisations are selective. They deploy immersive technologies where they add value and avoid them where they do not. This selectivity is a key indicator of maturity.

3.4.8 Synthesis: Problem-Led, not Platform-Led Adoption

Across all problem classes, a consistent pattern emerges. The metaverse delivers value when adoption is *problem-led rather than platform-led*. Organisations that begin with a clear understanding of their challenges are more likely to use immersive technologies effectively.

Conversely, organisations that adopt metaverse platforms without a clear purpose often struggle to sustain momentum. The technology becomes an experiment rather than a solution.

This distinction is central to separating hype from transformation. The metaverse is not transformative because it exists. It becomes transformative only when it addresses real problems better than existing alternatives.

3.5 WHERE METAVERSE ADOPTION FAILS OR STALLS

While parts of the metaverse demonstrate real and defensible value, a significant proportion of initiatives fail to progress beyond early experimentation. Understanding where and why adoption stalls is critical to evaluating whether the metaverse is over-hyped or simply uneven in its development.

Failure is rarely caused by a single factor. Instead, adoption stalls at the intersection of technology limitations, human behaviour, organisational structure, and economic reality. These constraints are often underplayed in early narratives, which focus on capability rather than context.

3.5.1 Usability and Human Limits

One of the most persistent barriers to adoption is usability. Immersive technologies demand more from users than conventional digital tools. They require physical engagement, spatial awareness, and sustained attention. For many users, this creates friction rather than efficiency.

Extended use of immersive environments can cause fatigue, discomfort, or disorientation. Even when hardware improves, these human limits remain relevant. Tasks that are quick and efficient on a laptop or mobile device often become slower in immersive settings.

This mismatch between task requirements and interaction models leads to selective usage. Users engage when immersion adds value and disengage when it does not. Many metaverse initiatives fail because they attempt to force immersion into contexts where it is unnecessary.

3.5.2 Cost and Sustainability Challenges

Cost is another major constraint. Developing immersive environments requires specialised skills, software, and hardware. Maintaining these environments over time adds further expense, particularly when content must be updated to remain relevant.

For organisations operating under budget pressure, immersive initiatives are vulnerable to reprioritisation. Projects that cannot demonstrate clear return on investment are often among the first to be scaled back. This is particularly true when economic conditions tighten.

The result is a pattern of enthusiastic launch followed by gradual decline. Without sustained funding and clear ownership, many initiatives fade quietly rather than failing visibly.

3.5.3 Organisational Resistance and Culture

Adoption also stalls due to organisational culture. Not all employees are comfortable with immersive technologies, particularly in professional settings. Concerns about appearance, privacy, and perceived seriousness influence willingness to participate.

Resistance is often passive rather than active. Users comply initially but revert to familiar tools over time. Without strong alignment between leadership intent and day-to-day practice, immersive initiatives struggle to gain traction.

Change management is therefore as important as technical capability. Organisations that underestimate this dimension often misinterpret stalled adoption as a technology problem rather than a cultural one.

3.5.4 Fragmentation and Uncertainty

The fragmented nature of the metaverse ecosystem further complicates adoption. Platforms are rarely interoperable, and standards remain immature. Organisations worry about investing in technologies that may not integrate with future systems or that may become obsolete.

This uncertainty encourages caution. Instead of committing fully, organisations run pilots and wait. While prudent, this approach slows progress and reinforces perceptions that the metaverse is perpetually experimental.

Taken together, these factors explain why many metaverse initiatives stall. They do not imply that the technology lacks potential, but they do challenge narratives of rapid, universal adoption. Table 3.5 summarises the main reasons for adoption failure, linking each failure category to its underlying cause and typical outcome.

As shown in Figure 3.5, adoption failure is typically cumulative rather than sudden, with multiple factors interacting over time.

3.6 SEPARATING HYPE METRICS FROM BUSINESS METRICS

A central reason the metaverse debate remains polarised is the misuse of metrics. Success is often measured using indicators that reflect attention

Table 3.5 Reasons for Adoption Failure

Failure Category	*Description*	*Typical Outcome*
Usability	Fatigue, discomfort	Low repeat usage
Cost	High build and upkeep	Budget withdrawal
Culture	Employee resistance	Passive abandonment
Fragmentation	Platform uncertainty	Pilot stagnation

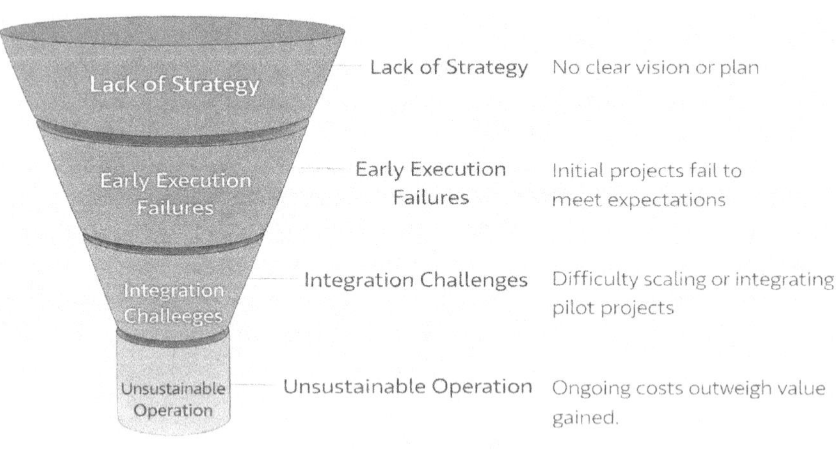

Figure 3.5 Adoption failure funnel.

Note: Adoption failure funnel showing how usability constraints, cost pressures, cultural resistance, and platform fragmentation progressively reduce sustained metaverse adoption.

rather than value. This conflation fuels hype and obscures meaningful assessment.

3.6.1 Hype-Driven Metrics

Hype metrics are designed to signal momentum. They include user registrations, virtual land sales, event attendance, media coverage, and social media engagement. While these indicators capture interest, they provide little insight into sustainability or impact.

Many metaverse initiatives show strong hype metrics early on, followed by rapid decline. This pattern reflects curiosity rather than commitment. When novelty fades, engagement drops, revealing the weakness of these measures.

3.6.2 Business-Relevant Metrics

Business metrics focus on outcomes. They include productivity improvements, cost savings, error reduction, training effectiveness, and operational resilience. These metrics are harder to measure but more meaningful.

When metaverse initiatives are evaluated against business metrics, results are mixed. In some contexts, particularly training and simulation, benefits are clear. In others, gains are marginal or difficult to isolate.

This divergence highlights the importance of aligning metrics with purpose. Initiatives framed around business problems are more likely to succeed than those driven by abstract engagement goals.

3.6.3 The Danger of Misalignment

Misaligned metrics create distorted incentives. Teams may optimise for visibility rather than value, leading to impressive demonstrations that fail to translate into impact. Over time, this undermines credibility and reinforces scepticism.

Separating hype metrics from business metrics is therefore essential for rational decision-making. Without this distinction, organisations risk mistaking attention for achievement. Table 3.6 distinguishes hype metrics from business metrics, showing that attention-based indicators are weak signals of value compared with operational and strategic measures.

Table 3.6 Hype Metrics versus Business Metrics

Metric Type	*Examples*
Hype Metrics	User sign-ups, land sales
Engagement Metrics	Event attendance
Business Metrics	Productivity, cost
Strategic Metrics	Integration, retention

3.7 INTERIM ASSESSMENT: IS THE METAVERSE OVER-PROMISED?

At this stage, it is reasonable to conclude that the metaverse has been over-promised in its most ambitious forms. Claims that it would rapidly replace existing digital platforms, transform everyday work, or become a dominant social environment have not materialised.

However, over-promise should not be confused with failure. Many transformative technologies experience similar trajectories. Early narratives overshoot reality, leading to disappointment before more grounded applications emerge.

The metaverse today is best understood as a set of evolving capabilities rather than a finished product. Its impact is incremental, context-dependent, and uneven. In this sense, it resembles earlier technology waves that eventually found stable roles after periods of exaggerated expectation.

This assessment suggests recalibration rather than rejection. The metaverse is not disappearing, but it is becoming more narrowly defined and practically oriented.

3.8 SECTOR-BY-SECTOR READINESS AND MATURITY ASSESSMENT

Readiness for metaverse adoption varies widely across sectors. This variation reflects differences in operational complexity, regulatory pressure, cultural norms, and economic incentives.

Sectors such as manufacturing, engineering, and professional training exhibit higher readiness. They face clear problems that immersive technologies can address and possess the technical maturity to integrate new tools.

Other sectors, including retail and consumer services, face lower readiness due to cost sensitivity, user behaviour, and limited differentiation. In these contexts, adoption remains selective.

Assessing readiness requires moving beyond enthusiasm to evaluate organisational capability, leadership commitment, and integration potential. Without these foundations, adoption efforts are unlikely to mature. As shown in Table 3.7, sector readiness for the metaverse is uneven, with some industries demonstrating greater maturity and clearer use-case alignment than others.

Figure 3.6 provides a visual synthesis of sector readiness, reinforcing the argument that metaverse value is highly context-dependent.

3.9 CONCLUSION: A CALIBRATED VIEW OF THE METAVERSE

The evidence presented in this chapter supports a balanced conclusion. The metaverse is neither an empty hype cycle nor an imminent revolution. It is a complex and evolving set of technologies whose value depends on how they are applied.

Table 3.7 Sector Readiness and Maturity Matrix

Sector	*Readiness Level*	*Maturity*
Manufacturing	High	Mature
Healthcare	Moderate	Targeted
Education	Moderate	Fragmented
Retail	Low	Experimental
Finance	Low	Controlled

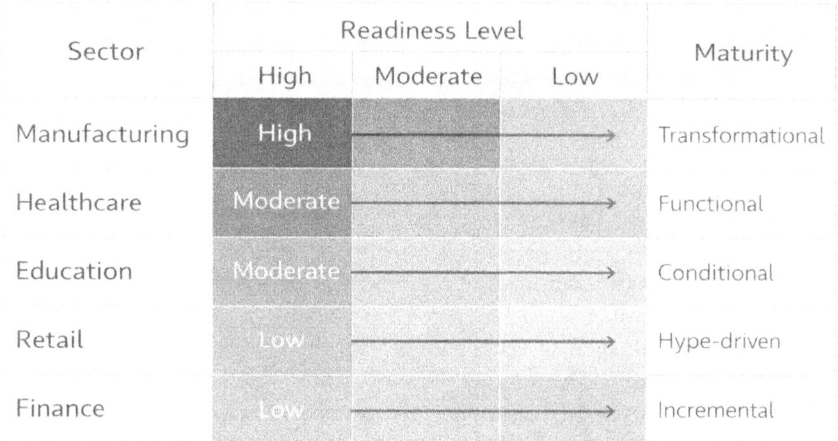

Figure 3.6 Sector readiness heatmap.

Note: Sector readiness heatmap illustrating relative preparedness and maturity levels for metaverse adoption across major industries.

Where the metaverse addresses real problems and aligns with organisational needs, it delivers tangible benefits. Where it is pursued for its own sake, it struggles to sustain momentum.

A calibrated view recognises both realities. It avoids sweeping claims and instead focuses on context, capability, and purpose. For organisations, the challenge is not whether to engage with the metaverse but how to do so selectively and responsibly.

BIBLIOGRAPHY

Dionisio, J. D. N., Burns, W. G., & Gilbert, R. (2013). 3D virtual worlds and the metaverse: Current status and future possibilities. *ACM Computing Surveys*, 45(3), 1–38.

Gartner. (2022). *Hype Cycle for Emerging Technologies*. Gartner Research.

McKinsey & Company. (2023). *The Business Case for the Metaverse*. McKinsey & Company.

PwC. (2022). *Seeing Is Believing: The Economic Impact of the Metaverse*. PwC.

Chapter 4

Metaverse – Is It a Hoax?

4.1 INTRODUCTION: WHY THE HOAX QUESTION EXISTS

The question "Is the metaverse a hoax?" did not arise because immersive technologies were exposed as fictional or fraudulent. Instead, it emerged because the distance between expectation and lived reality became too large to ignore. The word *hoax* reflects frustration, disappointment, and a breakdown of trust rather than a technical verdict on the existence or feasibility of immersive systems.

During the peak of metaverse enthusiasm, the concept was framed as an inevitable successor to the internet. Organisations were encouraged to believe that virtual worlds would soon become dominant environments for work, commerce, education, and social interaction. This framing created urgency and competitive anxiety. It also discouraged critical evaluation. Many organisations committed to metaverse initiatives before they had defined concrete objectives, understood technical and organisational constraints, or assessed whether immersive technologies were suitable for the problems they were trying to solve.

When early initiatives failed to produce visible or sustained value, the narrative shifted rapidly. What had been presented as transformative was now dismissed as empty hype. This abrupt reversal contributed significantly to the hoax label. Technologies that are genuinely deceptive tend to collapse suddenly when exposed. The metaverse did not collapse in this way. Instead, it stalled, fragmented, and lost momentum as attention moved elsewhere.

A key reason for this perception is that the metaverse is not a single technology or platform. It is an umbrella term that encompasses immersive interfaces, real-time three-dimensional environments, spatial computing, digital twins, virtual economies, and new models of social interaction. Treating this broad collection as a single product led to unrealistic expectations. Failures in one area were interpreted as evidence that the entire concept was flawed.

The hoax narrative also gained strength because high-profile investments did not translate into equally visible adoption. Corporate rebrands, public announcements, and large capital expenditures created the impression of imminent change. In practice, most users experienced little difference in their daily digital lives. Without tangible and repeatable benefits, trust eroded quickly.

 DOI: 10.1201/9781003405566-4

This chapter does not attempt to defend the metaverse uncritically, nor does it dismiss it outright. Instead, it explains why the hoax question exists and why it persists. The argument developed here is that the metaverse appears fraudulent when three conditions occur simultaneously. First, when organisations lack the educational and capability foundations required to apply immersive technology effectively. Second, when technological immaturity limits usability, scalability, and safety. Third, when immersive systems are applied to problems that do not benefit from immersion.

These conditions reinforce one another. Educational gaps lead to poor design and decision-making. Technology gaps magnify those mistakes. Misaligned use cases ensure that even well-engineered systems fail to deliver value. When these failures accumulate, scepticism hardens into outright dismissal.

The purpose of this chapter is diagnostic rather than promotional. It provides a structured explanation of how the hoax narrative emerged and why it is misleading. By unpacking the root causes, this chapter equips the reader to evaluate metaverse claims more critically and to distinguish between premature application and genuine lack of value.

This chapter first examines educational and capability gaps, then analyses technology gaps and immaturity, and finally explores how the metaverse has been misapplied to inappropriate businesses problems and growth ambitions. This chapter concludes by reframing the metaverse as a misunderstood and selectively useful set of technologies rather than a failed promise. Figure 4.1 illustrates how educational and capability gaps, technological immaturity, and poor problem selection can combine to create the perception that the metaverse is a hoax. Figure 4.2 shows how weak governance

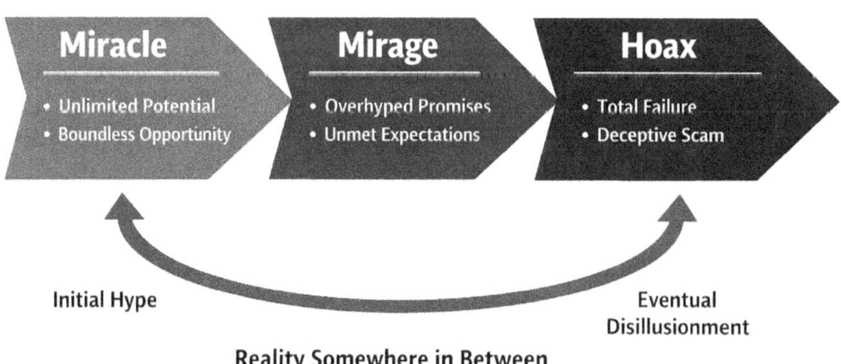

Figure 4.1 Perceptions of the Metaverse journey.

Note: Conceptual diagram showing the overlap between educational and capability gaps, technology gaps, and wrong problem selection, with the intersection labelled "hoax perception".

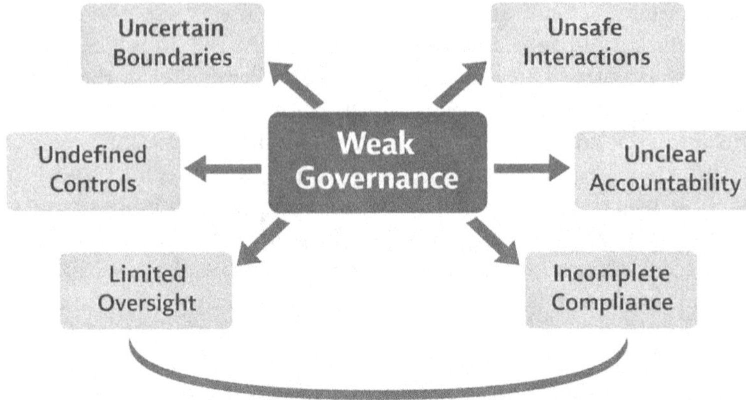

Figure 4.2 Governance gaps in Metaverse initiatives

Note: Conceptual diagram illustrating how weak governance in metaverse initiatives can result in undefined controls, limited oversight, uncertain boundaries, unsafe interactions, unclear accountability, and incomplete compliance.

Table 4.1 Common Misconceptions about the Metaverse

Misconception	*Why It Persists*	*Reality*
The metaverse is a single platform	Media narratives and vendor marketing	The metaverse is an ecosystem of technologies
Immersion automatically creates value	Visual novelty bias	Value depends on problem–solution fit
Consumer success predicts enterprise success	Social media precedent	Enterprise and consumer drivers differ
Hardware maturity guarantees adoption	Focus on devices	Organisational readiness is decisive
Early failure implies hoax	Short-term expectations	Maturity curves take years

in metaverse initiatives can lead to undefined controls, limited oversight, unclear accountability, unsafe interactions, and incomplete compliance.

Table 4.1 summarises common misconceptions about the metaverse, explains why they persist, and contrasts them with the underlying reality.

By the end of this chapter, the reader should be able to understand why the hoax narrative gained traction, recognise the warning signs of poorly conceived metaverse initiatives, and apply disciplined criteria when evaluating whether immersive technologies are appropriate for a given context.

4.2 EDUCATIONAL AND CAPABILITY GAPS IN METAVERSE TECHNOLOGY

One of the strongest drivers behind the perception of the metaverse as a hoax is the widespread educational and capability gap surrounding immersive technologies. This gap exists across leadership, delivery teams, and end users, and it affects not only how metaverse initiatives are designed but also how their outcomes are interpreted.

In many organisations, the decision to invest in the metaverse was made before there was a shared understanding of what the technology could realistically achieve. As a result, failure was often predetermined, not because the technology was unusable but because it was applied without the necessary intellectual and organisational foundations.

4.2.1 Leadership Misunderstanding and Strategic Misalignment

At senior leadership level, the metaverse was frequently introduced through high-level narratives rather than operational detail. Presentations focused on market size, future dominance, and competitive positioning. Less attention was given to constraints, trade-offs, or the conditions under which immersive technologies outperform existing digital tools.

This imbalance led many executives to treat the metaverse as a strategic destination rather than an experimental capability. Questions such as "How do we build a metaverse presence?" replaced more fundamental questions such as "What problem are we solving?" or "What would success look like in measurable terms?"

When objectives are framed in abstract or symbolic terms, accountability becomes weak. Projects are judged by their visibility rather than by outcomes. A virtual environment that looks impressive can be deemed a success even if it delivers no operational value. Over time, this disconnect fuels scepticism and reinforces the hoax narrative.

4.2.2 The Fragmented Capability Stack

Delivering sustainable metaverse solutions requires a combination of capabilities that are rarely mature within a single organisation. Immersive systems sit at the intersection of multiple disciplines, each of which introduces its own risks and dependencies.

These disciplines typically include immersive user experience design, real-time three-dimensional engineering, data instrumentation, security and identity management, governance and moderation, and operational support. Weakness in any one of these areas can undermine the entire initiative. Figure 4.3 summarises how technical constraints, scalability obstacles, interoperability challenges, user adoption barriers, and governance concerns collectively weaken the grand promise of universal virtual worlds.

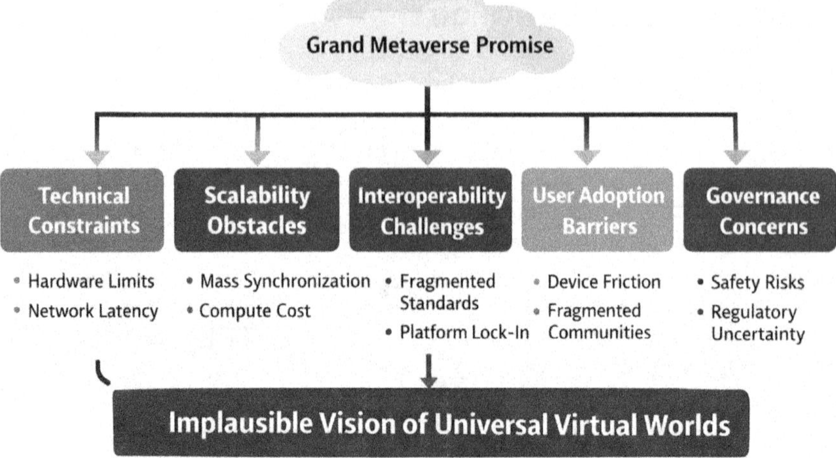

Figure 4.3 Visual mapping of the technical, scalability, interoperability, adoption, and governance constraints that challenge the grand metaverse promise.

Many organisations attempted to bridge these gaps by relying heavily on external vendors. While this accelerated early delivery, it created long-term dependency and limited internal learning. Teams struggled to evolve or scale solutions that they did not fully understand, leading to stagnation once the initial pilot phase ended.

4.2.3 Training Focused on Tools Rather Than Judgement

Where training existed, it often focused on tools rather than decision-making. Teams were taught how to use specific engines, platforms, or development environments but not how to assess whether immersive technology was appropriate in the first place.

This created technically competent teams delivering strategically weak solutions. Virtual environments were built because they could be built, not because they addressed a clearly defined need. When adoption failed, the technology was blamed rather than the decision process that led to its use.

Effective metaverse education must begin with judgement, not tooling. Practitioners need to understand where immersion adds value, where it introduces unnecessary friction, and where conventional digital tools remain superior. Table 4.2 outlines the educational and capability gaps that hinder metaverse adoption, linking specific weaknesses in leadership, architecture, governance, measurement, and product ownership to their practical impact on implementation.

Table 4.2 Educational and Capability Gaps in Metaverse Adoption

Capability Area	*Typical Gap*	*Impact on Adoption*
Leadership literacy	Poor understanding of immersive value	Misaligned investment decisions
Architecture knowledge	Over-simplified system assumptions	Scalability failure
Governance design	Late or missing controls	Trust collapse
Measurement	Weak KPIs	Inability to prove value
Product ownership	Pilot-centric thinking	Failure to scale

4.2.4 End-User Education and Expectation Failure

End users were often introduced to immersive environments without adequate preparation. Little effort was made to explain why a task was being moved into an immersive setting, what benefits users should expect, or how success would be measured.

For many users, early experiences were uncomfortable, unintuitive, or slower than existing tools. Without context or choice, these negative impressions became lasting. Once users disengaged, it was difficult to re-establish trust, even if later improvements were made.

This failure of expectation management is critical. Technologies that require behavioural change must offer clear and immediate benefits. When those benefits are not obvious, resistance is rational rather than conservative.

4.2.5 Measurement and Evaluation Capability Gaps

Another major educational gap lies in measurement. Many metaverse pilots were launched without baseline metrics, making it impossible to demonstrate improvement or justify continued investment.

In immersive contexts, measurement must extend beyond simple usage statistics. It should capture behavioural change, task efficiency, error reduction, learning retention, and safety outcomes. Without this data, discussions about value become subjective and politically charged.

When programmes cannot demonstrate value quantitatively, they become vulnerable to budget cuts and narrative reversal. The absence of measurement does not merely obscure success; it actively contributes to the perception of failure. Table 4.3 outlines the maturity levels of metaverse capability, showing how organisations progress from initial awareness and experimentation to operationalisation and optimisation.

4.2.6 Governance and Trust as Capability, not Compliance

In immersive environments, governance is not an afterthought. Identity, moderation, access control, and data protection are integral to the user experience. Weak governance undermines trust and accelerates disengagement. Figure 4.4

Table 4.3 Metaverse Capability Maturity Levels

Maturity Level	*Characteristics*	*Typical Outcomes*
Awareness	Conceptual familiarity only	Innovation theatre
Experimentation	Isolated pilots	Short-term novelty
Repeatability	Defined use cases	Selective success
Operationalisation	Integrated workflows	Sustainable value
Optimisation	Portfolio management	Competitive advantage

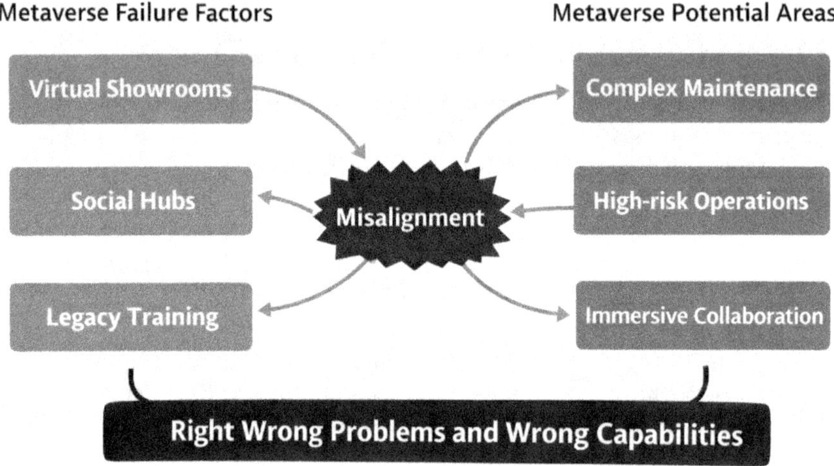

Figure 4.4 Misalignment of problems and capabilities in immersive initiatives.

illustrates how metaverse initiatives can fail when immersive capabilities are misaligned with the actual business problem, leading to solutions that are technically possible but strategically weak.

Many organisations treated governance as a compliance hurdle rather than as a design requirement. As a result, immersive environments felt unsafe, unregulated, or inappropriate for professional use. Incidents involving harassment or misuse quickly overshadowed any potential benefits.

Strong governance capability requires dedicated roles, clear policies, and technical enforcement mechanisms. Without these, immersive systems struggle to gain legitimacy.

4.2.7 Capability Gaps as a Reinforcing Cycle

Educational and capability gaps do not operate in isolation. They form a reinforcing cycle. Poor understanding leads to weak design choices. Weak design choices produce poor outcomes. Poor outcomes reinforce scepticism. Scepticism reduces investment in education and capability development.

This cycle explains why many organisations now dismiss the metaverse outright, even though the same organisations successfully use immersive technologies in narrow, well-defined contexts such as simulation or specialist training. Breaking this cycle requires deliberate investment in education, disciplined problem selection, and realistic expectation-setting.

4.2.8 Section Summary

The educational and capability gap is a primary driver of the hoax narrative. Organisations that lack the intellectual and organisational foundations required to apply immersive technologies effectively are unlikely to see value, regardless of the maturity of the technology itself.

Without shared understanding, disciplined training, robust measurement, and strong governance, metaverse initiatives become symbolic rather than functional. In such conditions, failure is not surprising. What is surprising is how often it is attributed to the technology rather than to the way it was applied.

4.2.9 Capability Maturity and Organisational Readiness

A recurring failure across metaverse initiatives is the absence of an explicit capability maturity assessment. Organisations often assume readiness based on isolated skills or prior digital transformation experience. In reality, metaverse readiness requires a specific and uncommon combination of competencies.

Capability maturity can be described across five levels.

- At the first level, awareness exists but understanding is superficial. Organisations recognise the term "metaverse" and associate it with VR or digital worlds, but lack clarity on use cases, constraints, or risks.
- At the second level, experimentation occurs. Small pilots are launched, typically vendor-led, with limited internal ownership. Measurement is weak, and outcomes are largely qualitative.
- At the third level, repeatability emerges. Organisations begin to build internal capability, define evaluation criteria, and apply immersive technologies to a narrow set of problems with increasing confidence.
- At the fourth level, operational adoption takes place. Immersive systems are integrated into workflows, supported by governance, and funded beyond innovation budgets.
- At the fifth level, scaling and optimisation occur. Multiple use cases coexist, standards are established, and immersive technologies are treated as part of the enterprise digital fabric.

Most organisations that experienced metaverse disappointment were operating at levels one or two while planning as if they were at level four. This mismatch is a primary driver of failure.

4.2.10 Leadership Literacy versus Technical Training

Another overlooked distinction is between leadership literacy and technical training. Many organisations focused on training engineers and designers while neglecting leadership education. As a result, decision-makers lacked the conceptual tools to ask the right questions.

Leadership literacy includes understanding:

- When immersion adds value
- What trade-offs exist between fidelity, scale, and cost
- How governance and trust shape adoption
- Why some use cases fail regardless of execution quality

Without this literacy, leaders may approve initiatives that are technically impressive but strategically unsound. This reinforces the perception that the technology itself is flawed.

Leadership education does not require deep technical detail. It requires structured frameworks, comparative examples, and exposure to failure patterns. Where this is absent, organisations repeat the same mistakes.

4.3 TECHNOLOGY GAPS AND IMMATURITY IN THE METAVERSE

Even when organisations invest in education and capability development, they often encounter hard technological limits that constrain what immersive systems can deliver. These limits form the second major pillar of the hoax narrative. The metaverse has failed not because it is imaginary but because it has been expected to operate at levels of scale, fidelity, and reliability that current technology stacks cannot consistently support.

Technology gaps matter because they shape user experience, cost, and risk. When these gaps are not acknowledged openly, they are misinterpreted as evidence that the entire concept is fundamentally flawed.

4.3.1 Hardware Availability, Comfort, and Adoption Friction

Immersive experiences depend heavily on hardware. Head-mounted displays, controllers, sensors, and supporting devices are central to many metaverse visions. However, widespread adoption of this hardware has proven uneven and slow.

From a user perspective, immersive hardware introduces friction. Devices are more intrusive than smartphones or laptops, require setup and calibration, and may cause discomfort during extended use. For some users, motion sickness, eye strain, or fatigue make immersive sessions undesirable or impossible.

From an organisational perspective, hardware introduces operational challenges. Devices must be purchased, managed, cleaned, supported, and replaced. In shared environments, hygiene and availability become additional concerns. These practical issues often receive little attention during strategy discussions but quickly dominate real-world deployment.

When access to hardware is inconsistent, adoption becomes fragmented. Some users experience the system as intended, while others encounter degraded or limited functionality. This inconsistency undermines collaboration and reinforces scepticism.

4.3.2 Performance, Latency, and Real-Time System Constraints

Immersive environments are fundamentally real-time systems. They must respond instantly to user movement, gestures, and interactions. Even small delays can break immersion and create discomfort.

Delivering low-latency performance at scale is technically demanding. It requires high-performance compute resources, efficient networking, and careful optimisation of rendering and simulation workloads. Trade-offs are unavoidable. Systems optimised for visual fidelity may struggle with scalability. Systems optimised for scale may sacrifice realism.

Many early metaverse narratives ignored these trade-offs. Persistent, shared worlds were presented as near-term realities without acknowledging the engineering complexity involved. When users encountered lag, glitches, or inconsistent behaviour, the gap between promise and experience became visible. Table 4.4 summarises the principal technology gaps affecting metaverse platforms, linking each category of limitation to its practical consequence for immersion, interoperability, security, compliance, and cost.

Table 4.4 Technology Gaps Affecting Metaverse Platforms

Gap Category	*Description*	*Consequence*
Latency	Real-time interaction limits	Reduced immersion
Interoperability	Closed ecosystems	Vendor lock-in
Identity	Fragmented controls	Security risk
Privacy	Behavioural data sensitivity	Regulatory exposure
Cost	Infrastructure scaling	Financial unsustainability

4.3.3 Content Creation Cost and Tooling Limitations

High-quality immersive environments are expensive to build and maintain. Creating three-dimensional assets, scripting interactions, optimising performance, and testing across devices requires specialised skills and significant time investment.

Although development tools have improved, they remain complex. Unlike traditional digital content, immersive assets often need to be rebuilt or heavily modified for different platforms. Reuse is limited, and iteration cycles are slow.

This has important economic implications. Many organisations underestimate ongoing content costs and treat pilots as finished products. Over time, environments become outdated or repetitive, reducing user engagement. When budgets tighten, content quality is often the first casualty.

Low-quality content reinforces negative perceptions. Users associate poor visuals or awkward interactions with a lack of seriousness or value, even if the underlying concept is sound.

4.3.4 Interoperability and Ecosystem Fragmentation

A central promise of the metaverse is continuity. Users expect identities, assets, and experiences to persist across environments. In practice, most platforms operate as isolated ecosystems.

This fragmentation has both technical and commercial roots. Differences in engines, data formats, physics models, and identity systems make interoperability difficult. Platform providers also have limited incentives to support portability that could reduce user lock-in.

For organisations, fragmentation increases risk. Investments made in one platform may not translate to others. Skills, assets, and data become trapped in specific ecosystems. This undermines confidence and discourages long-term commitment.

Without interoperability, the metaverse lacks network effects. Instead of a shared digital space, it becomes a collection of disconnected experiences, each requiring separate investment and governance.

4.3.5 Safety, Privacy, and Governance as Technical Challenges

Immersive environments generate richer and more sensitive data than traditional digital platforms. Movement patterns, spatial behaviour, voice interactions, and proximity information can all reveal personal characteristics.

Protecting this data and ensuring safe interaction is technically complex. Real-time moderation, identity verification, and abuse prevention are difficult to implement, particularly in dynamic, user-generated environments. Figure 4.5 illustrates the typical lifecycle of innovation-led metaverse initiatives, showing how projects can move from early exploration and

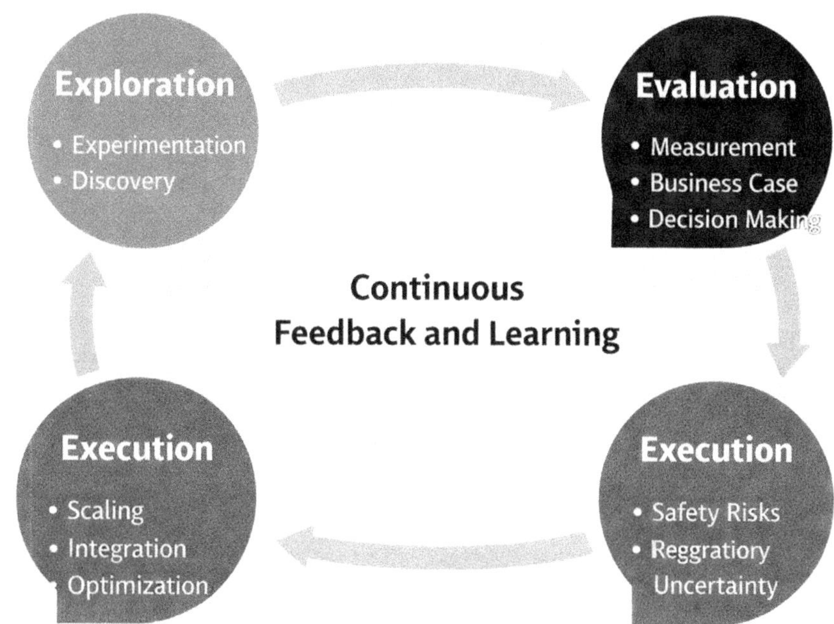

Figure 4.5 Innovation initiative lifecycle.

Note: The innovation initiative lifecycle highlights how emphasis on demonstration over operability contributes to stalled metaverse programmes.

demonstration to stalled adoption when operational readiness, governance, measurement, and scaling plans are not in place.

Many early platforms underestimated the importance of trust and safety. Incidents involving harassment or misuse quickly overshadowed potential benefits. For organisations operating in regulated or reputation-sensitive sectors, these risks were unacceptable.

Governance failures are often interpreted as cultural or behavioural problems. In reality, they are frequently technical problems. Without robust identity systems, moderation tools, and audit mechanisms, enforcing policy becomes impractical.

4.3.6 Economic Sustainability and Scaling Limits

Beyond feasibility lies economic reality. Immersive platforms are expensive to build and operate. Infrastructure costs, content production, moderation, and support all contribute to a high-cost base.

Revenue models remain uncertain, particularly for consumer-focused platforms. Virtual goods, subscriptions, and advertising have produced inconsistent results. Enterprise use cases can justify higher per-user costs, but only when value is clearly measurable.

High-profile investments and subsequent losses have made these economics visible. When returns do not materialise quickly, confidence declines. This financial pressure contributes directly to the hoax narrative, even though long development horizons are common for foundational technologies.

4.3.7 Technology Gaps as Misinterpreted Signals

Taken together, these technology gaps explain why many metaverse initiatives struggled to scale. However, they are often misinterpreted. Limitations are treated as evidence of deception rather than immaturity.

This misinterpretation matters. Technologies mature unevenly. Some applications become viable earlier than others. The metaverse's challenge is not that it cannot work but that it cannot yet support all the use cases it was promised to enable.

Understanding this distinction allows organisations to adopt a more disciplined approach. Instead of asking whether the metaverse is real, they can ask which applications are feasible given current constraints and which should be deferred.

4.3.8 Section Summary

The technology gap in the metaverse spans hardware adoption, performance constraints, content economics, interoperability, safety, and financial sustainability. These gaps do not invalidate immersive technology, but they sharply limit its near-term scope.

When these limitations are ignored, disappointment follows. When they are acknowledged and planned for, immersive systems can deliver value in focused, well-governed contexts. The hoax narrative emerges not from technical impossibility but from expecting immature systems to behave like mature platforms.

4.3.9 Architectural Complexity and Layered System Constraints

Metaverse platforms are often discussed as if they were single, unified systems. In practice, they are layered architectures composed of multiple interacting components, each with its own constraints and failure modes. Understanding these layers is essential to understanding why many metaverse initiatives struggle to meet expectations.

At the outermost layer are client devices and interfaces. These include head-mounted displays, controllers, sensors, and in some cases desktop or mobile access points. Device capability determines rendering fidelity, interaction latency, and user comfort. Variability at this layer introduces inconsistent experiences across users, undermining collaboration and trust.

Beneath the client layer lies the networking and synchronisation layer. This layer is responsible for maintaining shared state across participants. As the number of concurrent users increases, synchronisation complexity grows non-linearly. Trade-offs must be made between consistency, responsiveness, and scale.

The simulation and state management layer governs how virtual environments behave over time. Persistence, physics, and interaction logic are computationally expensive. Maintaining a coherent shared world under real-time constraints places significant demands on infrastructure.

Identity, access control, and entitlements form another critical layer. Decisions made here affect security, moderation, privacy, and user friction. Strong identity controls increase trust but may reduce anonymity and accessibility. Weak controls increase risk and undermine governance.

Finally, data, analytics, and observability layers determine whether behaviour can be measured and improved. Without robust instrumentation, organisations cannot evaluate effectiveness, diagnose issues, or justify continued investment.

Design choices at any one layer impose constraints on all others. This interdependence explains why "simple" metaverse visions often prove infeasible in practice.

4.3.10 Latency as a Technical and Economic Constraint

Latency is frequently discussed as a technical performance metric, but it also has profound economic implications. Immersive experiences require low latency to maintain realism and user comfort. Achieving this at scale is costly.

Low latency demands geographically distributed infrastructure, efficient networking, and continuous optimisation. As user numbers grow, maintaining performance becomes increasingly expensive. The cost curve is steep, particularly for consumer-scale platforms where willingness to pay is limited.

In enterprise contexts, the economics can be more favourable. When immersive systems reduce accidents, improve training outcomes, or accelerate complex decision-making, higher infrastructure costs can be justified. In consumer contexts, where value is primarily experiential, the same costs are harder to recover.

Latency economics therefore shape viable use cases. Applications that tolerate delay or asynchronous interaction are easier to scale. Applications requiring tight real-time coordination are limited to smaller audiences or controlled environments.

Table 4.5 Latency Requirements and Viable Use Cases

Latency Tolerance	*Example Use Case*	*Viability*
Very low	Collaborative simulation	Limited scale
Low	Training environments	Enterprise viable
Medium	Asynchronous design review	Broad viability
High	Virtual tours	Mass deployment

Failure to account for these economics leads to unrealistic growth assumptions and subsequent disappointment. Table 4.5 relates latency tolerance to viable metaverse use cases, showing how technical responsiveness shapes the scale and practicality of deployment.

4.3.11 Data Privacy and Behavioural Sensitivity in Immersive Environments

Immersive systems generate data that is qualitatively different from traditional digital platforms. Beyond clicks and keystrokes, they capture behavioural signals such as movement patterns, gaze direction, proximity interactions, and voice characteristics.

These signals can reveal sensitive information about users, including physical condition, emotional state, and behavioural tendencies. As a result, privacy risks are amplified. Data that appears innocuous in isolation may become sensitive when aggregated.

Many early metaverse platforms treated immersive telemetry as an extension of conventional analytics. This approach underestimates both regulatory risk and user concern. Privacy expectations in immersive environments are often higher because the experience feels more personal and embodied.

Organisations operating in regulated sectors face additional constraints. Data collection, storage, and processing must comply with existing privacy frameworks, even when those frameworks were not designed with immersive systems in mind.

Failure to address privacy proactively undermines trust and limits adoption. In extreme cases, it can halt programmes entirely.

4.3.12 Interoperability Myths and Standardisation Reality

Interoperability is frequently cited as a defining feature of the metaverse. Users and organisations expect identities, assets, and experiences to move seamlessly across environments. In practice, this vision remains largely aspirational.

Technical barriers include incompatible asset formats, differing physics models, and inconsistent identity systems. Even where standards exist, implementation varies widely. Commercial incentives further complicate

Table 4.6 Interoperability Barriers and Strategic Risk

Barrier	*Cause*	*Strategic Impact*
Asset incompatibility	Proprietary formats	Content lock-in
Identity fragmentation	Platform silos	User friction
Physics mismatch	Engine variation	Inconsistent experience
Commercial incentives	Walled gardens	Limited portability

the picture. Platform providers benefit from ecosystem lock-in and may resist portability.

For organisations, lack of interoperability increases risk. Investments made in one platform may not be transferable. Skills and content become stranded. This uncertainty discourages long-term commitment.

The gap between interoperability rhetoric and reality contributes to scepticism. When promised openness fails to materialise, trust erodes. Table 4.6 summarises the main interoperability barriers affecting metaverse platforms, linking each barrier to its underlying cause and strategic impact.

4.3.13 Operational Integration and Enterprise Architecture Friction

Metaverse initiatives rarely fail in isolation. They fail when they collide with existing enterprise architecture. Identity systems, security policies, data pipelines, and compliance controls impose constraints that are often overlooked during pilot phases.

Integration challenges include authentication alignment, network security restrictions, data residency requirements, and device management policies. Addressing these issues late in the process can stall or terminate programmes.

Successful initiatives engage enterprise architects and security teams early. They treat immersive systems as part of the broader digital estate rather than as standalone experiments. Ignoring integration reality creates a false sense of progress during pilots, followed by abrupt failure during attempted scaling.

4.3.14 Summary

The technology gaps affecting the metaverse are not limited to hardware or performance. They span architecture, economics, privacy, interoperability, and enterprise integration. These gaps interact, amplifying risk and constraining scale.

When these constraints are not acknowledged, immersive technologies appear to overpromise and underdeliver. When they are understood and planned for, the metaverse becomes a toolset with clear boundaries rather than an all-encompassing platform. Figure 4.6 shows the relationship between organisational capability maturity and metaverse value realisation, highlighting why the

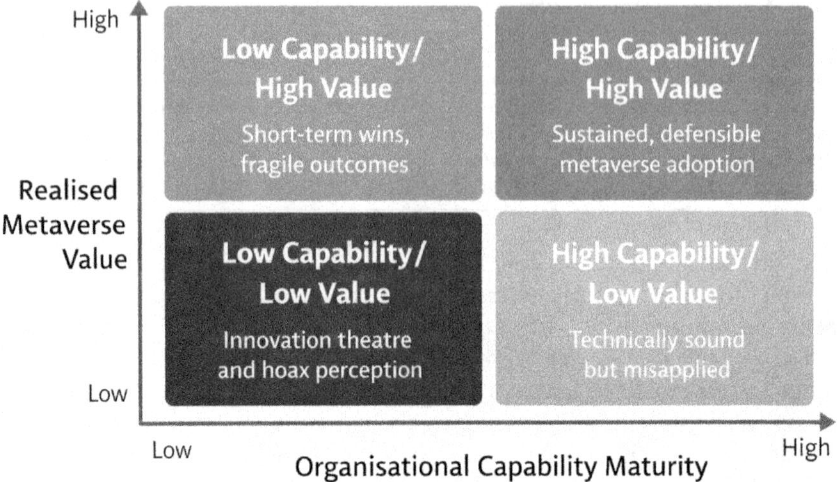

Relationship between organisational capability maturity and realised metaverse value, higblighting why immature adoption often results in hoax perceptions

Figure 4.6 Capability maturity versus Metaverse value realisation.

Note: Capability maturity versus metaverse value realisation explains why similar technologies produce radically different outcomes across organisations.

same immersive technologies can produce very different outcomes depending on readiness, governance, measurement, and use-case alignment.

The hoax narrative emerges when immaturity is mistaken for impossibility. A more productive response is selective adoption informed by architectural and economic reality.

4.4 USE OF THE METAVERSE FOR THE WRONG BUSINESS PROBLEMS OR GROWTH PROSPECTS

The perception of the metaverse as a hoax is strongest when immersive technologies are applied to problems they are poorly suited to solve. Even when organisations partially address educational and technology gaps, initiatives often fail because they start from the wrong question. Instead of asking "Where does immersion create measurable advantage?", organisations ask "How do we use the metaverse?"

This inversion is critical. Technologies do not create value on their own. Value emerges when a technology is applied to a problem whose characteristics align with its strengths. When this alignment is missing, even sophisticated systems appear pointless or wasteful.

4.4.1 Platform-First Thinking and Innovation Theatre

Platform-first thinking treats the metaverse as a destination rather than a capability. Organisations feel pressure to demonstrate participation, often driven by competitive anxiety or board-level curiosity. The result is a focus on visibility rather than utility.

Common platform-first statements include:

- "We need a metaverse strategy."
- "We need a presence in virtual worlds."
- "Our competitors are investing in this space."

These statements generate activity but not clarity. They encourage organisations to build environments before defining outcomes. When success is measured by launch rather than impact, initiatives quickly become innovation theatre.

Innovation theatre creates artefacts that look impressive but do not change behaviour. Virtual offices sit empty. Branded spaces attract curiosity but no repeat engagement. Internal pilots become demonstrations for executives rather than tools for employees.

Over time, these failures reinforce the belief that the metaverse has no practical value. The problem is not that immersive technology cannot deliver value but that it was never asked to solve a meaningful problem.

4.4.2 The Catalogue of Wrong Problems

Certain problem types consistently produce poor outcomes when addressed with immersive technology. These patterns appear across industries and geographies, suggesting structural rather than contextual causes.

One common misapplication is routine communication. Meetings, status updates, and information sharing are already well served by videoconferencing and collaboration tools. Introducing immersion adds friction without corresponding benefit.

Another frequent mistake is generic retail browsing. Most consumers value speed and convenience. Immersive shopping environments require more effort and time, which only makes sense for complex or high-involvement products. When applied indiscriminately, virtual retail feels inefficient rather than innovative.

A third pattern is brand-led experimentation without a community strategy. Virtual spaces are launched as marketing statements rather than as ecosystems. Without reasons to return, these spaces quickly become empty, reinforcing scepticism.

Finally, forced internal adoption often backfires. Employees who are required to use immersive tools without understanding the benefit may perceive them as intrusive, uncomfortable, or performative. Resistance is rational in such cases. As shown in Analytical Case Box 4.1, many virtual showroom initiatives failed not because of poor execution, but because immersion was applied to a weak problem–solution fit.

ANALYTICAL CASE BOX 4.1: THE VIRTUAL SHOWROOM FALLACY

Many early metaverse initiatives took the form of virtual showrooms. These environments replicated physical retail or exhibition spaces in three-dimensional form, often with high visual fidelity and brand-specific design elements. The underlying assumption was that immersion itself would drive engagement and conversion.

In practice, most virtual showrooms suffered from low repeat visitation and weak commercial impact. Users visited once out of curiosity, explored briefly, and did not return. Unlike physical showrooms, virtual environments lacked social pressure, tactile engagement, and immediacy of transaction. Unlike conventional e-commerce, they introduced friction rather than convenience.

The core failure was not technical execution. Many of these environments were visually impressive and functionally stable. The failure lay in problem selection. The task being addressed, browsing standard products, did not benefit meaningfully from immersion. Users could accomplish the same goal faster using familiar two-dimensional interfaces.

This case illustrates a common pattern in metaverse adoption: translating a physical experience into a virtual form without reassessing its value proposition. Immersion was treated as an inherent benefit rather than as a tool that must justify its cost and complexity.

The lesson is clear. Immersive environments must do something fundamentally different, not merely look different. When immersion does not reduce friction, improve understanding, or create new capability, it becomes novelty rather than value.

4.4.3 Growth Prospect Myths and Unrealistic Expectations

Several growth narratives amplified disappointment and contributed to the hoax perception. These narratives were often repeated without sufficient scrutiny and became implicit assumptions in business cases.

One myth is that the metaverse would rapidly become a universal consumer destination. This assumes widespread hardware adoption, low friction access, and strong habit formation. In reality, immersive environments demand more effort from users than most mainstream digital platforms.

Another myth is that virtual goods and digital assets would create stable new revenue streams. While such economies can exist, they depend on strong social gravity and active creator ecosystems. Without these conditions, monetisation remains speculative and volatile.

A third myth is that early presence guarantees long-term advantage. In practice, presence without pull offers no protection. If users do not return, being early only increases cost and exposure. Table 4.7 identifies the types of business problems that are well suited to immersive technologies, linking each problem type to the specific advantage immersion can provide.

When these growth assumptions fail, organisations often conclude that the entire concept is fraudulent. In reality, the failure lies in the assumptions, not in the technology itself.

4.4.4 The Immersion Advantage Test

A practical way to avoid wrong-problem adoption is to apply an immersion advantage test before funding any initiative. This test forces teams to articulate why immersion is necessary rather than merely possible. Figure 4.7 compares the expectation curve surrounding metaverse adoption with the slower and more uneven reality of actual capability development, helping to explain why early optimism later shifted into scepticism.

Table 4.7 Business Problems Well Suited to Immersive Technologies

Problem Type	*Immersive Advantage*
Complex spatial training	Improved retention
Hazard simulation	Risk-free rehearsal
Design prototyping	Shared spatial context
Remote expert guidance	Presence and clarity
Scenario-based learning	Behavioural realism

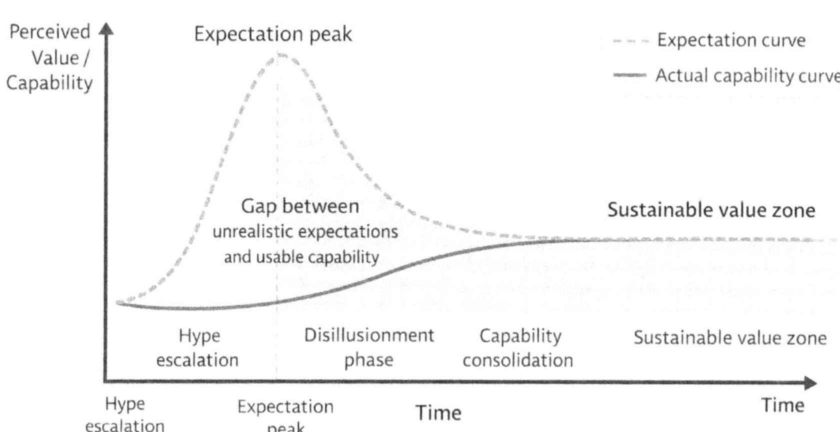

Figure 4.7 Metaverse adoption timeline versus expectation curve.

Note: This figure contextualises current scepticism within broader technology adoption cycles by showing the divergence between expectations and actual capability over time.

A problem is likely to benefit from immersive technology if one or more of the following conditions apply:

- Spatial understanding is central to decision-making.
- Physical risk makes real-world rehearsal expensive or unsafe.
- Systems are complex and require simulation before change.
- Collaboration depends on shared three-dimensional context.
- Errors are costly and practice can reduce their likelihood.

If none of these conditions apply, immersive technology is unlikely to outperform conventional digital tools.

4.4.5 Why Valid Use Cases Still Fail to Scale

Even when organisations select appropriate problems, many initiatives stall after the pilot phase. This is often interpreted as evidence that the metaverse cannot scale. In reality, the causes are usually organisational rather than technical.

Common scaling barriers include lack of instrumentation, making it impossible to prove value; slow and expensive content updates, leading to stale experiences; inadequate device management; incomplete governance; and unclear ownership beyond the innovation team.

Pilots that are not designed for scale should not be judged as failed technologies. They are incomplete products. Without a path to operationalisation, even strong use cases cannot progress. As shown in Analytical Case Box 4.2, many enterprise metaverse pilots fail not because the technology is inherently incapable, but because the pilots were designed for demonstration rather than integration, measurement, and scale.

ANALYTICAL CASE BOX 4.2: THE DEMO TRAP IN ENTERPRISE METAVERSE PILOTS

A recurring enterprise failure pattern is the "demo trap". Organisations commission metaverse pilots designed primarily to impress senior stakeholders rather than to function as scalable systems. These pilots prioritise visual appeal, scripted interactions, and controlled demonstrations.

Such pilots often succeed in their immediate objective. Executives are impressed, innovation teams receive recognition, and the initiative is perceived as a success. However, the underlying system is rarely designed for integration, measurement, or ongoing operation.

Key characteristics of demo-trap pilots include hard-coded scenarios, limited user roles, lack of analytics, and absence of governance controls. When attempts are made to extend these pilots into real operational contexts, they collapse under their own limitations.

The demo trap contributes directly to the hoax narrative. When a highly visible pilot fails to scale, observers conclude that the technology itself is incapable. In reality, the pilot was never designed to scale.

This case highlights the importance of defining pilot success criteria carefully. A successful pilot is not one that looks impressive but one that can be measured, iterated, and either scaled or terminated based on evidence.

4.4.6 Case-Pattern Analysis of Failure

Rather than listing vendor case studies, it is more instructive to analyse recurring failure patterns.

One pattern is the showroom problem. A visually impressive environment is launched but offers no ongoing utility. Engagement drops rapidly, and the initiative is quietly abandoned.

Another pattern is the demo trap. A pilot is built to impress stakeholders rather than to integrate with systems, measure outcomes, or support updates. Scaling proves impossible.

A third pattern is trust collapse. Weak moderation or identity controls allow misuse, leading to reputational damage and programme shutdown.

A fourth pattern is hidden operating cost. The full cost of content maintenance, device support, and governance becomes apparent only after launch. Budgets are withdrawn, and the initiative stalls. As shown in Analytical Case Box 4.3, failures in moderation, safety, and behavioural governance can rapidly undermine trust and halt metaverse adoption, regardless of technical sophistication.

ANALYTICAL CASE BOX 4.3: TRUST COLLAPSE AND THE COST OF WEAK MODERATION

Several metaverse initiatives failed abruptly following incidents related to harassment, impersonation, or misuse. In many cases, the technology functioned as intended, but governance mechanisms were insufficient to manage human behaviour in immersive spaces.

Immersive environments amplify social presence. Interactions feel more personal and immediate than in text-based or video-based systems. As a result, negative behaviour has a disproportionate emotional impact. When moderation is slow or ineffective, trust collapses rapidly.

In enterprise contexts, a single incident can halt adoption entirely. Employees may refuse to engage with the platform, and risk-averse leadership may withdraw support. In consumer contexts, reputational damage spreads quickly and discourages new users.

This case demonstrates that trust and safety are not optional features. They are foundational capabilities. Treating moderation as a secondary concern almost guarantees failure, regardless of technical sophistication.

The broader lesson is that immersive technologies intensify existing social risks. Organisations must plan for this intensification rather than assuming that digital norms will transfer unchanged.

4.4.7 The Correct Operating Model for Metaverse Initiatives

Successful metaverse programmes treat immersive environments as products, not experiments. This requires a clear operating model with defined ownership and accountability. Key components include product ownership tied to outcomes, content operations with a regular update cadence, device lifecycle management, trust and safety governance, observability and analytics, and explicit scale and stop criteria.

Without this structure, immersive initiatives remain fragile and dependent on enthusiasm rather than evidence. As shown in Analytical Case Box 4.4, some metaverse programmes are abandoned not because the concept lacks value but because ongoing operating costs were underestimated during the pilot phase.

ANALYTICAL CASE BOX 4.4: HIDDEN OPERATING COSTS AND PROGRAMME ABANDONMENT

Another frequent failure mode is programme abandonment due to unexpected operating costs. During pilot phases, budgets often focus on development and launch. Ongoing costs related to content updates, device management, user support, and governance are underestimated or ignored.

As pilots transition toward wider use, these costs become visible. Content must be refreshed to remain relevant. Devices must be maintained and replaced. Support requests increase. Governance processes require staffing and tooling.

When these costs are revealed, programmes are often judged retrospectively as uneconomic. Funding is withdrawn, and the initiative is quietly shut down. Observers interpret this outcome as evidence that the metaverse is inherently too expensive.

In reality, the issue is incomplete cost modelling. Any digital product incurs ongoing operational expense. Metaverse initiatives are no different, but the costs are distributed across unfamiliar categories.

This case reinforces the importance of treating immersive systems as products rather than experiments. Product thinking requires full lifecycle cost awareness, not just upfront investment.

4.4.8 Section Summary

The metaverse appears to be a hoax most clearly when it is used to chase fashionable growth narratives or applied to problems that do not benefit from immersion. These failures are not random. They follow predictable patterns driven by platform-first thinking, weak assumptions, and lack of operational discipline.

By shifting focus from presence to purpose, organisations can avoid these traps. The technology itself is rarely the limiting factor. The choice of problem and the design of the operating model determine whether immersive systems deliver value or disappointment.

4.4.9 Enterprise versus Consumer Metaverse Misalignment

A major contributor to failed metaverse initiatives is the persistent conflation of enterprise and consumer use cases. Although both are often grouped under the same terminology, they operate under fundamentally different success criteria, adoption dynamics, and economic constraints.

Enterprise metaverse use cases are evaluated primarily on functional outcomes. Organisations adopt immersive technologies to reduce errors, improve training effectiveness, enhance safety, or enable complex spatial collaboration. In these contexts, adoption is driven by mandate, measurable performance improvement, and integration into existing workflows.

Consumer metaverse use cases, by contrast, depend on voluntary participation. Success is determined by engagement, enjoyment, habit formation, and social pull. Friction must be minimised, and the perceived value must be immediate and emotionally resonant.

When organisations apply consumer growth assumptions to enterprise deployments, they underinvest in governance, measurement, and operational support. Conversely, when enterprise discipline is imposed on consumer platforms, experiences often become rigid, over-regulated, and unattractive to users.

Many metaverse initiatives failed because they attempted to serve both domains simultaneously. Virtual environments were designed to be entertaining yet secure, open yet controlled, scalable yet personalised. These goals are often incompatible within a single system.

Recognising the distinction between enterprise and consumer contexts is therefore essential. Without this clarity, organisations misjudge adoption signals and draw incorrect conclusions about the viability of immersive technologies. Table 4.8 compares enterprise and consumer metaverse models across adoption drivers, success metrics, risk tolerance, governance, and scale economics.

Table 4.8 Enterprise versus Consumer Metaverse Comparison

Dimension	*Enterprise*	*Consumer*
Adoption driver	Mandated	Voluntary
Success metric	Performance	Engagement
Risk tolerance	Low	High
Governance	Strict	Flexible
Scale economics	Controlled	Network-driven

4.4.10 The Cost of Misaligned Growth Narratives

Growth narratives played a decisive role in shaping expectations around the metaverse. These narratives often borrowed language from previous platform shifts, particularly social media and mobile computing. Terms such as "network effects", "first-mover advantage", and "winner-takes-all" were applied without sufficient scrutiny.

In reality, immersive platforms face very different constraints. Network effects are weaker when access requires specialised hardware. First-mover advantage is limited when content creation costs are high and interoperability is low. Winner-takes-all dynamics are unlikely in fragmented ecosystems with incompatible standards.

Misaligned growth narratives encourage premature scaling. Organisations attempt to grow user bases before solving fundamental issues related to usability, governance, and value delivery. When growth stalls, confidence collapses, and the hoax narrative gains traction.

This pattern mirrors earlier technology cycles in which infrastructure was mistaken for product-market fit. The lesson is not that growth is impossible but that it must follow demonstrated value rather than precede it.

4.4.11 Decision Discipline as an Antidote to Innovation Theatre

The most effective way to avoid misuse of the metaverse is not technical sophistication but decision discipline. Organisations that succeed with immersive technologies tend to apply explicit evaluation frameworks before committing resources.

Such frameworks require teams to justify why immersion is necessary, how value will be measured, and under what conditions the initiative will be stopped. They also force early consideration of governance, adoption friction, and long-term operating cost.

Decision discipline shifts the conversation from enthusiasm to evidence. It makes it acceptable to conclude that a problem does not warrant immersive technology. This, paradoxically, increases trust in the initiatives that do proceed.

Without such discipline, organisations drift into innovation theatre. Projects are launched to signal modernity rather than to solve problems. When these projects fail, the technology is blamed, reinforcing the hoax narrative.

4.5 WHY THE METAVERSE IS NOT A HOAX

Having examined the educational, capability, technological, and problem-selection failures that fuel scepticism, it is now possible to address the hoax question directly. The metaverse is not a hoax in the literal sense. The underlying technologies exist, they function, and in specific contexts they deliver measurable value. What has failed is not the concept itself but the way it has been framed and applied.

Calling the metaverse a hoax implies intentional deception. In most cases, this is not accurate. What occurred instead was a convergence of inflated expectations, premature scaling attempts, and limited organisational readiness. The result was disappointment rather than exposure. Figure 4.8 summarises the main conditions under which metaverse initiatives are more likely to create genuine value, particularly where immersive capability is aligned with a clear business problem, measurable outcomes, appropriate governance, and operational readiness.

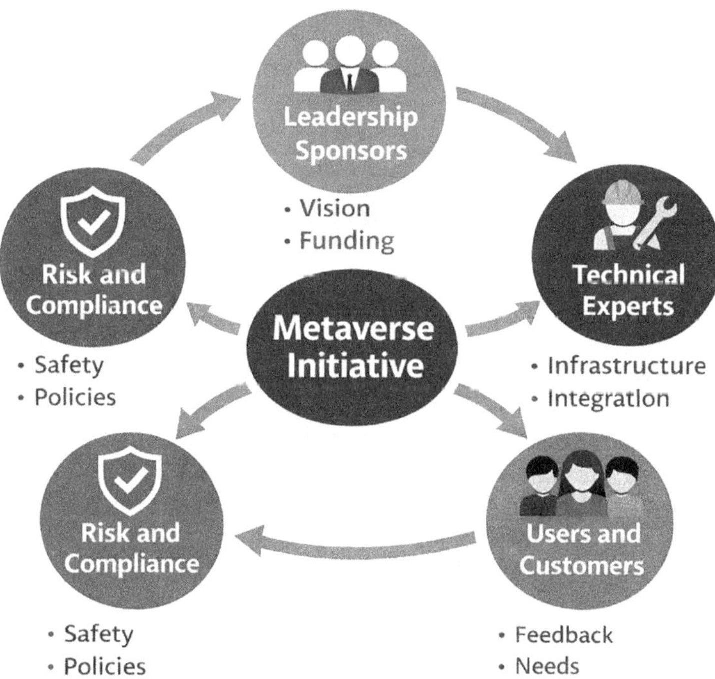

Figure 4.8 Engaging stakeholders in a Metaverse initiative.

The metaverse is better understood as a set of enabling technologies rather than as a finished platform. Immersive interfaces, spatial computing, and real-time simulation have clear applications in areas such as training, design, remote assistance, and digital twins. In these contexts, value is often incremental but tangible. Errors are reduced, understanding improves, and risk can be managed more effectively.

The perception of fraud emerges when these narrow, realistic applications are conflated with grand narratives about universal virtual worlds. When promises exceed capability, trust erodes. This erosion is then misattributed to deception rather than to misalignment.

Another reason the hoax narrative persists is comparison. The rise of generative artificial intelligence demonstrated what rapid, visible impact looks like. AI tools delivered immediate productivity gains without requiring new devices or major behavioural change. Against this backdrop, the metaverse appeared slow, awkward, and expensive. This comparison is misleading. Different technologies mature at different speeds and address different classes of problems.

Importantly, the metaverse has already delivered value in domains that do not attract mass attention. Simulation-based training, safety rehearsal, and spatial planning often occur away from public view. These successes are rarely celebrated because they are operational rather than spectacular.

The conclusion from this analysis is straightforward. The metaverse is not a hoax, but it is frequently presented and pursued in ways that guarantee disappointment. Recognising this distinction allows organisations to move beyond defensive or dismissive reactions and towards more disciplined experimentation.

4.6 HOAX, HYPE, OR MISUNDERSTOOD TECHNOLOGY?

The hoax debate can be resolved by reframing the question. Instead of asking whether the metaverse is real or fake, it is more productive to ask whether it is misunderstood. In most cases, misunderstanding is the most accurate description.

Misunderstanding arises when the metaverse is treated as a singular entity rather than as a spectrum of technologies and applications. Some parts of this spectrum are mature enough to deliver value today. Others remain experimental or speculative. Treating all of them as equally ready leads to confusion and misallocation of resources.

A useful way to conceptualise this is through a simple two-dimensional model. One axis represents organisational capability maturity, ranging from low to high. The other represents use case fit, ranging from poor alignment to strong alignment. This creates four distinct outcomes. Figure 4.9 summarises the disciplined evaluation approach required to distinguish weak metaverse initiatives from genuinely viable use cases, focusing on problem fit, capability maturity, governance readiness, technical feasibility, and measurable value.

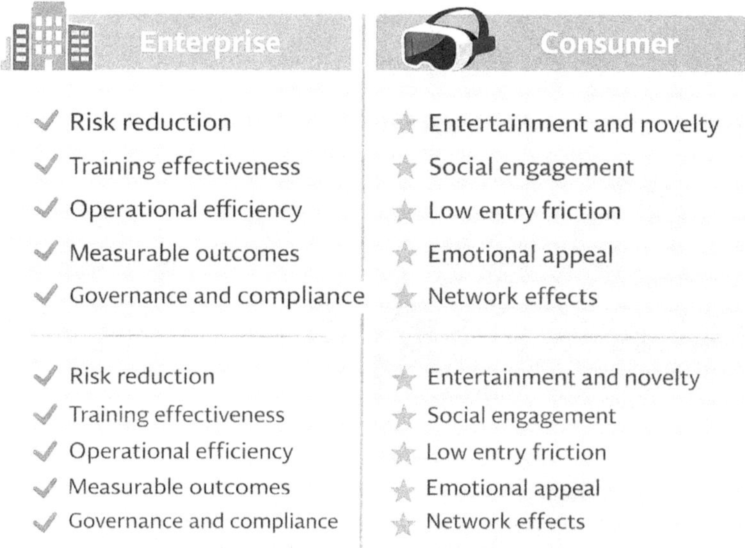

Figure 4.9 Enterprise versus consumer Metaverse value drivers.

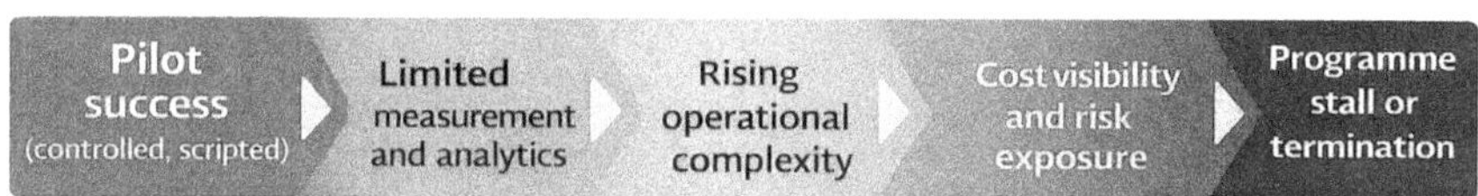

Figure 4.10 Pilot-to-scale barriers in Metaverse programmes.

When capability maturity is low and use case fit is poor, initiatives almost always fail. These failures generate the strongest hoax narratives. When capability is low but use case fit is strong, pilots may struggle but still produce learning. When capability is high but use case fit is poor, organisations can deliver impressive systems that nevertheless fail to generate value. Only when both capability and use case fit are high does scalable value emerge. Figure 4.10 shows how metaverse initiatives should be assessed through a structured decision lens, moving from the initial business problem through capability, technology, governance, user adoption, and measurable value before any scaling decision is made.

This model explains why different organisations reach different conclusions about the metaverse. Their experiences are shaped less by the technology itself and more by where they sit within this matrix.

Misunderstanding also arises from time horizons. Many metaverse ambitions require ecosystem-level coordination, standardisation, and behavioural change. These developments take time. When expectations are set on short-term cycles, long-term technologies appear to fail.

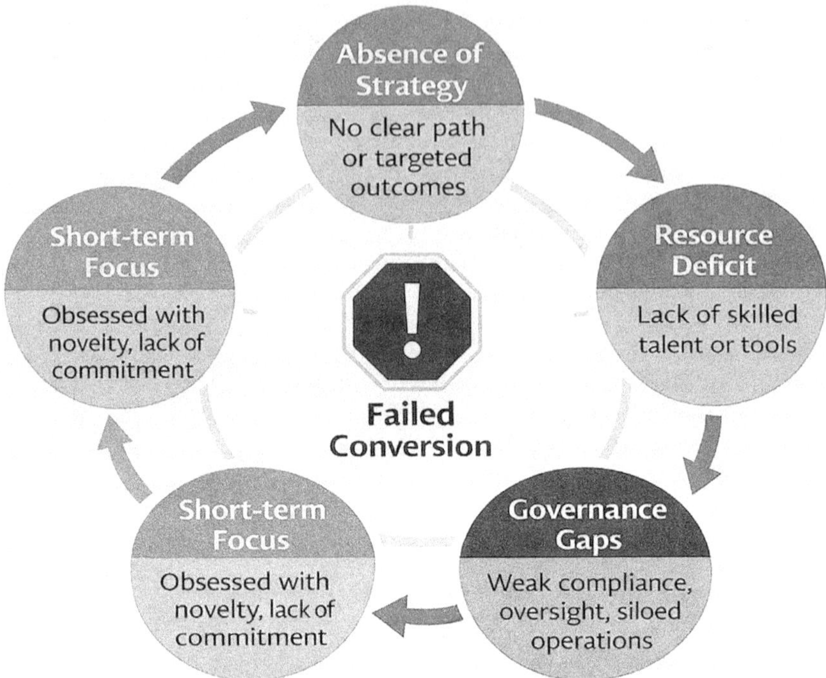

Figure 4.11 Common pitfalls in Metaverse pilot-to-scale conversion.

Note: This figure illustrates recurring reasons why metaverse pilots fail to convert into scalable operational initiatives.

The hoax narrative is therefore a warning sign. It signals that expectations, capability, and application are misaligned. Organisations that recognise this can recalibrate. Those that do not may abandon potentially valuable tools prematurely. Figure 4.11 brings together the main reasons why the metaverse is often perceived as a hoax, showing how weak capability, immature technology, poor use-case selection, unrealistic expectations, and weak governance can collectively undermine trust in metaverse initiatives.

4.7 CHAPTER SUMMARY AND TRANSITION

This chapter set out to answer a provocative question: *Is the metaverse a hoax?* The analysis shows that the answer is neither a simple yes nor a simple no. The metaverse is not a fabricated illusion, but it has been promoted and adopted in ways that obscure its real value and limitations.

Three root causes underpin the hoax perception. Educational and capability gaps lead to weak decision-making and unrealistic objectives. Technology gaps and immaturity constrain usability, scalability, and safety.

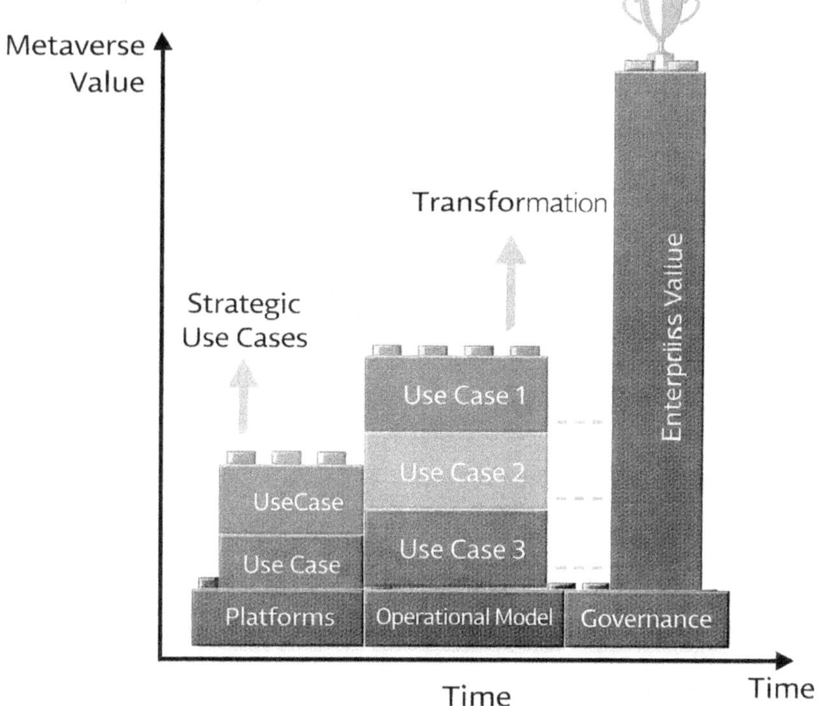

Figure 4.12 Building reliable Metaverse value over time.

Note: This figure illustrates how reliable metaverse value is built progressively over time through foundational platforms, operating models, governance, and strategically layered use cases.

Misapplication to inappropriate business problems and exaggerated growth narratives ensure that even functional systems fail to deliver perceived value.

These factors interact. When combined, they create a powerful narrative of disappointment that is easily labelled as fraud or deception. In reality, the failures are predictable and largely preventable. Figure 4.12 summarises the chapter's final position by distinguishing between the metaverse as a failed over-promoted narrative and the metaverse as a selectively useful set of immersive, spatial and simulation technologies when applied to the right problems.

This chapter also demonstrates that immersive technologies can deliver value when applied selectively and governed effectively. The challenge is not to prove that the metaverse is real but to decide where it is worth using and where it is not.

The implications for practitioners and decision-makers are clear. Metaverse initiatives should begin with problem definition, capability assessment, and realistic expectation-setting. They should be instrumented for measurement, designed for governance, and evaluated continuously. Programmes that do not meet these criteria should be stopped early rather than defended indefinitely.

This chapter provides the conceptual foundation for such disciplined decision-making. It clears away inflated narratives and replaces them with a structured understanding of why the metaverse appears to fail and how value can still be extracted responsibly.

The next chapter builds on this foundation by examining the architectural and enabling technologies that underpin the metaverse. By understanding how immersive systems are constructed, readers can better assess feasibility, cost, interoperability, and risk before committing resources.

BIBLIOGRAPHY

Ball, M. (2022). *The Metaverse: And How It Will Revolutionize Everything*. New York: Liveright Publishing.

Citi GPS. (2022). *Metaverse and Money: Decrypting the Future*. New York: Citigroup Global Perspectives & Solutions. Available at: https://www.citigroup.com/global/insights/metaverse (Accessed: 10 January 2026).

Dionisio, J. D. N., Burns, W. G., & Gilbert, R. (2013). 3D virtual worlds and the metaverse: Current status and future possibilities. *ACM Computing Surveys*, 45(3), 1–38.

Gartner. (2023). *Emerging Technologies: Hype Cycle for the Metaverse*. Stamford, CT: Gartner Research. Available at: https://www.gartner.com (Accessed: 10 January 2026).

IDC. (2023). *Worldwide Augmented and Virtual Reality Spending Guide*. Framingham, MA: International Data Corporation. Available at: https://www.idc.com (Accessed: 10 January 2026).

McKinsey & Company. (2022). *Value Creation in the Metaverse*. Available at: https://www.mckinsey.com (Accessed: 10 January 2026).

Meta Platforms, Inc. (2021). *Founder's Letter: The Metaverse*. Available at: https://about.meta.com (Accessed: 10 January 2026).

Nadella, S. (2021). *The Metaverse and the Future of Work*. Microsoft Official Blog. Available at: https://blogs.microsoft.com (Accessed: 10 January 2026).

PwC. (2022). *Seeing Is Believing: The Economic Impact of the Metaverse*. London: PricewaterhouseCoopers. Available at: https://www.pwc.com (Accessed: 10 January 2026).

Radoff, J. (2021). *The Metaverse Value Chain*. Available at: https://medium.com/building-the-metaverse (Accessed: 10 January 2026).

Stephenson, N. (1992). *Snow Crash*. New York: Bantam Books.

Chapter 5

Architectural Foundations and Enabling Technologies of the Metaverse

5.1 INTRODUCTION

Following the critical examination of hype, misapplication, and failure narratives in Chapter 4, this chapter focuses on the architectural and technological foundations that underpin the metaverse. Rather than treating the metaverse as a singular platform or destination, this chapter frames it as a composite system composed of multiple interdependent technologies, each with distinct capabilities, constraints, and maturity levels.

The purpose of this chapter is not to speculate on future visions but to describe what is technically achievable today, what remains structurally constrained, and how architectural decisions shape outcomes. In doing so, it provides a grounded reference point for practitioners, architects, and decision-makers seeking to evaluate metaverse initiatives realistically.

Architecture matters because immersive systems are inherently complex. Unlike conventional digital applications, metaverse environments must coordinate real-time interaction, spatial simulation, identity, security, and data flows across distributed infrastructure. Weakness or immaturity in any one component can undermine the entire system.

This chapter therefore decomposes the metaverse into its core architectural layers and enabling technologies. Each layer is examined in isolation and in relation to others, highlighting trade-offs and integration challenges. The focus is deliberately neutral and technical, avoiding promotional narratives in favour of structural clarity.

The scope of this chapter includes infrastructure, simulation engines, identity and trust mechanisms, content systems, client devices, and the technologies that enable them to function together. Speculative concepts, social visions, and economic models are intentionally excluded, as these are addressed elsewhere in this book.

DOI: 10.1201/9781003405566-5

5.2 CORE ARCHITECTURAL LAYERS OF THE METAVERSE

At a technical level, metaverse systems are best understood as layered architectures. Each layer performs a distinct function and imposes constraints on the layers above and below it. Effective design depends on recognising these dependencies rather than assuming seamless integration. This section outlines the core architectural layers common to most metaverse implementations, regardless of platform or use case.

5.2.1 Infrastructure and Compute Foundations

The foundation of any metaverse system is its underlying infrastructure. This includes compute resources, storage, networking, and acceleration hardware such as GPUs. Unlike traditional web applications, immersive systems are computationally intensive and sensitive to latency.

Cloud infrastructure plays a central role in providing scalable compute and storage. However, reliance on centralised cloud regions introduces latency that can degrade immersive experiences. To mitigate this, many architectures incorporate edge computing, placing processing closer to users to reduce round-trip delays.

Networking is equally critical. Real-time interaction requires low-latency, high-bandwidth connections with predictable performance. Packet loss, jitter, and congestion have a direct impact on user comfort and interaction fidelity. As a result, metaverse platforms often impose stricter network requirements than conventional applications.

Infrastructure design also affects cost. High-performance compute, especially GPU-backed workloads, is expensive to operate at scale. Architectural decisions at this layer therefore influence not only technical feasibility but also economic sustainability.

5.2.2 Simulation and State Management

Above the infrastructure layer sits the simulation and state management layer. This layer is responsible for maintaining the behaviour, physics, and persistence of the virtual environment.

Simulation engines calculate object movement, collision, and interaction in real time. In multi-user environments, these calculations must be synchronised across participants to maintain a coherent shared experience. As the number of concurrent users increases, synchronisation complexity grows rapidly.

State management determines how changes in the environment are recorded and propagated. Decisions must be made about what state is authoritative, how conflicts are resolved, and how persistence is maintained across sessions. These decisions affect scalability, consistency, and fault tolerance.

Trade-offs are unavoidable. Strong consistency improves realism but limits its scale. Eventual consistency allows larger audiences but can introduce perceptible inconsistencies. Architectural choices in this layer directly shape the types of experiences that can be delivered reliably.

5.2.3 Identity, Access, and Trust Mechanisms

Identity is a foundational component of metaverse architecture. Users must be authenticated, represented, and authorised to interact within environments. Unlike conventional systems, identity in immersive environments is embodied through avatars, spatial presence, and behavioural signals.

Authentication mechanisms establish who a user is. Authorisation mechanisms determine what actions they can perform and which spaces they can access. These controls must be enforced consistently across distributed systems.

Trust mechanisms extend beyond access control. They include moderation tools, reporting processes, and behavioural enforcement. Weak trust systems expose platforms to impersonation, harassment, and misuse, undermining adoption and legitimacy.

Identity design also intersects with privacy. Decisions about persistent identity versus anonymity have implications for safety, compliance, and user acceptance. Architectural choices in this layer therefore carry both technical and ethical weight.

5.2.4 Content and Experience Layer

The content and experience layer defines what users see, hear, and interact with. This includes three-dimensional assets, interaction logic, scripting, and experience orchestration.

Content creation is resource-intensive. High-quality assets require specialised skills and tooling. Managing content at scale introduces challenges related to versioning, performance optimisation, and compatibility across devices.

Experience orchestration governs how users move through environments, how interactions are triggered, and how narratives or workflows unfold. Poorly designed experiences can negate the benefits of sophisticated infrastructure and simulation.

This layer is often where pilot projects focus their effort, sometimes at the expense of underlying architectural robustness. As discussed in Chapter 4, visually impressive experiences that lack integration, governance, or measurement rarely scale successfully.

5.2.5 Client Devices and Interfaces

The top layer of the architecture consists of client devices and interfaces. These include head-mounted displays, controllers, sensors, and in some cases desktop or mobile interfaces used as fallbacks.

Device capabilities vary widely in terms of processing power, display quality, field of view, and interaction fidelity. This variability introduces inconsistency in user experience and complicates testing and support.

Human factors are particularly important at this layer. Comfort, ergonomics, and accessibility influence adoption more strongly than technical specifications. Motion sickness, fatigue, and cognitive load remain significant barriers for some users.

Architectural decisions must therefore account for heterogeneous devices and user tolerance. Systems designed for a narrow class of hardware may deliver high fidelity but exclude large portions of the potential user base.

5.2.6 Interdependencies between Layers

While each architectural layer can be described independently, metaverse systems function as tightly coupled wholes. Decisions made at one layer constrain options at others.

For example, choices about identity persistence affect data storage, privacy controls, and moderation tooling. Decisions about simulation fidelity influence infrastructure cost and network requirements. Device limitations shape interaction design and content complexity.

Understanding these interdependencies is essential for realistic planning. Many failed initiatives underestimated the cumulative impact of small architectural compromises made in isolation.

5.2.7 Section Summary

The metaverse is not a monolithic platform but a layered system composed of infrastructure, simulation, identity, content, and client technologies. Each layer introduces specific constraints and trade-offs that shape what is feasible.

Architectural clarity is therefore a prerequisite for meaningful adoption. Organisations that treat the metaverse as an abstract concept rather than as a concrete system risk repeating the misalignments explored in Chapter 4.

The next section builds on this foundation by examining the specific technologies that enable these architectural layers to function, and by assessing their current maturity and limitations. Figure 5.1 illustrates the layered architecture of the metaverse, showing how infrastructure, networking, spatial computing, content, and experience layers depend on supporting elements such as identity, governance, and user interfaces.

5.3 ENABLING TECHNOLOGIES OF THE METAVERSE

The architectural layers described in the previous section are enabled by a collection of underlying technologies that together make immersive

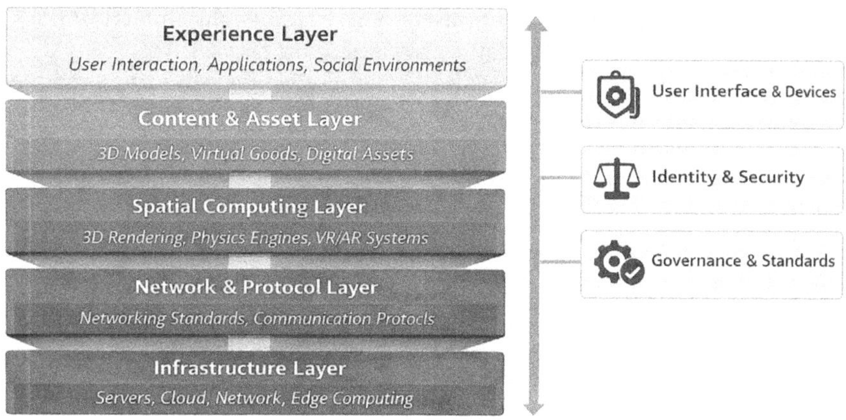

Figure 5.1 Layered architecture of the Metaverse.

Note: Layered architectural view of a metaverse system, illustrating infrastructure, simulation, identity, content, and client layers and their interdependencies.

environments technically feasible. These technologies differ significantly in maturity, stability, and suitability for enterprise use. Understanding their capabilities and limitations is essential for evaluating what the metaverse can realistically deliver today.

This section examines the principal enabling technologies underpinning metaverse systems, focusing on their functional role, current constraints, and implications for large-scale deployment. The discussion avoids platform-specific promotion and instead concentrates on structural characteristics common across implementations.

5.3.1 Virtual Reality Technologies

VR technologies provide fully immersive environments by replacing the user's visual and auditory perception of the physical world with a computer-generated alternative. VR systems rely on head-mounted displays, motion tracking, rendering engines, and low-latency input pipelines to create a sense of presence.

From a technical perspective, VR is one of the more mature immersive technologies. Commercial hardware platforms are widely available, and rendering engines can produce high-fidelity environments. However, maturity at the device level does not automatically translate into readiness for enterprise-scale deployment.

Key constraints include hardware ergonomics, session duration limitations, and user tolerance. Extended VR use can lead to discomfort, fatigue, or motion sickness for a subset of users. These factors place practical limits on how VR can be used in sustained business workflows.

Performance requirements are also demanding. High frame rates and low latency are essential to maintain immersion and avoid discomfort. Achieving these requirements consistently across diverse network conditions and device capabilities remains challenging. As a result, VR is best suited to bounded use cases such as training simulations, design reviews, or controlled collaborative sessions, rather than as a general-purpose work environment.

5.3.2 Augmented and Mixed Reality Technologies

AR and mixed reality technologies overlay digital information onto the physical environment rather than replacing it entirely. This allows users to remain aware of their surroundings while interacting with virtual objects and data.

From an architectural standpoint, AR and MR systems introduce additional complexity. They require accurate spatial mapping, environmental understanding, and alignment between physical and digital coordinates. Errors in tracking or calibration can quickly degrade usability.

Compared to VR, AR and MR are generally better tolerated for longer sessions, as they do not isolate users from the physical world. This makes them attractive for enterprise scenarios such as maintenance, guided workflows, and on-site collaboration.

However, hardware limitations remain significant. Field of view constraints, battery life, device weight, and cost all limit widespread adoption. In addition, AR and MR systems often depend on continuous sensor input, raising privacy and data governance concerns.

These technologies are therefore promising but uneven in maturity. Their suitability varies strongly by context, and architectural designs must accommodate gradual adoption rather than assume universal deployment.

5.3.3 Real-Time 3D Engines

Real-time 3D engines form the core execution environment for most metaverse experiences. They are responsible for rendering graphics, processing interaction logic, simulating physics, and managing scene composition.

Modern 3D engines are powerful and flexible, enabling complex environments to be constructed relatively quickly. However, they were originally designed for gaming and entertainment contexts rather than enterprise systems.

This heritage introduces challenges. Enterprise requirements such as deterministic behaviour, long-term maintainability, auditability, and integration with existing systems are not always first-class concerns in engine design.

Scaling real-time engines beyond small groups of users also presents difficulties. As concurrency increases, maintaining synchronised state and consistent behaviour becomes computationally expensive. Architectural compromises are often required, such as reducing interaction fidelity or partitioning users into smaller instances.

As a result, 3D engines are a necessary but insufficient component. They must be embedded within broader architectures that address governance, observability, and lifecycle management.

5.3.4 Networking and Synchronisation Technologies

Networking technologies underpin all multi-user metaverse experiences. They are responsible for transmitting state updates, user actions, and environmental changes between participants in real time.

Low latency is critical. Even small delays can disrupt interaction and reduce the sense of shared presence. To mitigate this, metaverse systems often use predictive techniques, local interpolation, and selective state replication.

Synchronisation introduces trade-offs between consistency and scalability. Strong consistency ensures that all users observe the same state but limits the number of participants. Weaker consistency models improve scalability but can introduce perceptible divergence.

Network reliability and variability further complicate design. Consumer-grade networks are subject to congestion, packet loss, and fluctuating performance. Architectures must therefore be resilient to imperfect conditions rather than assume ideal connectivity. These constraints make networking one of the most significant limiting factors for large-scale, shared metaverse environments.

5.3.5 Spatial Audio and Interaction Systems

Spatial audio and interaction systems contribute significantly to immersion by providing directional sound cues and intuitive interaction mechanisms. These systems enhance presence and situational awareness but add additional computational and design complexity.

Accurate spatial audio requires real-time processing of sound sources relative to user position and orientation. In multi-user environments, this processing scales with the number of participants and sound events.

Interaction systems, such as gesture recognition and haptic feedback, depend on sensor accuracy and user behaviour. Variability in user movement, lighting conditions, and device calibration can affect reliability.

From an enterprise perspective, these systems must balance immersion against robustness. Overly complex interaction models can increase training requirements and reduce accessibility.

5.3.6 Enterprise Deployment Lens

When enabling technologies are evaluated through an enterprise lens, additional considerations emerge. Stability, supportability, and lifecycle management become as important as raw capability.

Enterprises require predictable upgrade paths, long-term vendor support, and clear responsibility boundaries. Many immersive technologies evolve rapidly, with frequent hardware and software changes that can disrupt deployed systems.

Integration with existing identity systems, data platforms, and security controls is also essential. Technologies that operate in isolation may succeed in pilots but fail to scale across organisations. This gap between technological possibility and organisational readiness is a recurring theme in metaverse adoption.

5.3.7 Technology Maturity and Risk Profile

The enabling technologies of the metaverse occupy different positions on the maturity spectrum. Some, such as real-time rendering and basic VR hardware, are relatively stable. Others, including large-scale synchronisation and enterprise-grade AR, remain emergent.

Risk arises not only from immaturity but from uneven maturity across components. Architectures that assume all enabling technologies are equally ready often encounter unexpected bottlenecks. Effective design therefore requires explicit assessment of maturity and risk at each layer, rather than reliance on aggregate narratives about technological readiness.

5.3.8 Section Summary

The metaverse is enabled by a diverse set of technologies, each contributing specific capabilities while introducing distinct constraints. No single technology determines success or failure; outcomes emerge from their interaction within a broader architectural context.

Understanding these enabling technologies in detail is essential for realistic planning. Overestimating maturity or underestimating integration complexity leads to the misalignments explored in earlier chapters. The next section examines how these technologies generate and consume data, and why analytics and observability are critical to managing immersive systems at scale.

5.4 DATA, ANALYTICS, AND OBSERVABILITY IN IMMERSIVE SYSTEMS

Immersive systems fundamentally change the nature, scale, and sensitivity of data generated by digital platforms. Unlike traditional enterprise systems, where data is largely transactional or document-based, metaverse environments continuously capture spatial, behavioural, and interactional signals. These signals are produced in real time, often at high frequency, and are tightly coupled to user embodiment and presence.

As a result, data, analytics, and observability are not optional supporting functions in metaverse architectures. They are core structural components that determine whether immersive systems can be operated safely, scaled reliably, and governed responsibly. This section examines the data characteristics of immersive systems, the analytical challenges they introduce, and the architectural requirements for observability at scale.

5.4.1 Nature and Characteristics of Metaverse Data

Metaverse platforms generate multiple overlapping categories of data, each with distinct properties and implications. At the most basic level, system telemetry captures infrastructure metrics such as CPU usage, memory consumption, network latency, and rendering performance. These metrics are similar in form to those collected by conventional cloud applications, but their tolerances are much tighter due to real-time interaction requirements.

Beyond system telemetry, immersive platforms produce continuous streams of spatial data. This includes user position, orientation, movement trajectories, gaze direction, and proximity to other users or objects. Such data is inherently high-dimensional and time-sensitive.

Interaction data adds further complexity. Gestures, voice input, object manipulation, and environmental changes are recorded as events or state transitions. These interactions are often ambiguous without contextual interpretation, as the same physical action may have different meanings depending on environment design and user intent.

Finally, many immersive systems capture environmental context, such as room geometry, lighting conditions, and physical obstacles. This information blurs the boundary between digital and physical domains, raising new architectural and governance considerations.

5.4.2 Behavioural and Embodied Analytics

One of the most frequently cited benefits of immersive environments is their ability to capture embodied behaviour. Proponents argue that such data enables richer insight into learning effectiveness, collaboration patterns, and decision-making processes.

In practice, behavioural analytics in immersive environments are fraught with interpretive challenges. User behaviour is shaped not only by task objectives but also by device ergonomics, interface affordances, and user familiarity with immersive interaction. Early-stage users often exhibit exploratory or compensatory behaviours that do not reflect stable patterns.

Architectures must therefore distinguish between signal and noise. This requires explicit modelling of interaction constraints and learning curves. Without such modelling, analytics outputs risk overstating engagement, mischaracterising performance, or reinforcing design biases.

Moreover, behavioural data in immersive systems is highly personal. Movement patterns, reaction times, and spatial preferences can reveal physical condition, cognitive load, and emotional state. This elevates the ethical and regulatory stakes of behavioural analytics well beyond those associated with conventional usage data.

5.4.3 Real-Time Analytics versus Post-Session Analysis

Architectural decisions must be made regarding when and how data is analysed. Some insights are only useful in real time, such as detecting performance degradation, unsafe interactions, or policy violations. Other analyses, such as learning outcomes or workflow optimisation, are more appropriately conducted after sessions conclude. Table 5.1 summarises the

Table 5.1 Categories of Data Generated in Immersive Systems

Data Category	*Description*	*Typical Sources*	*Architectural Implications*
System Telemetry	Operational metrics describing platform performance and health	Cloud infrastructure, rendering engines, network services	Requires real-time monitoring, low-latency ingestion, and correlation across layers
Spatial Data	Continuous position, orientation, and movement information	Head-mounted displays, controllers, tracking sensors	High-volume, high-frequency data requiring efficient streaming and sampling strategies
Interaction Data	User actions such as gestures, object manipulation, and navigation	Input devices, interaction engines	Context-dependent interpretation; requires event normalisation and state awareness
Behavioural Data	Patterns inferred from repeated interactions over time	Analytics pipelines, session logs	Sensitive and privacy-critical; must be governed and purpose-limited
Communication Data	Voice and text interactions between users	Audio systems, messaging services	Requires encryption, moderation support, and retention controls
Environmental Context Data	Physical and virtual environment attributes	Sensors, spatial mapping services	Blurs digital–physical boundary; introduces compliance and privacy considerations

Note: This table presents categories of data generated by metaverse platforms, highlighting data characteristics, sources, and architectural implications.

key interoperability and standards considerations that influence whether metaverse platforms can operate as isolated environments or as part of a wider, connected digital ecosystem.

Real-time analytics impose stringent performance requirements. Data must be processed with minimal latency and without disrupting rendering or interaction pipelines. This often necessitates edge processing or selective sampling rather than full data capture.

Post-session analysis allows for richer processing and aggregation but introduces delays between behaviour and insight. Architects must therefore balance immediacy against depth, deciding which signals justify real-time treatment and which can be deferred. Poorly considered choices in this area can either overload systems or deprive operators of timely visibility into critical issues.

5.4.4 Observability as an Architectural Requirement

Observability refers to the ability to infer the internal state of a system from its external outputs. In immersive systems, observability extends beyond infrastructure health to encompass user experience, interaction quality, and synchronisation integrity.

Traditional monitoring tools are insufficient on their own. Metrics such as average latency or CPU utilisation do not capture frame drops, motion-to-photon delay, or perceptual inconsistencies that directly affect immersion.

Architectures must therefore incorporate immersive-specific observability signals, including frame timing stability, synchronisation divergence between participants, and interaction latency distributions. These signals must be correlated across layers, from infrastructure to client devices.

Without comprehensive observability, immersive platforms become operationally opaque. Issues may be detected only after users report discomfort or disengagement, by which point trust may already be eroded.

5.4.5 Data Volume, Cost, and Retention Trade-Offs

The continuous nature of immersive data generation creates significant storage and processing costs. Capturing high-frequency spatial and behavioural data for large numbers of users quickly becomes economically unsustainable.

Architects must therefore make explicit decisions about data retention, aggregation, and disposal. Not all data can or should be retained indefinitely. Decisions must be guided by analytical value, regulatory requirements, and ethical considerations.

Data minimisation is particularly important given the sensitivity of embodied data. Retaining detailed behavioural traces without a clear purpose increases privacy risk and compliance burden. Well-designed architectures treat data lifecycle management as a first-class concern rather than an afterthought.

5.4.6 Data Quality, Bias, and Representativeness

Data generated in immersive environments is subject to multiple sources of bias. Device capabilities influence interaction fidelity, meaning that users with lower-end hardware may appear less engaged or capable. Network conditions can distort performance metrics and behavioural signals.

Selection bias is also significant. Users willing or able to engage with immersive systems may not represent the broader population. Conclusions drawn from immersive analytics must therefore be contextualised carefully.

Architectures should support data quality assessment, calibration, and validation against external benchmarks. Without these safeguards, immersive analytics risk reinforcing flawed assumptions.

5.4.7 Enterprise Governance and Accountability

In enterprise contexts, data accountability extends beyond technical correctness to include governance, auditability, and explainability. Decision-makers must be able to understand how immersive data is collected, processed, and used.

This requires clear data ownership, documented processing logic, and transparent reporting mechanisms. Black-box analytics are particularly problematic when immersive data informs training outcomes, performance evaluation, or compliance decisions. Architectural designs must therefore align data and analytics pipelines with existing enterprise governance frameworks rather than operating as isolated systems.

5.4.8 Implications for Metaverse Architecture

The data and analytics characteristics of immersive systems reinforce the importance of architectural discipline. Immersive platforms that prioritise experience design without equal attention to observability and governance are unlikely to scale sustainably.

Architects must treat data as a core design axis, balancing insight generation against cost, risk, and ethical responsibility. Doing so enables immersive systems to deliver value while maintaining trust and operational control. Figure 5.2 illustrates data flow and observability layers within a metaverse architecture, showing how telemetry, behavioural data, and system metrics propagate across infrastructure and application layers.

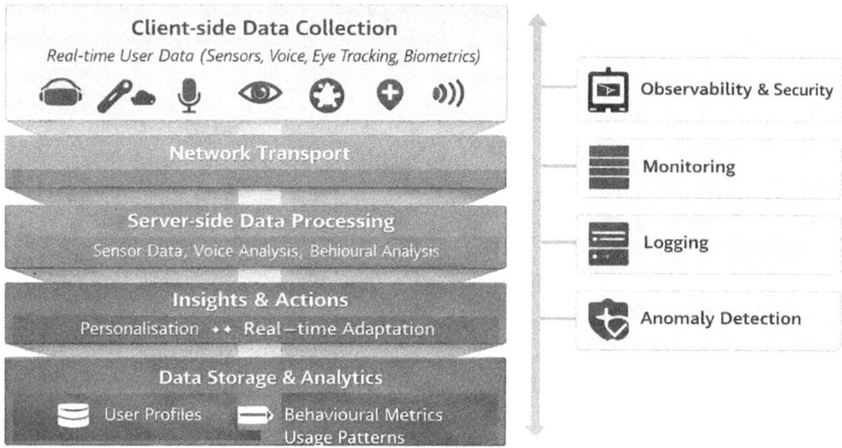

Figure 5.2 Data flow and observability layers within a Metaverse architecture, illustrating how telemetry, behavioural data, and system metrics propagate across infrastructure and application layers.

5.4.9 Section Summary

Data, analytics, and observability are foundational to the operation of immersive systems. The richness of immersive data offers significant potential but also introduces complexity, cost, and risk.

Effective metaverse architectures explicitly address these challenges through careful design of data pipelines, analytics strategies, and observability mechanisms. Without this foundation, immersive initiatives are prone to failure regardless of their experiential quality.

5.5 SECURITY, PRIVACY, AND GOVERNANCE FOUNDATIONS

Security, privacy, and governance challenges in the metaverse are qualitatively different from those encountered in traditional digital systems. This difference arises from the embodied nature of interaction, the persistence of shared environments, and the sensitivity of the data generated through immersive engagement. As a result, conventional security models and governance frameworks, while necessary, are insufficient on their own.

This section examines the structural security and governance requirements of immersive systems, focusing on identity, data protection, behavioural control, and regulatory alignment. The emphasis is on architectural implications rather than platform-specific implementations.

5.5.1 Security Characteristics of Immersive Environments

Immersive environments expand the attack surface beyond conventional application boundaries. In addition to accounts and data, attackers may target avatars, spatial presence, communication channels, and interaction mechanisms.

Unlike text-based or transactional systems, immersive platforms involve continuous interaction. Security incidents can therefore unfold in real time, affecting multiple users simultaneously. This increases both the speed and impact of potential breaches.

Furthermore, immersive systems often integrate heterogeneous components, including hardware devices, local sensors, network services, and cloud platforms. Each component introduces its own vulnerabilities, and weaknesses at any layer can compromise the system as a whole. Security architecture must therefore adopt a holistic view, addressing threats across devices, networks, platforms, and user behaviour.

5.5.2 Identity Security and Authentication

Identity is central to immersive interaction. Users are represented through avatars that act as proxies for presence, agency, and social identity. Compromise of identity in immersive environments can have consequences that extend beyond data access to include impersonation, harassment, and reputational harm.

Authentication mechanisms must balance security with usability. Excessively intrusive controls may disrupt immersion, while weak authentication exposes platforms to abuse. Architectural designs must therefore integrate identity verification seamlessly into the interaction flow.

In enterprise contexts, immersive identity systems must integrate with existing identity and access management frameworks. Standalone identity silos increase administrative burden and create inconsistencies in access control and auditability.

Persistent identity raises additional questions. While persistence enables continuity and accountability, it also increases privacy risk and may discourage participation. Architectural decisions must make these trade-offs explicit.

5.5.3 Authorisation and Access Control in Spatial Contexts

Traditional access control models are typically role-based and action-oriented. In immersive environments, access control also has a spatial dimension. Users may be authorised to enter certain areas, interact with specific objects, or engage with particular groups.

Spatial authorisation introduces complexity. Permissions must be evaluated continuously as users move and interact. Static access rules are insufficient in dynamic environments.

Architectures must therefore support context-aware access control that accounts for location, proximity, and interaction state. This increases system complexity but is essential for maintaining safety and confidentiality in shared spaces.

5.5.4 Privacy Risks of Embodied and Behavioural Data

Immersive systems capture data that is deeply personal. Movement patterns, gestures, voice characteristics, and spatial behaviour can reveal physical condition, emotional state, and cognitive responses.

Unlike conventional personal data, embodied data is difficult to anonymise without destroying its analytical value. Even when identifiers are removed, behavioural patterns may allow re-identification.

Architectural approaches to privacy must therefore prioritise data minimisation and purpose limitation. Collecting data simply because it is technically feasible increases risk without necessarily delivering value.

Consent mechanisms must be clear and meaningful. Users must understand what data is collected, how it is used, and how long it is retained. In immersive environments, conveying this information without breaking immersion presents a design challenge.

5.5.5 Moderation, Safety, and Behavioural Governance

Behavioural governance is more complex in immersive environments than in text-based platforms. Proximity, gesture, and voice can be used to intimidate or harass in ways that are difficult to moderate after the fact.

Effective governance requires a combination of preventive design, real-time monitoring, and responsive intervention. Architectural designs must support mechanisms for reporting, evidence capture, and enforcement without imposing excessive friction on legitimate users.

Automation plays an important role, but it has limits. Behavioural cues are context-dependent, and false positives can undermine trust. Human oversight therefore remains necessary, particularly in sensitive or high-stakes environments. Failure to address behavioural governance adequately can rapidly erode user trust and lead to reputational damage. Table 5.2 maps security and privacy risks across the architectural layers of the metaverse, linking each layer to its key vulnerabilities and governance considerations.

Table 5.2 Security and Privacy Risks by Architectural Layer

Architectural Layer	*Key Security Risks*	*Privacy Risks*	*Governance Considerations*
Infrastructure Layer	Cloud misconfiguration, denial-of-service attacks, dependency failures	Indirect exposure through logs and telemetry	Alignment with enterprise cloud security standards and incident response processes
Network Layer	Interception, latency manipulation, traffic analysis	Inference of user behaviour through traffic patterns	Network segmentation, encryption, and monitoring requirements
Identity Layer	Credential theft, impersonation, unauthorised access	Linkage of virtual identity to real-world identity	Strong authentication, access logging, and identity lifecycle management
Simulation and Engine Layer	Exploitation of engine vulnerabilities, state manipulation	Behavioural inference from interaction patterns	Patch management, code governance, and validation controls
Content and Interaction Layer	Malicious content injection, harassment, moderation bypass	Exposure of personal expression and social behaviour	Content governance, moderation policies, and enforcement mechanisms
Client Device Layer	Device compromise, sensor abuse, firmware vulnerabilities	Capture of biometric and environmental data	Device management, update controls, and user consent mechanisms

Note: This table presents security and privacy risks across metaverse architectural layers, illustrating threat exposure and governance considerations.

5.5.6 Device and Endpoint Security

Client devices represent a critical security boundary. Head-mounted displays, controllers, and sensors collect and transmit sensitive data and may operate outside controlled enterprise environments.

Device compromise can enable surveillance, data leakage, or manipulation of user perception. Architectural designs must therefore consider secure device provisioning, update mechanisms, and lifecycle management.

In enterprise deployments, device security policies must align with existing endpoint management frameworks. Consumer-grade device assumptions may not meet organisational risk thresholds.

5.5.7 Regulatory and Legal Considerations

Metaverse platforms intersect with multiple regulatory domains, including data protection, workplace safety, accessibility, and sector-specific compliance. These obligations vary by jurisdiction and use case.

Architectural decisions determine whether compliance can be enforced systematically or relies on manual controls. For example, data residency requirements may necessitate regional infrastructure deployment, while accessibility standards may influence interaction design.

Regulatory uncertainty further complicates planning. As immersive technologies evolve, regulatory frameworks are likely to adapt, potentially introducing new obligations. Architectures that lack flexibility may struggle to accommodate such changes.

5.5.8 Governance Models and Accountability

Effective governance requires clear allocation of responsibility. In immersive systems, accountability may be shared across platform providers, content creators, and operators.

Ambiguity in governance models is a common cause of failure. When incidents occur, unclear responsibility delays response and undermines confidence.

Architectural designs must therefore support governance structures that define roles, escalation paths, and decision rights. This includes logging, audit trails, and reporting mechanisms that enable oversight. In enterprise contexts, governance must align with existing risk management and compliance processes rather than operating as an exception.

5.5.9 Security Economics and Trade-Offs

Security controls impose cost, complexity, and sometimes friction. In immersive environments, these trade-offs are particularly acute, as excessive controls can disrupt experience quality.

Architects must balance risk reduction against usability and scalability. Not all risks can be eliminated, and attempting to do so may render systems unusable or economically unviable. Explicit risk acceptance, supported by transparent governance, is therefore a necessary component of realistic metaverse architecture.

5.5.10 Implications for Sustainable Adoption

Security, privacy, and governance are not barriers to metaverse adoption; they are prerequisites for sustainability. Platforms that neglect these foundations may achieve short-term engagement but are unlikely to maintain trust over time.

Architectural designs that embed security and governance from the outset enable more resilient and adaptable systems. Conversely, retrofitting controls after incidents occur is costly and often ineffective.

5.5.11 Section Summary

Immersive environments introduce new security, privacy, and governance challenges that extend beyond those of traditional digital systems. Addressing these challenges requires architectural approaches that integrate identity, access control, data protection, and behavioural governance across all layers of the system.

Without such foundations, metaverse initiatives risk becoming operationally fragile, ethically questionable, and ultimately unsustainable. Figure 5.3 illustrates the security and governance overlay across metaverse architectural layers, showing how risk controls span infrastructure, identity, content, and interaction domains.

5.6 INTEROPERABILITY AND STANDARDS

Interoperability is frequently cited as a defining aspiration of the metaverse, yet it remains one of the most technically and commercially unresolved challenges. While popular narratives often assume seamless movement of users, identities, and assets across virtual environments, the practical reality is far more constrained. Interoperability is not a single problem but a collection of interrelated technical, organisational, and economic challenges. This section examines interoperability from an architectural perspective, focusing on why it is difficult to achieve, how standards efforts have evolved, and what realistic expectations should guide system design.

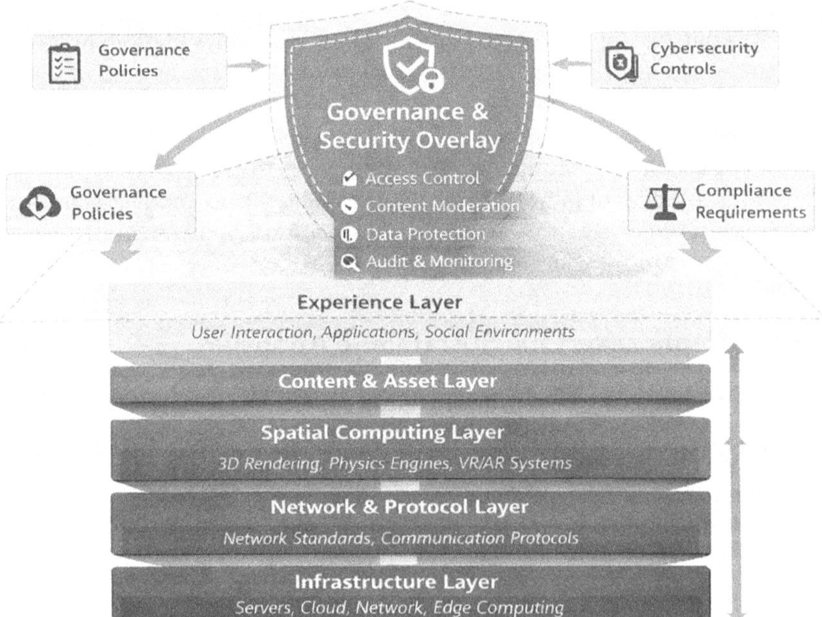

Figure 5.3 Security and governance overlay across Metaverse architectural layers, highlighting how risk controls span infrastructure, identity, content, and interaction domains.

5.6.1 Dimensions of Interoperability in Immersive Systems

Interoperability in the metaverse spans multiple dimensions. At the most basic level, it concerns the ability to exchange data between systems. More advanced forms involve the portability of digital assets, identities, behaviours, and even social relationships.

Data interoperability involves shared formats, schemas, and semantics. Asset interoperability extends this to three-dimensional models, textures, animations, and interaction logic. Identity interoperability raises additional complexity, requiring consistent representation of users across platforms with differing trust models.

Behavioural interoperability, which would allow actions and capabilities to persist across environments, is the most ambitious and least realised dimension. Achieving this would require alignment not only of technical standards but also of design philosophies and governance rules. Architectural designs must therefore clarify which dimensions of interoperability are required for a given use case, rather than assuming comprehensive portability as a default goal.

5.6.2 Technical Barriers to Interoperability

Technical barriers to interoperability are substantial. Immersive platforms often rely on proprietary asset formats, physics engines, and rendering pipelines optimised for specific performance characteristics. Even when open formats are used, differences in implementation can lead to inconsistent behaviour.

State synchronisation poses additional challenges. Persistent virtual environments maintain complex internal state that may not map cleanly between systems. Translating this state risks loss of fidelity or semantic meaning.

Network architectures also differ. Some platforms are designed for small-group interaction, while others prioritise large-scale audiences. These architectural assumptions influence data models and interaction patterns, further complicating interoperability. As a result, technical interoperability often requires compromise, abstraction, or loss of functionality.

5.6.3 Standards Bodies and Industry Initiatives

Multiple organisations are engaged in developing standards relevant to immersive technologies. These include efforts focused on file formats, identity frameworks, interaction models, and network protocols.

Standards bodies provide a forum for coordination, but progress is often incremental. Achieving consensus across diverse stakeholders with competing commercial interests is inherently slow. Moreover, standards may lag behind rapidly evolving technologies, limiting their immediate applicability.

Industry-led initiatives sometimes move faster but may prioritise the interests of dominant platforms. This can result in de facto standards that lack openness or long-term stability. Architects must therefore evaluate standards not only on technical merit but also on governance, adoption momentum, and alignment with strategic objectives.

5.6.4 Commercial Incentives and Strategic Resistance

Interoperability is not purely a technical challenge; it is also an economic one. Platform providers may have limited incentive to enable portability that reduces user lock-in or commoditises unique capabilities.

Walled-garden strategies can be commercially attractive, particularly in early stages of market development. Interoperability may be deferred until ecosystems mature or competitive pressure increases.

From an enterprise perspective, this creates strategic risk. Dependence on closed platforms can limit flexibility and increase switching costs. Architectural designs must therefore account for the likelihood of partial or delayed interoperability.

5.6.5 Interoperability and Governance Complexity

Interoperability introduces governance challenges alongside technical ones. When assets, identities, or users move across platforms, questions arise regarding policy enforcement, liability, and dispute resolution.

For example, content moderation rules may differ between environments. An action permitted in one platform may violate policies in another. Resolving such conflicts requires coordination mechanisms that extend beyond technical interfaces.

Architectural designs must therefore consider not only how systems connect but also how rules and responsibilities are aligned across boundaries.

5.6.6 Enterprise Implications of Limited Interoperability

Enterprises often operate across multiple platforms and vendors. Limited interoperability complicates integration, increases operational overhead, and constrains strategic choice.

In practice, enterprises may prioritise internal interoperability within their own ecosystems over broad cross-platform portability. This may involve standardising on specific tools or building abstraction layers that shield internal systems from external variability.

Such approaches can mitigate risk but may reduce flexibility. Architects must weigh the benefits of control against the costs of reduced openness. Table 5.3 summarises the main interoperability barriers affecting metaverse

Table 5.3 Interoperability Barriers and Strategic Impact

Interoperability Dimension	*Primary Barriers*	*Technical Impact*	*Strategic Implications*
Identity Interoperability	Proprietary identity systems, incompatible trust models	Fragmented user identities across platforms	Increased administrative overhead and reduced user mobility
Asset Interoperability	Non-standard 3D formats, engine-specific behaviours	Loss of fidelity or functionality during asset transfer	Higher content creation costs and platform lock-in
Data Interoperability	Inconsistent schemas and semantics	Complex data transformation and integration pipelines	Reduced analytical consistency and governance complexity
Interaction Models	Platform-specific physics and interaction logic	Inconsistent user experience across environments	Limits cross-platform usability and training portability
Networking Protocols	Divergent synchronisation and latency models	Difficulty maintaining shared state	Constrains multi-platform collaboration
Governance Alignment	Differing content and conduct policies	Policy conflicts and enforcement gaps	Increased legal and reputational risk

Note: This table presents key interoperability barriers in metaverse platforms and their strategic implications for organisations.

systems, linking each interoperability dimension to its technical impact and strategic implications.

5.6.7 Architectural Strategies for Managing Interoperability Risk

Given the challenges outlined, architectural strategies for interoperability should be pragmatic. These may include:

- Designing modular systems with well-defined interfaces
- Using open formats where feasible while planning for conversion costs
- Avoiding over-reliance on platform-specific features
- Maintaining exit strategies and migration pathways

Rather than aiming for full interoperability from the outset, architectures can support incremental progress as standards mature and ecosystems evolve.

5.6.8 Interoperability versus Innovation Trade-Offs

Pursuing interoperability can constrain innovation. Strict adherence to standards may limit the ability to experiment with novel interaction models or performance optimisations.

Conversely, excessive divergence can fragment ecosystems and undermine long-term viability. Architectural decisions must therefore balance short-term innovation against long-term compatibility. Explicit recognition of this trade-off enables more informed decision-making and reduces the risk of misaligned expectations.

5.6.9 Future Trajectories and Uncertainty

The trajectory of interoperability in the metaverse remains uncertain. Technological advances, regulatory intervention, and market dynamics will all influence outcomes.

Architectures that assume rapid convergence may prove brittle. Those that accommodate uncertainty through flexibility and modularity are more likely to remain viable over time.

5.6.10 Section Summary

Interoperability is a multifaceted challenge that encompasses technical, commercial, and governance dimensions. While it is often presented as a defining feature of the metaverse, achieving meaningful interoperability remains difficult in practice.

Architectural designs must therefore adopt a realistic stance, recognising current limitations while preparing for gradual progress. By doing so, organisations can avoid overcommitting to assumptions that may not materialise. Figure 5.4 illustrates the interoperability and standards landscape for the metaverse, categorising the identity, virtual asset, spatial, and communication layers that support cross-platform functionality.

5.7 INTEGRATION WITH ENTERPRISE ARCHITECTURE

For the metaverse to transition from experimental deployments to sustained enterprise capability, immersive platforms must integrate coherently with existing enterprise architecture. This requirement is frequently underestimated, particularly during early pilots where metaverse initiatives are treated as isolated innovation efforts rather than as components of the wider technology estate.

Enterprise architecture integration determines whether immersive systems can be governed, secured, supported, and scaled in line with organisational

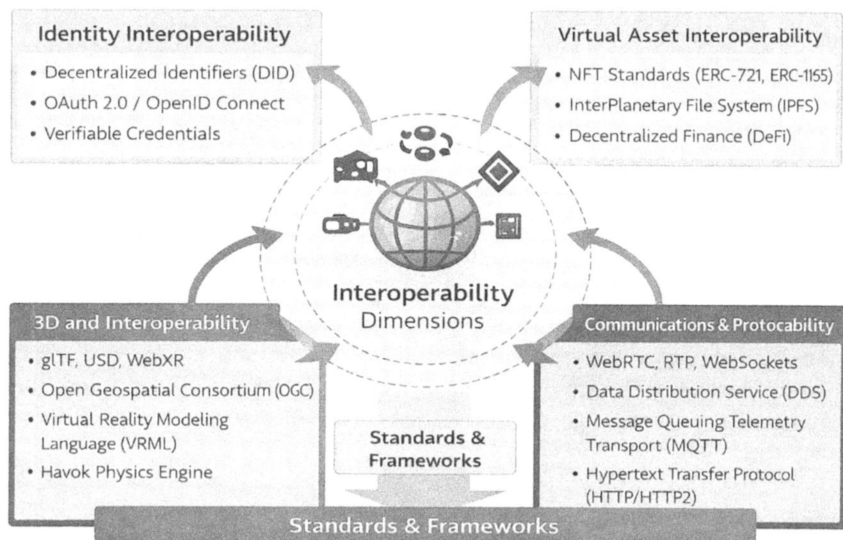

Figure 5.4 Interoperability and standards landscape for the Metaverse, categorising identity, virtual asset, spatial, and communication layers that enable cross-platform functionality.

standards. Without such integration, metaverse deployments risk becoming operational anomalies that are difficult to justify economically, manage operationally, or retire strategically. This section examines the principal architectural touchpoints between metaverse platforms and enterprise systems, focusing on identity, networking, security, data, applications, and operational ownership.

5.7.1 Role of Enterprise Architecture in Metaverse Adoption

Enterprise architecture provides the structural framework through which technology initiatives are aligned with business objectives, risk tolerance, and operational constraints. Metaverse platforms that bypass this framework may achieve short-term visibility but often struggle to deliver sustained value.

From an architectural perspective, immersive systems must be evaluated in terms of how they interact with core enterprise domains, including identity management, network infrastructure, security controls, data platforms, and application ecosystems. Each domain introduces dependencies that shape feasibility, cost, and risk. Treating the metaverse as an architectural domain rather than a standalone product enables more realistic planning and reduces the likelihood of strategic misalignment.

5.7.2 Identity and Access Management Integration

Identity and access management is one of the most critical integration points for enterprise metaverse deployments. Most organisations operate centralised identity platforms that govern authentication, authorisation, and auditability across systems.

Immersive platforms that introduce separate identity silos increase administrative overhead and weaken security posture. Users may be required to manage multiple credentials, while security teams lose unified visibility into access patterns.

Architectural integration with enterprise identity systems enables single sign-on, role-based access control, and consistent policy enforcement. It also supports compliance requirements by ensuring that access to immersive environments is traceable and revocable.

5.7.3 Network Architecture and Connectivity Constraints

Metaverse platforms impose distinctive demands on enterprise networks. Real-time interaction, high-bandwidth media streams, and sensitivity to latency challenge network architectures optimised for transactional systems and asynchronous communication.

Introducing immersive traffic can expose capacity limitations, increase congestion, and complicate quality-of-service management. Network performance variability directly affects user experience, potentially undermining confidence in immersive systems.

Architectural planning must therefore address network segmentation, prioritisation, and capacity planning explicitly. Failure to do so may result in degraded immersive experiences or unintended disruption to other critical services.

5.7.4 Security Architecture and Trust Boundaries

Integrating immersive platforms into enterprise environments extends organisational trust boundaries. Data flows between metaverse systems and enterprise back-end services must be protected against interception, manipulation, and misuse.

Security architectures must define clear trust zones, authentication points, and monitoring mechanisms. Immersive platforms that operate outside established security controls introduce blind spots that increase organisational risk.

In regulated industries, security integration is non-negotiable. Architectural designs must demonstrate how immersive systems align with internal security policies and external regulatory obligations.

5.7.5 Data Platform and Analytics Integration

Enterprises typically rely on centralised data platforms to support reporting, analytics, and decision-making. Metaverse platforms that generate large volumes of behavioural and spatial data must integrate with these platforms to avoid fragmentation and governance gaps.

Integration challenges include data format compatibility, ingestion pipelines, and metadata management. Immersive data often differs substantially from traditional enterprise data, requiring transformation and contextualisation.

Architectural designs should clearly define which immersive data is integrated into enterprise platforms, which remains local to the metaverse system, and how data quality and lineage are maintained.

5.7.6 Application Ecosystem and Workflow Integration

For immersive platforms to deliver operational value, they must connect meaningfully to existing enterprise applications and workflows. These may include learning management systems, design and engineering tools, asset repositories, or collaboration platforms.

Isolated immersive experiences that do not feed into downstream processes often fail to demonstrate measurable impact. Integration enables immersive activity to contribute to tangible business outcomes. Architectural planning must therefore identify application and workflow integration points early, rather than treating them as secondary enhancements.

5.7.7 Operational Ownership and Support Models

Operational ownership of metaverse platforms is frequently unclear. Responsibilities may be distributed across innovation teams, IT functions, security departments, and business units.

Without clear ownership, issues such as incident response, maintenance, updates, and user support can be neglected. This undermines reliability and erodes stakeholder trust.

Enterprise architecture frameworks can clarify ownership by defining operational models, escalation paths, and service-level expectations. Immersive platforms must be treated as operational systems rather than experimental artefacts.

5.7.8 Change Management and Organisational Readiness

Integration challenges extend beyond technical considerations. Immersive platforms introduce new interaction paradigms that require user training, support, and cultural adaptation.

Change management must address user expectations, accessibility concerns, and adoption barriers. Without adequate preparation, users may resist or misuse immersive systems, regardless of their technical quality. Architectural planning should therefore incorporate organisational readiness alongside technical integration to support sustainable adoption.

5.7.9 Integration Risks and Mitigation Approaches

Common integration risks include identity fragmentation, network saturation, data silos, and unclear accountability. These risks are often amplified when immersive platforms are deployed rapidly or without architectural oversight.

Mitigation approaches include phased integration, architectural governance reviews, and alignment with established enterprise standards. Explicitly identifying integration risks early enables more controlled and resilient deployment. Table 5.4 outlines the main enterprise integration challenges associated with metaverse systems, linking each integration domain to its architectural impact and mitigation approach.

Table 5.4 Enterprise Integration Challenges and Mitigation Approaches

Integration Domain	*Common Challenges*	*Architectural Impact*	*Mitigation Approaches*
Identity and Access	Separate credential stores, inconsistent role models	Fragmented access control and audit gaps	Integration with enterprise IAM, single sign-on, role mapping
Network Infrastructure	Latency sensitivity, bandwidth spikes	Degraded immersive experience and network congestion	Traffic prioritisation, segmentation, capacity planning
Security Controls	Extension of trust boundaries	Increased exposure to cyber threats	Zero-trust principles, continuous monitoring, defined trust zones
Data Platforms	Non-standard data formats, high data volume	Data silos and governance complexity	Defined ingestion pipelines, data minimisation, metadata management
Application Integration	Lack of workflow connectivity	Limited operational value	API integration, workflow mapping, downstream system linkage
Operations and Support	Unclear ownership and escalation paths	Slow incident resolution	Defined operating models, service ownership, SLAs

Note: This table presents common enterprise integration challenges for metaverse platforms and architectural mitigation strategies.

5.7.10 Section Summary

Integration with enterprise architecture is a prerequisite for sustainable metaverse adoption. Immersive platforms that operate outside established architectural frameworks are unlikely to scale effectively or maintain organisational trust.

By embedding immersive systems within existing identity, security, network, and data architectures, organisations can reduce risk, improve governance, and align metaverse initiatives with strategic objectives. Figure 5.5 summarises the primary enterprise integration touchpoints discussed in this section, highlighting where immersive platforms intersect with established enterprise architecture domains.

5.8 ARCHITECTURAL TRADE-OFFS AND DESIGN DECISIONS

Architectural design of metaverse systems is defined less by ideal solutions and more by unavoidable trade-offs. Unlike conventional enterprise applications, immersive platforms must balance competing demands across performance, scalability, usability, governance, and cost. No single architecture can optimise for all dimensions simultaneously.

Understanding these trade-offs is essential for realistic planning. Many metaverse initiatives fail not because the underlying technologies are

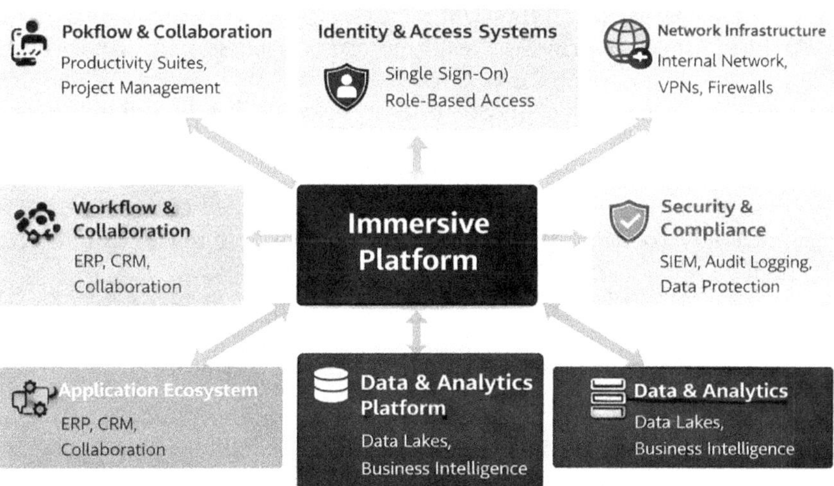

Figure 5.5 Key enterprise integration touchpoints for Metaverse platforms, illustrating alignment with identity, security, network, data, application, and operational domains.

inadequate but because architectural decisions implicitly prioritise certain outcomes while neglecting others. This section examines the most significant trade-offs encountered in metaverse architecture and their practical implications.

5.8.1 Fidelity versus Scalability

One of the most fundamental trade-offs in metaverse architecture is between experiential fidelity and system scalability. High-fidelity environments offer detailed graphics, realistic physics, and rich interaction, but they impose heavy computational and network demands.

As the number of concurrent users increases, maintaining such fidelity becomes increasingly expensive and technically challenging. Architects are often forced to simplify environments, reduce interaction complexity, or segment users into smaller instances.

Conversely, architectures optimised for large-scale participation typically sacrifice detail and interactivity. While such environments may support broader access, they may fail to deliver the immersive qualities that justify the use of metaverse technologies in the first place. Architectural decisions must therefore align fidelity targets with intended scale and use case, rather than attempting to maximise both simultaneously.

5.8.2 Real-Time Interaction versus System Stability

Immersive environments prioritise real-time interaction to create a sense of presence and immediacy. However, real-time systems are inherently less tolerant of latency, jitter, and transient failures.

Architectures that prioritise real-time responsiveness may reduce buffering, redundancy, or validation checks to minimise delay. While this improves immediacy, it can also increase susceptibility to instability and error propagation.

Alternatively, architectures that emphasise stability may introduce delays or constraints that reduce interaction fluidity. This trade-off must be managed carefully, particularly in enterprise contexts where reliability and predictability are critical.

5.8.3 Openness versus Control

Open architectures encourage innovation, extensibility, and ecosystem growth. They enable third parties to contribute content, tools, and integrations, potentially accelerating platform development.

However, openness complicates governance. Managing security, quality, and compliance becomes more difficult as control is distributed. In immersive environments, where interactions are embodied and real-time, governance challenges are amplified.

Closed architectures offer greater control and consistency but may limit flexibility and long-term adaptability. Organisations must weigh the benefits of openness against the risks and costs of governance complexity.

5.8.4 Customisation versus Standardisation

Customised immersive solutions can be tailored closely to specific workflows, environments, or organisational cultures. Such customisation may improve user acceptance and perceived value.

However, custom solutions are more expensive to develop, harder to maintain, and less portable. They may also impede interoperability and complicate future integration efforts.

Standardised architectures, by contrast, benefit from reuse and consistency but may fail to address specialised requirements. Architectural decisions must therefore balance the desire for differentiation against the efficiencies of standardisation.

5.8.5 Cost Efficiency versus Performance Optimisation

Performance optimisation in immersive systems often requires specialised hardware, high-performance networking, and extensive tuning. These measures improve experience quality but significantly increase operational cost.

Cost-efficient architectures may rely on shared infrastructure, reduced fidelity, or asynchronous interaction models. While more economical, such approaches may limit the range of viable use cases.

Decision-makers must therefore consider not only technical feasibility but also long-term cost sustainability. Optimising for peak performance without regard to cost frequently leads to initiatives that cannot be scaled or maintained.

5.8.6 Innovation Speed versus Architectural Stability

The metaverse domain evolves rapidly, with frequent advances in hardware, software, and interaction models. Architectures designed for rapid innovation may prioritise flexibility and experimentation.

However, frequent change can undermine stability, increase technical debt, and complicate governance. In enterprise environments, excessive volatility may be unacceptable.

Architectural designs must strike a balance between accommodating innovation and maintaining stable, supportable systems. This often involves modular design, clear interfaces, and controlled experimentation.

5.8.7 User Experience versus Governance Controls

Strong governance controls are essential for security, privacy, and compliance. However, excessive controls can disrupt immersion, increase friction, and reduce usability.

For example, frequent authentication prompts or intrusive monitoring may undermine user comfort and engagement. Conversely, insufficient controls expose platforms to misuse and risk. Architectural decisions must therefore integrate governance mechanisms in ways that minimise disruption while maintaining effectiveness.

5.8.8 Centralisation versus Distribution

Centralised architectures simplify management and governance but may introduce latency and single points of failure. Distributed architectures improve resilience and performance but increase complexity.

In immersive systems, distribution is often necessary to achieve acceptable latency. However, distributed architectures complicate synchronisation, monitoring, and compliance. Architects must evaluate where centralisation is appropriate and where distribution is necessary, based on performance, risk, and operational considerations.

5.8.9 Trade-Offs across Organisational Contexts

The optimal balance of trade-offs varies by organisational context. Consumer platforms, enterprise training systems, and industrial simulations face different priorities and constraints.

Architectures that succeed in one context may fail in another. Applying architectural patterns without regard to context is a common source of misalignment. Effective architectural design therefore requires explicit articulation of priorities and acceptance of trade-offs, rather than pursuit of idealised solutions.

5.8.10 Section Summary

Architectural trade-offs are inherent in metaverse system design. Attempts to avoid or obscure these trade-offs often result in unrealistic expectations and fragile implementations.

By recognising and managing trade-offs explicitly, architects and decision-makers can design immersive systems that align with organisational goals, constraints, and risk tolerance. Such clarity is essential for sustainable adoption and long-term value creation. Table 5.5 summarises the principal architectural trade-offs in metaverse design, comparing alternative design choices and their practical implications for fidelity, scalability, latency, stability, openness, and control.

Table 5.5 Architectural Trade-offs in Metaverse Design

Design Dimension	*Option A*	*Option B*	*Practical Implications*
Fidelity versus Scalability	High-fidelity immersive environments	Large-scale multi-user environments	Higher fidelity limits concurrency; higher scale often reduces immersion
Real-time Interaction versus Stability	Low-latency, immediate interaction	Buffered, resilient processing	Real-time designs risk instability; stable designs may reduce immersion
Openness versus Control	Open ecosystems and extensibility	Closed, tightly governed platforms	Openness enables innovation but increases governance complexity
Customisation versus Standardisation	Tailored immersive solutions	Standardised platforms and components	Customisation improves fit but increases cost and maintenance burden
Cost versus Performance	High-performance specialised infrastructure	Cost-optimised shared infrastructure	Performance gains often come with disproportionate cost increases
Centralisation versus Distribution	Centralised control and management	Distributed processing and delivery	Distribution improves latency but complicates governance and monitoring

Note: This table presents key architectural trade-offs in metaverse system design and their practical implications.

Figure 5.6 illustrates the architectural trade-offs in metaverse design, showing the tensions between performance, security, usability, and cost in immersive system architecture.

5.9 CHAPTER SUMMARY

This chapter examined the architectural foundations and enabling technologies that underpin the metaverse, shifting the discussion from conceptual narratives to practical system design considerations. Rather than treating the metaverse as a singular platform or product, this chapter framed it as a layered and interdependent set of technologies, architectural decisions, and governance mechanisms.

The analysis demonstrated that immersive systems depend on a complex interaction between infrastructure, networking, identity, security, data platforms, and user-facing technologies. Each layer introduces constraints and

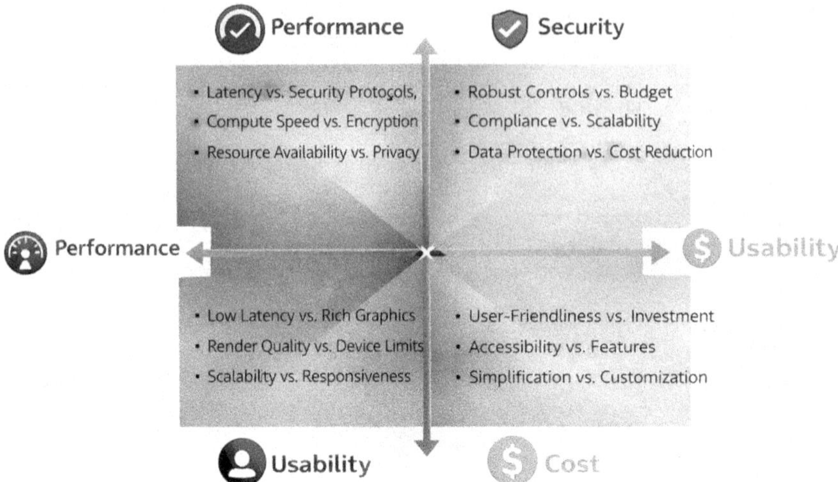

Figure 5.6 Architectural trade-offs in Metaverse design, illustrating tensions between performance, security, usability, and cost in immersive system architecture.

trade-offs that shape feasibility, cost, and user experience. Architectural coherence across these layers is therefore essential for any metaverse initiative seeking to move beyond experimentation.

Key challenges were identified across scalability, interoperability, enterprise integration, and governance. These challenges are not merely technical but organisational and economic in nature. Misalignment between immersive platforms and existing enterprise architecture was shown to be a common cause of stalled or abandoned initiatives.

This chapter also highlighted that architectural decisions inevitably involve trade-offs. Attempts to maximise fidelity, openness, performance, and scale simultaneously are rarely sustainable. Instead, successful implementations require explicit prioritisation aligned with business objectives and risk tolerance.

By grounding the metaverse in architectural reality, this chapter provides a foundation for the strategic and operational frameworks developed in subsequent chapters. The focus now shifts from how immersive systems are built to how organisations assess, justify, and govern their adoption in practice.

BIBLIOGRAPHY

Ball, M. (2022). *The Metaverse: And How It Will Revolutionize Everything*. New York: Liveright Publishing.

Carmigniani, J., & Furht, B. (2011). Augmented reality: An overview. *Handbook of Augmented Reality*. New York: Springer.

IEEE Standards Association. (2023). *IEEE Virtual Worlds and Metaverse Standards*. IEEE.

ISO/IEC. (2022). *Information Technology – Virtual World Interoperability and Data Exchange*. ISO/IEC JTC 1.

Jerald, J. (2015). *The VR Book: Human-Centered Design for Virtual Reality*. New York: ACM Books.

Krevelen, D. W. F. van, & Poelman, R. (2010). A survey of augmented reality technologies. *The Visual Computer*, 26(6–8), 395–409.

NVIDIA Corporation. (2023). *Real-Time Simulation and Omniverse Architecture*. NVIDIA Technical White Paper.

OpenXR Working Group. (2023). *OpenXR Specification*. Khronos Group.

Perry, T., & Sniderman, P. (2021). Observability in distributed systems. *Communications of the ACM*, 64(8), 54–61.

Zuboff, S. (2019). *The Age of Surveillance Capitalism*. London: Profile Books.

Chapter 6

Metaverse Decision Framework

6.1 INTRODUCTION TO THE METAVERSE DECISION FRAMEWORK

The metaverse has been widely discussed as a transformative technological paradigm, yet its adoption across enterprises has been inconsistent and often disappointing. While some organisations report tangible benefits from immersive technologies, many others struggle to translate experimentation into sustained value. This disparity is rarely caused by the technology itself. More commonly, it reflects weaknesses in problem definition, decision discipline, and value assessment.

This chapter introduces a structured decision framework designed to assist business leaders, product owners, and transformation teams in evaluating whether, when, and how the metaverse should be applied within a specific business context. Rather than assuming that immersive technologies are inherently beneficial, the framework begins from a more cautious premise: the metaverse should only be adopted where it demonstrably improves outcomes relative to existing, non-immersive alternatives.

The purpose of this framework is not to promote the metaverse but to *reduce decision risk*. By providing a systematic and repeatable method for assessing suitability, readiness, and value, it addresses one of the most common causes of failure in metaverse initiatives: starting with technology rather than with the business problem.

6.1.1 Why a Dedicated Metaverse Framework Is Required

Conventional technology assessment frameworks are poorly suited to immersive systems. Traditional digital investments are typically evaluated using metrics such as automation efficiency, cost reduction, or system consolidation. In contrast, metaverse initiatives often target experiential outcomes, behavioural change, or qualitative improvements that are harder to quantify and easier to overstate.

DOI: 10.1201/9781003405566-6

Immersive technologies also introduce additional layers of complexity. These include user comfort and accessibility, organisational change, operational support, and new categories of security and governance risk. Without a structured approach, decision-makers may overestimate potential benefits while underestimating implementation challenges.

A dedicated framework is therefore required to:

- Identify business problems for which immersive technologies may be appropriate
- Distinguish incremental improvements from genuinely transformational claims
- Assess organisational readiness in a realistic and evidence-based manner
- Quantify value in a way that supports defensible investment decisions

This framework responds directly to these requirements.

6.1.2 Business-First, Technology-Second Principle

A central principle of the framework is that *business problems must be identified and validated before any consideration of metaverse technology.* Many unsuccessful initiatives begin with a predetermined solution and then attempt to justify it retrospectively.

The framework deliberately reverses this sequence. It starts with business objectives, constraints, and performance gaps, and only later evaluates whether immersive technologies offer advantages over conventional solutions.

This principle ensures that:

- Metaverse adoption is driven by necessity rather than novelty
- Alternative non-metaverse solutions are evaluated fairly
- Technology choices remain proportionate to the problem being addressed

By anchoring decisions in business reality, the framework reduces the risk of misaligned or unjustified investment.

6.1.3 Intended Audience and Scope

The framework is designed for use by a broad range of stakeholders, including senior executives, product owners, programme managers, and consultants. It does not assume deep technical expertise in immersive systems and is intentionally platform-agnostic.

Its scope spans both strategic and operational decision-making. The framework can be applied to:

- Individual use cases or pilot initiatives
- Departmental or functional transformation programmes
- Organisation-wide metaverse strategies

The framework is scalable and adaptable, allowing it to be used consistently across different sectors and organisational contexts.

6.1.4 Overview of the End-to-End Framework Flow

The metaverse decision framework follows a structured, end-to-end sequence designed to minimise bias and surface constraints early. Each stage builds on the outputs of the previous one, ensuring that assumptions are tested rather than carried forward unchallenged.

At a high level, the framework consists of the following stages:

- Business problem identification
- Baseline maturity and readiness assessment
- Value chain gap analysis
- Value quantification without metaverse intervention
- Incremental value quantification using metaverse technologies
- Consolidation into a metaverse fit score

This sequence is intentionally linear. Skipping stages or reordering steps undermines the integrity of the assessment and increases the likelihood of optimistic but unsustainable conclusions. Figure 6.1 illustrates an end-to-end metaverse decision framework, showing the sequential assessment stages from business problem identification through to evaluation of metaverse fit.

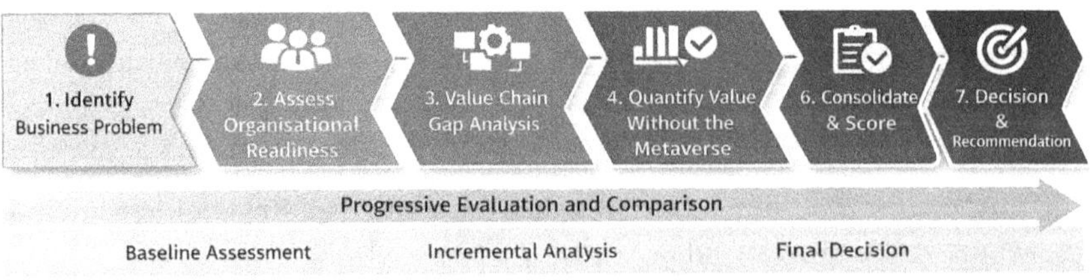

Figure 6.1 End-to-end Metaverse decision framework illustrating the sequential assessment stages from business problem identification through to the Metaverse fit score.

6.1.5 Relationship to Earlier Chapters

This chapter builds directly on the analytical groundwork established earlier in this book. The examination of hype, misalignment, and failure modes in previous chapters informs the framework's emphasis on discipline, realism, and evidence-based decision-making.

Insights incorporated include:

- The gap between technological capability and organisational readiness
- The risks of applying immersive technologies to poorly defined problems
- The architectural and governance constraints that shape feasibility

By embedding these lessons into a practical framework, this chapter translates critique into actionable guidance.

6.1.6 What the Framework Does not Attempt to Do

It is important to clarify the limits of the framework. It does not attempt to:

- Predict future market winners or dominant platforms
- Provide detailed system architecture designs
- Replace full business case development or programme planning

Instead, it functions as a *decision filter*. Its purpose is to determine whether a metaverse initiative is justified in principle, and under what conditions it may be worth pursuing further. Subsequent chapters build on this foundation by addressing strategy, business cases, and applied examples.

6.1.7 Structure of this Chapter

The remainder of this chapter expands each stage of the framework in detail. Diagnostic tools, assessment models, and evaluation criteria are introduced progressively, enabling readers to apply the framework step by step.

Where appropriate, tables and visual models are used to support clarity, repeatability, and comparison. This chapter concludes with a consolidated metaverse fit score that provides a clear decision outcome. Readers are encouraged to work through this chapter sequentially, as later sections depend on the logic and outputs of earlier stages.

6.1.8 Section Summary

This section has established the rationale, scope, and structure of the metaverse decision framework. By adopting a business-first, technology-second approach, the framework addresses the root causes of misaligned and underperforming metaverse initiatives. The sections that follow translate this intent into a structured assessment model designed to support informed, defensible decision-making.

6.2 BUSINESS PROBLEM IDENTIFICATION

Effective application of the metaverse begins with disciplined identification of the business problem to be addressed. This principle may appear self-evident, yet it is routinely violated in practice. Many metaverse initiatives originate from strategic curiosity, competitive anxiety, or vendor influence rather than from a clearly articulated operational need. As a result, immersive technologies are often deployed in search of a problem, rather than as a response to one.

Business problem identification is therefore positioned as the first substantive stage of the metaverse decision framework. Its purpose is to ensure that any consideration of immersive technologies is grounded in organisational reality, measurable outcomes, and explicit constraints. Without this foundation, subsequent assessments of readiness, value, and feasibility are likely to be distorted.

6.2.1 Importance of Problem Clarity

Problem clarity establishes a shared understanding of what is not working and why it matters. In complex organisations, different stakeholders frequently hold divergent interpretations of the same issue. What appears as a skills gap to one group may be perceived as a process failure or resource constraint by another.

In metaverse initiatives, lack of clarity is particularly dangerous because immersive solutions are experiential and visually compelling. Early demonstrations can create the illusion of progress, even when they do not address the root cause of the problem. Clear problem definition acts as a stabilising reference point, preventing momentum from substituting for evidence. A well-articulated problem enables consistent evaluation, reduces ambiguity in success criteria, and supports objective decision-making throughout the lifecycle of the initiative.

6.2.2 Differentiating Business Problems from Technology Opportunities

A recurring pattern in unsuccessful metaverse initiatives is the conflation of technology opportunities with business problems. Statements such as "we should explore immersive collaboration" or "the metaverse could transform our operations" describe possibilities rather than deficiencies.

Business problems are characterised by unmet objectives, inefficiencies, risks, or performance gaps. They can be articulated independently of any

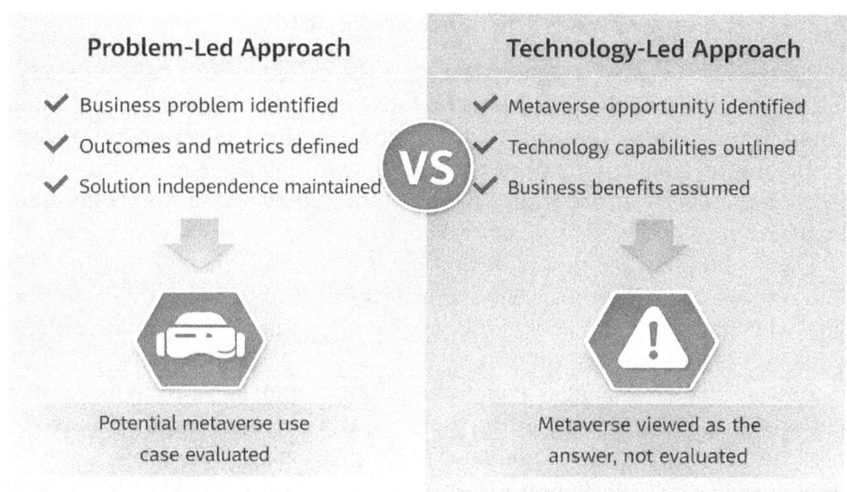

Figure 6.2 Comparison between business-problem-led and technology-led approaches to Metaverse adoption.

proposed solution. Technology opportunities, by contrast, describe what could be done rather than what must be fixed.

The framework therefore requires that problem identification be conducted without reference to immersive technologies. This constraint forces stakeholders to articulate the problem in operational terms and prevents premature commitment to a particular solution path. Figure 6.2 compares business-problem-led and technology-led approaches to metaverse adoption, highlighting the difference between value-driven evaluation and solution-first experimentation.

6.2.3 Categories of Business Problems Relevant to the Metaverse

Not all business problems are equally suited to immersive solutions. While the framework avoids prescriptive mappings, certain categories of problems are more likely to benefit from the characteristics of immersive technologies.

These include problems involving spatial reasoning, such as design review or layout optimisation; challenges requiring experiential learning, such as safety training or behavioural rehearsal; and scenarios where physical access is constrained by cost, distance, or risk.

Conversely, problems that are primarily transactional, rule-based, or data-processing oriented are unlikely to justify immersive approaches. Identifying the category of problem early provides a preliminary filter that reduces wasted effort.

6.2.4 Problem Ownership and Stakeholder Alignment

Clear ownership of the problem is essential for accountability and decision continuity. Problems that lack a defined owner often reflect organisational ambiguity or competing priorities. In such cases, metaverse initiatives may be championed enthusiastically but abandoned when responsibility becomes unclear.

The problem owner should be accountable for both current performance and future improvement. This individual or function must be able to articulate why the problem exists, how it affects organisational outcomes, and what constraints limit resolution.

Stakeholder alignment is equally important. Immersive initiatives often cut across functional boundaries, making early alignment critical to avoiding resistance or fragmentation later in the process.

6.2.5 Establishing a Baseline of Current-State Performance

Any assessment of improvement requires a baseline. In practice, many organisations lack robust measures of current performance, particularly for experiential or behavioural outcomes. This absence of baseline data creates fertile ground for overclaiming benefits.

The framework therefore requires explicit documentation of the current state, even if measurement is approximate. This may include qualitative assessments, proxy metrics, or expert judgement, provided assumptions are clearly stated.

Establishing a baseline not only supports later value quantification but also surfaces gaps in measurement capability that may need to be addressed regardless of whether a metaverse solution is adopted.

6.2.6 Identifying Constraints and Boundary Conditions

Business problems do not exist in isolation; they are shaped by constraints such as budget limits, regulatory requirements, workforce capabilities, and organisational culture. Ignoring these constraints during problem identification leads to solutions that are theoretically attractive but practically infeasible.

Immersive technologies introduce additional boundary conditions, including hardware availability, user tolerance, accessibility requirements, and support capacity. These factors must be acknowledged early rather than treated as implementation details. Explicitly documenting constraints ensures that later stages of the framework operate within realistic bounds and reduces the risk of late-stage rejection.

6.2.7 Constructing a Well-Formed Problem Statement

The problem statement is the primary output of this stage. It should be concise yet sufficiently detailed to guide evaluation. A well-formed problem statement typically describes the current situation, the negative impact of the problem, and the desired improvement.

Crucially, it should avoid embedding assumptions about solutions. Statements that imply a particular technology bias the assessment and undermine objectivity. Neutral language preserves flexibility and supports comparative evaluation.

Problem statements should be reviewed and validated by key stakeholders to ensure shared understanding and commitment. Table 6.1 provides a practical tool for ensuring that problem statements are outcome-oriented and solution-agnostic.

6.2.8 Common Failure Modes in Problem Definition

Poor problem definition manifests in predictable ways. These include vague objectives, shifting scope, and reliance on anecdotal evidence. In metaverse

Table 6.1 Business Problem Definition Checklist

Checklist Dimension	*Guiding Question*	*Yes/No*	*Notes*
Problem clarity	Is the problem stated clearly and unambiguously?		
Outcome focus	Is the problem expressed in terms of outcomes rather than solutions?		
Ownership	Is there a clearly accountable business owner?		
Stakeholder alignment	Are all key stakeholders aligned on the problem definition?		
Baseline understanding	Is current-state performance understood or estimated?		
Constraints identified	Are regulatory, budgetary, and organisational constraints documented?		
Solution neutrality	Does the problem statement avoid implying specific technologies?		

Note: This table presents a checklist for validating clarity and completeness of business problem definitions.

initiatives, such weaknesses are often masked by early enthusiasm or impressive demonstrations.

Another common failure mode is addressing symptoms rather than causes. For example, low engagement in training may reflect organisational incentives rather than instructional design. Applying immersive technology in such cases may improve experience without improving outcomes. Recognising these failure modes helps organisations apply the framework rigorously rather than superficially.

6.2.9 Outputs of the Problem Identification Stage

The problem identification stage produces a structured set of artefacts that feed directly into subsequent stages of the framework. These include a validated problem statement, identified owner, key stakeholders, baseline indicators, and documented constraints.

These outputs create a shared reference point and enable consistent evaluation as the framework progresses. They also provide traceability, allowing later decisions to be revisited and reassessed if assumptions change.

6.2.10 Section Summary

Business problem identification is the cornerstone of the metaverse decision framework. By insisting on clarity, ownership, baseline understanding, and constraint recognition, this stage reduces the likelihood of misaligned or unjustified adoption.

Only when a problem has been clearly defined and validated should immersive technologies be evaluated as a potential response. This discipline distinguishes purposeful application from exploratory experimentation.

6.3 BASELINE MATURITY AND READINESS ASSESSMENT

Once a business problem has been clearly identified and validated, the next step in the metaverse decision framework is to assess organisational maturity and readiness. This stage evaluates whether the organisation is realistically capable of addressing the problem at all, regardless of whether immersive technologies are involved. In many cases, metaverse initiatives fail not because the technology is unsuitable but because the organisation lacks the foundational capabilities required to implement and sustain any meaningful change.

The readiness assessment therefore acts as a second critical filter. It prevents organisations from progressing to value quantification and solution design when more fundamental gaps remain unresolved.

6.3.1 Purpose of the Readiness Assessment

The primary purpose of the readiness assessment is to establish a factual baseline of current organisational capability. This baseline enables decision-makers to distinguish between problems that are constrained by technology and those that are constrained by process, skills, governance, or culture.

Without this assessment, organisations may incorrectly attribute poor performance to lack of technological sophistication. In reality, many issues stem from inconsistent processes, unclear ownership, or insufficient capability development. Introducing immersive technologies into such contexts often amplifies existing weaknesses rather than resolving them. The readiness assessment ensures that metaverse adoption is considered only when foundational capabilities are sufficiently mature.

6.3.2 Dimensions of Organisational Readiness

Readiness is multidimensional and cannot be reduced to a single metric. The framework evaluates readiness across several interrelated dimensions, including process maturity, people capability, technology infrastructure, governance structures, and change capacity.

Process maturity refers to the degree to which business processes are defined, documented, and consistently executed. Immersive technologies cannot compensate for poorly understood or unstable processes.

People capability encompasses skills, experience, and capacity within the organisation. This includes not only technical skills but also the ability to design, operate, and adapt new ways of working.

Technology infrastructure readiness addresses the availability and reliability of supporting systems, networks, and devices required to enable immersive solutions.

Governance and change capacity relate to decision-making structures, risk management, and the organisation's ability to absorb change without disruption. Figure 6.3 illustrates the core organisational readiness dimensions that influence successful metaverse adoption, including the capabilities and conditions required for effective implementation.

6.3.3 Process Maturity Assessment

Process maturity is often overlooked in technology-driven initiatives. Yet immersive solutions frequently depend on well-defined workflows to deliver value. For example, training simulations require clear learning objectives, assessment criteria, and integration with existing learning management processes.

The framework assesses whether relevant processes are documented, stable, and measured. Processes that vary significantly across teams or locations are difficult to standardise through immersive platforms. Low process

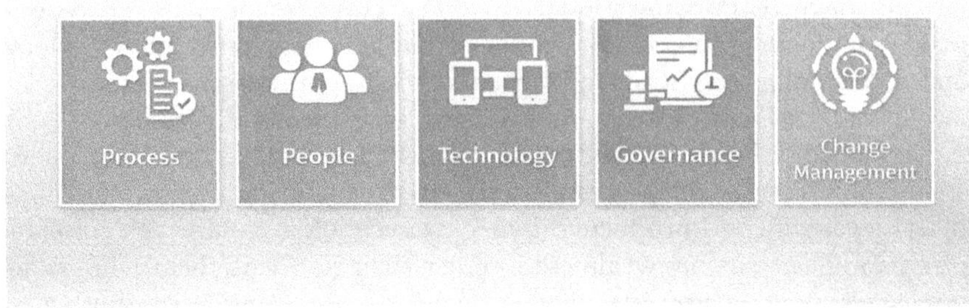

Figure 6.3 Core organisational readiness dimensions influencing successful Metaverse adoption.

maturity suggests that improvement efforts should focus on process clarification and optimisation before considering immersive technologies.

6.3.4 People Capability and Skills Readiness

Immersive technologies introduce new skill requirements across design, facilitation, support, and governance. Organisations must assess whether they possess or can realistically acquire these capabilities.

Skills gaps may exist among both end users and support teams. Users may require training to interact effectively in immersive environments, while support teams must manage devices, platforms, and user issues.

Capability readiness also includes organisational bandwidth. Teams already operating at capacity may struggle to absorb additional initiatives, regardless of their potential value.

6.3.5 Technology and Infrastructure Readiness

Technology readiness extends beyond possession of hardware or software. It includes network capacity, device management, security controls, and integration with existing systems.

Immersive platforms are sensitive to latency, bandwidth variability, and device performance. Organisations with constrained or inconsistent infrastructure may experience degraded experiences that undermine adoption. The framework therefore evaluates whether existing infrastructure can support immersive workloads reliably and at scale, or whether significant investment would be required.

6.3.6 Governance, Risk, and Compliance Readiness

Governance readiness assesses whether the organisation has mechanisms to manage risk, enforce policies, and ensure accountability. Immersive technologies introduce new categories of risk, including behavioural, privacy, and safety concerns.

Organisations lacking clear governance structures may struggle to respond to incidents or regulatory scrutiny. Introducing immersive systems without adequate governance increases exposure and reputational risk. The readiness assessment examines whether decision rights, escalation paths, and compliance processes are defined and operational.

6.3.7 Change Capacity and Organisational Resilience

Even well-designed solutions fail if the organisation cannot absorb change. Change capacity reflects the organisation's ability to adapt processes, behaviours, and roles without excessive disruption.

Factors influencing change capacity include leadership support, communication effectiveness, and prior experience with transformation initiatives. Organisations experiencing change fatigue may resist additional initiatives, regardless of merit. Assessing change capacity helps determine whether the timing of a metaverse initiative is appropriate or whether sequencing adjustments are needed.

6.3.8 Diagnostic Tools and Assessment Methods

The framework encourages the use of structured diagnostic tools to support readiness assessment. These may include questionnaires, workshops, interviews, and document reviews.

Quantitative scoring can support comparison across dimensions, but qualitative judgement remains essential. Readiness assessments should be transparent, with assumptions documented and validated.

Overly optimistic scoring undermines the purpose of the assessment and increases downstream risk. Table 6.2 supports structured evaluation of readiness gaps and highlights areas requiring preparatory action.

6.3.9 Interpreting Readiness Assessment Outcomes

Readiness assessment outcomes should not be interpreted as pass or fail. Instead, they indicate where preparatory work is required and which risks must be managed.

Low readiness in certain dimensions does not automatically preclude metaverse adoption, but it may necessitate phased implementation or complementary capability-building efforts. The framework emphasises honest interpretation over aspirational scoring.

6.3.10 Outputs of the Readiness Assessment Stage

The outputs of this stage include a documented maturity profile across assessed dimensions, identified gaps, and recommended preparatory actions.

Table 6.2 Organisational Readiness Assessment Matrix

Readiness Dimension	*Low Maturity Indicators*	*Medium Maturity Indicators*	*High Maturity Indicators*
Process	Processes undocumented or inconsistent	Processes defined but variably applied	Processes standardised and measured
People	Skills gaps and limited capacity	Partial capability with reliance on specialists	Broad capability and internal expertise
Technology	Fragmented or constrained infrastructure	Adequate infrastructure with limitations	Scalable, reliable infrastructure
Governance	Unclear decision rights and controls	Partial governance with gaps	Clear governance and accountability
Change capacity	High resistance to change	Mixed change adoption history	Strong change management capability

Note: This table presents the organisational readiness assessment matrix across process, people, technology, governance, and change dimensions.

These outputs feed directly into the next stage of the framework, which examines value chain gaps and opportunities for improvement.

6.3.11 Section Summary

Baseline maturity and readiness assessment provides a reality check for metaverse adoption decisions. By evaluating organisational capability across multiple dimensions, this stage prevents premature or misaligned investment. Only when readiness is understood and addressed should organisations proceed to value chain analysis and value quantification.

6.4 VALUE CHAIN GAP ANALYSIS

Once a business problem has been clearly identified and organisational readiness assessed, the next stage of the metaverse decision framework is value chain gap analysis. This stage examines how value is currently created, delivered, and captured within the relevant business process, and where structural gaps or inefficiencies exist.

The purpose of value chain gap analysis is to determine whether meaningful improvement is possible and, critically, where that improvement should occur. Without this step, organisations risk applying immersive technologies to isolated activities rather than to points of leverage within the broader system.

6.4.1 Role of the Value Chain in Decision-Making

A value chain represents the sequence of activities through which an organisation transforms inputs into outcomes. In the context of the metaverse framework, it provides a structured lens for understanding where problems originate and how they propagate across processes, teams, and systems.

Many metaverse initiatives focus on highly visible activities, such as training delivery or collaboration sessions, without examining upstream or downstream dependencies. Value chain analysis ensures that interventions are positioned where they can influence outcomes rather than symptoms.

6.4.2 Mapping the Current-State Value Chain

The first step in this stage is to map the current-state value chain associated with the identified business problem. This mapping should be sufficiently detailed to capture handoffs, decision points, and dependencies, while remaining focused on the scope of the problem.

Current-state mapping reveals how work actually occurs, which may differ significantly from documented processes. Informal practices, workarounds, and shadow systems often emerge during this exercise and should be documented explicitly.

Understanding the current state is essential for identifying realistic improvement opportunities. Figure 6.4 illustrates a value chain mapping model used to identify structural gaps and value leakage points relevant to metaverse evaluation.

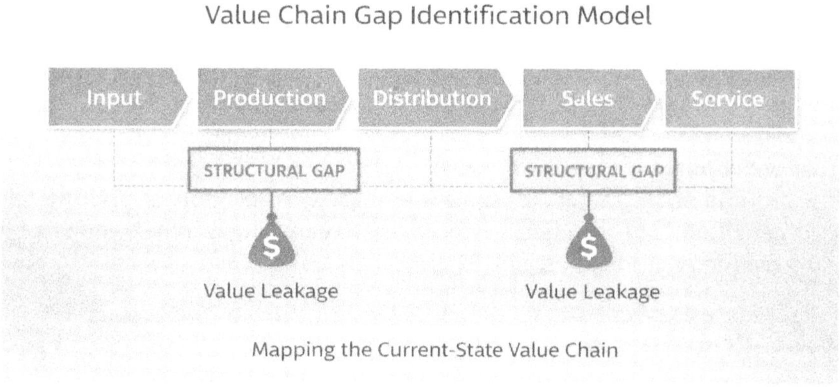

Figure 6.4 Value chain mapping model used to identify structural gaps and value leakage points relevant to Metaverse evaluation.

6.4.3 Identifying Value Leakage and Inefficiencies

Value leakage occurs when effort, time, or resources fail to translate into desired outcomes. Common sources include rework, delays, miscommunication, and misaligned incentives.

In immersive initiatives, value leakage often arises from poor integration with existing processes or insufficient alignment with performance metrics. For example, immersive training may improve engagement but fail to reduce errors if assessment and reinforcement mechanisms remain unchanged. Identifying sources of leakage allows organisations to target improvements more precisely.

6.4.4 Gap Identification across Value Chain Stages

Gaps are defined as discrepancies between current performance and desired outcomes. These gaps may exist at individual stages of the value chain or at the interfaces between stages.

The framework encourages systematic examination of each stage, asking whether it contributes effectively to the overall objective. Gaps may be structural, behavioural, informational, or technological in nature.

Importantly, not all gaps warrant intervention. Some gaps may be tolerable given constraints, while others may require prioritisation due to their disproportionate impact.

6.4.5 Differentiating Process Gaps from Capability Gaps

A critical distinction in value chain analysis is between process gaps and capability gaps. Process gaps arise from unclear workflows, inconsistent execution, or poor coordination. Capability gaps reflect missing skills, tools, or infrastructure.

Immersive technologies are often proposed as solutions to capability gaps but are less effective at addressing poorly designed processes. Applying metaverse solutions without addressing underlying process gaps risks reinforcing inefficiency.

The framework therefore requires explicit classification of each identified gap. Table 6.3 distinguishes between structural gap types, supporting targeted intervention strategies.

6.4.6 Prioritisation of Value Chain Gaps

Not all gaps can or should be addressed simultaneously. Prioritisation is necessary to focus effort where it yields the greatest benefit.

The framework suggests evaluating gaps based on impact, feasibility, and alignment with strategic objectives. Gaps that are high-impact but low-feasibility may require preparatory work, while low-impact gaps may be

Table 6.3 Value Chain Gap Classification

Gap Type	*Description*	*Typical Symptoms*	*Suitable Intervention*
Process gap	Inefficient or unclear workflows	Delays, rework, inconsistency	Process redesign
Capability gap	Missing skills or tools	Errors, dependency on experts	Training or tooling
Information gap	Poor visibility or feedback	Late decisions, misalignment	Analytics or reporting
Coordination gap	Weak handoffs between teams	Duplication, miscommunication	Governance or collaboration
Experience gap	Limited experiential understanding	Low engagement, poor retention	Immersive solutions (selectively)

Note: This table presents the classification of value chain gaps relevant to metaverse decision-making.

deferred. Prioritisation supports disciplined decision-making and prevents scope expansion.

6.4.7 Role of Non-Metaverse Interventions

A distinctive feature of the framework is its explicit consideration of non-metaverse interventions at this stage. Many value chain gaps can be addressed through process redesign, training, or policy changes without immersive technologies.

By identifying these opportunities, the framework ensures that the metaverse is evaluated as one option among many, rather than as a default solution. This step also establishes a baseline against which the incremental value of immersive solutions can later be assessed.

6.4.8 Documenting Assumptions and Dependencies

Value chain analysis inevitably involves assumptions about causality and behaviour. These assumptions should be documented explicitly, along with dependencies between activities and stakeholders.

Transparent documentation enables later validation and adjustment as new information emerges. It also supports stakeholder alignment by making reasoning visible rather than implicit. Failure to document assumptions increases the risk of misinterpretation and dispute in later stages.

6.4.9 Outputs of the Value Chain Gap Analysis

The outputs of this stage include a mapped current-state value chain, a list of identified gaps, classification of gap types, and prioritised improvement opportunities. These outputs provide the foundation for subsequent value quantification stages, enabling comparison between non-metaverse and metaverse-enabled interventions.

6.4.10 Section Summary

Value chain gap analysis translates abstract business problems into concrete improvement opportunities. By examining where value is created and lost, this stage ensures that immersive technologies, if considered, are applied where they can influence outcomes meaningfully. Only after gaps have been identified and prioritised should organisations proceed to quantify value and assess the incremental contribution of the metaverse.

6.5 QUANTIFYING VALUE WITHOUT THE METAVERSE

Before assessing the incremental value of immersive technologies, the framework requires explicit quantification of value achievable without the metaverse. This step is critical. It ensures that organisations do not attribute improvements to immersive technologies that could have been achieved through conventional means. In many cases, significant value can be unlocked through process optimisation, capability development, or policy changes alone. By quantifying non-metaverse value first, the framework establishes a defensible baseline against which any additional benefit from immersive solutions can be measured.

6.5.1 Rationale for Non-Metaverse Value Assessment

Organisations often underestimate the extent to which existing processes can be improved without introducing new technologies. Enthusiasm for immersive solutions may obscure simpler, lower-risk interventions that address the same problem more effectively.

This step forces decision-makers to confront an uncomfortable but necessary question: if the problem can be solved without the metaverse, why introduce additional complexity? Only when non-metaverse interventions are insufficient should immersive technologies be considered. The assessment therefore acts as a safeguard against technology-driven bias.

6.5.2 Identifying Conventional Improvement Levers

Conventional improvement levers include process redesign, role clarification, training enhancements, automation, and performance management adjustments. These levers are typically less costly and less disruptive than immersive technologies.

The framework encourages systematic identification of such levers for each prioritised value chain gap. For example, a training effectiveness issue may be addressed through curriculum redesign, improved assessment, or better instructor support. Explicit consideration of these levers provides a more complete understanding of improvement potential.

6.5.3 Establishing Measurement Metrics

Quantifying value requires clear metrics. These metrics should align with the problem definition and reflect outcomes rather than activity. Examples include error rates, time to competence, throughput, or customer satisfaction.

In many cases, existing metrics may be incomplete or inconsistent. The framework therefore allows for the use of proxy measures, provided assumptions are documented.

The emphasis is on comparability rather than precision. Metrics must enable meaningful comparison between current state, improved non-metaverse state, and metaverse-enabled scenarios.

6.5.4 Estimating Improvement Potential

Once improvement levers and metrics have been identified, the next step is to estimate the improvement potential achievable without immersive technologies. This may involve benchmarking, pilot studies, or expert judgement.

Estimates should be conservative and grounded in evidence. Overly optimistic projections undermine the credibility of the assessment and bias later comparisons. Where uncertainty exists, ranges or scenarios may be used to reflect variability.

6.5.5 Cost and Effort Considerations

Value quantification must consider not only benefits but also costs and effort. Conventional interventions may require investment in training, process redesign, or system changes.

The framework requires that these costs be estimated alongside benefits, even if only at a high level. Ignoring costs creates a distorted view of value and may lead to unrealistic expectations. Comparing cost-benefit profiles across intervention types supports rational prioritisation.

6.5.6 Time to Realisation

Time is a critical dimension of value. Some improvements can be realised quickly, while others require sustained effort over extended periods. The framework therefore includes assessment of time to realisation for non-metaverse interventions. Faster improvements may be preferable even if absolute benefits are lower. Time considerations also inform sequencing decisions and help manage stakeholder expectations. Table 6.4 establishes the baseline against which incremental metaverse value is assessed.

Table 6.4 Non-Metaverse Value Quantification Template

Improvement Lever	*Expected Benefit*	*Measurement Metric*	*Estimated Value*	*Cost/Effort*	*Time to Realisation*
Process redesign					
Training enhancement					
Automation					
Policy change					
Capability development					

Note: This table presents the template for estimating value achievable without metaverse intervention.

6.5.7 Risk and Implementation Complexity

Non-metaverse interventions are not risk-free. Process changes may encounter resistance, training initiatives may fail to achieve desired outcomes, and automation may introduce unintended consequences.

Assessing risk and complexity provides a more realistic view of improvement potential. High-risk interventions may warrant reconsideration or phased implementation. This assessment also establishes a baseline for comparing the relative risk of immersive solutions.

6.5.8 Documenting the Non-Metaverse Value Baseline

The output of this stage is a documented baseline of achievable value without immersive technologies. This baseline includes expected benefits, costs, timeframes, and risks.

Documentation should be transparent and auditable, enabling later review and adjustment. This discipline supports accountability and reduces the likelihood of post-hoc rationalisation.

The non-metaverse baseline becomes a reference point for evaluating incremental value. Figure 6.5 compares value achievable through non-metaverse interventions with the incremental value that immersive technologies may add.

6.5.9 Implications for Metaverse Consideration

If non-metaverse interventions are sufficient to address the problem effectively, the framework may recommend deferring or rejecting immersive solutions. This outcome should be viewed as success rather than failure.

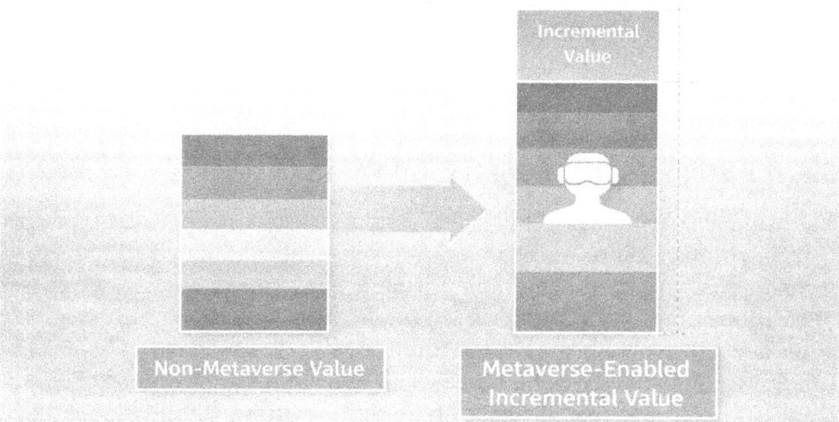

Figure 6.5 Non-Metaverse vs Metaverse value comparison.

Note: Comparative view of value achievable through non-metaverse interventions versus incremental value enabled by immersive technologies.

Conversely, if residual gaps remain after non-metaverse improvements, immersive technologies may be considered as potential enhancers rather than primary drivers of value. This distinction preserves the integrity of the decision-making process.

6.5.10 Section Summary

Quantifying value without the metaverse establishes a disciplined baseline for comparison. By identifying improvement potential, costs, timeframes, and risks associated with conventional interventions, this stage ensures that immersive technologies are evaluated on their incremental contribution rather than on aspiration alone. Only after this baseline has been established should organisations proceed to assess the additional value offered by the metaverse.

6.6 QUANTIFYING INCREMENTAL VALUE USING THE METAVERSE

Once the baseline value achievable without immersive technologies has been established, the next stage of the framework assesses the *incremental value* that may be realised through the use of the metaverse. This stage is deliberately comparative rather than aspirational. Its purpose is not to justify metaverse adoption but to determine whether immersive technologies deliver additional benefits that outweigh their costs, risks, and complexity. Incremental value is defined as the measurable improvement achieved beyond what could reasonably be delivered through conventional interventions alone.

6.6.1 Rationale for Incremental Value Assessment

Many metaverse initiatives fail because value is evaluated in isolation rather than in comparison to alternatives. Improvements attributed to immersive technologies are often achievable through non-immersive means, yet this distinction is rarely made explicit.

By assessing incremental value, the framework ensures that immersive solutions are justified on their *marginal contribution*, not on absolute outcomes. This discipline protects organisations from overinvestment and post-hoc rationalisation. Incremental assessment also clarifies whether the metaverse is essential, optional, or unnecessary for addressing the identified problem.

6.6.2 Identifying Metaverse-Specific Value Drivers

Incremental value arises only where immersive technologies offer capabilities that conventional solutions cannot easily replicate. These capabilities include spatial immersion, embodied interaction, real-time simulation, and shared presence.

The framework requires explicit identification of which of these capabilities are relevant to the problem at hand. For example, immersive simulation may enable safe rehearsal of rare or hazardous scenarios, while spatial collaboration may enhance understanding of complex three-dimensional systems.

If no metaverse-specific value drivers can be identified, incremental value is likely to be limited. Figure 6.6 maps core metaverse-specific capabilities to the mechanisms through which they can create incremental value.

6.6.3 Mapping Metaverse Capabilities to Value Chain Gaps

Incremental value must be traced back to specific gaps identified in the value chain analysis. This mapping ensures that immersive technologies are applied purposefully rather than opportunistically.

For each prioritised gap, the framework evaluates whether immersive capabilities directly address the root cause or merely enhance experience without affecting outcomes. This mapping exercise often reveals that some gaps are unsuitable for immersive intervention, reinforcing the importance of selectivity.

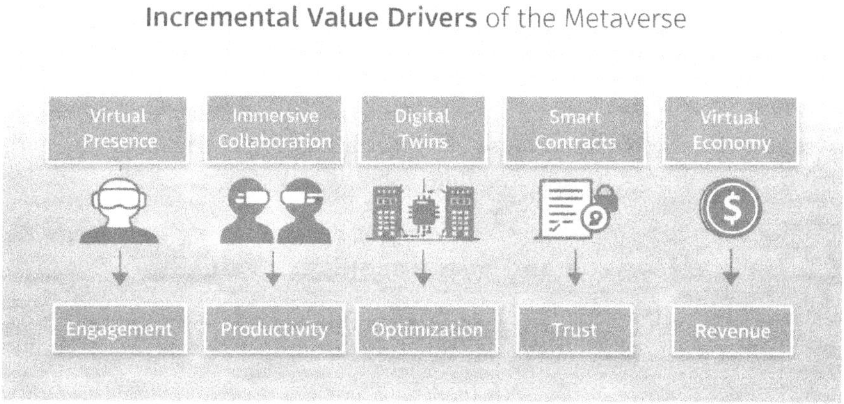

Figure 6.6 Incremental value drivers of the Metaverse.

Note: Core metaverse-specific capabilities mapped to incremental value creation mechanisms.

6.6.4 Estimating Incremental Benefits

Incremental benefits may be quantitative, such as reduced error rates or faster time to competence, or qualitative, such as improved confidence or situational awareness. Where possible, benefits should be expressed using the same metrics established in the non-metaverse baseline.

Estimation should be conservative and evidence-based. Pilot studies, controlled trials, or external benchmarks may inform projections, but assumptions must be documented clearly. Overestimation of benefits undermines credibility and increases the risk of disappointment.

6.6.5 Assessing Incremental Costs

Immersive solutions introduce additional costs beyond those associated with conventional interventions. These may include hardware procurement, platform licensing, content development, support infrastructure, and ongoing maintenance.

The framework requires that these costs be identified and estimated explicitly. Hidden or deferred costs, such as device replacement or user support, are common sources of underestimation. Comparing incremental costs against incremental benefits provides a more realistic view of net value.

6.6.6 Evaluating Risk and Uncertainty

Incremental value assessment must account for uncertainty and risk. Immersive technologies may introduce adoption risks, usability challenges, or unforeseen operational issues.

The framework encourages explicit evaluation of risk factors, including technological maturity, user acceptance, and dependency on vendors or platforms.

Where uncertainty is high, scenario analysis or sensitivity testing may be used to explore potential outcomes. Table 6.5 enables structured comparison between immersive and non-immersive approaches.

6.6.7 Time Horizon and Sustainability of Value

Incremental value should be assessed over an appropriate time horizon. Short-term gains may be offset by long-term costs or declining engagement.

The framework therefore considers whether immersive benefits are sustainable and whether they scale beyond pilot contexts. Solutions that deliver initial impact but fail to integrate into routine operations may offer limited long-term value. Time horizon analysis supports more balanced investment decisions.

6.6.8 Comparison with Non-Metaverse Baseline

The culmination of this stage is a direct comparison between the non-metaverse baseline and the metaverse-enabled scenario. This comparison highlights the marginal contribution of immersive technologies.

Where incremental value is modest or uncertain, the framework may recommend deferral or limited experimentation rather than full-scale adoption. Where incremental value is substantial and defensible, immersive technologies may warrant further consideration.

6.6.9 Decision Implications

Incremental value assessment informs, but does not determine, the final decision. It provides evidence that feeds into synthesis and scoring in the subsequent stage.

Table 6.5 Incremental Metaverse Value Assessment

Value Dimension	*Non-Metaverse Baseline*	*Metaverse-Enabled Scenario*	*Incremental Impact*
Performance improvement			
User engagement			
Error reduction			
Time efficiency			
Risk exposure			
Cost profile			

Note: This table presents the incremental value assessment comparing benefits, costs, risks, and time horizons of metaverse-enabled solutions

Importantly, a finding of limited incremental value should be viewed as a valid and valuable outcome. Avoiding unnecessary complexity is a positive result of disciplined assessment.

6.6.10 Section Summary

Quantifying incremental value using the metaverse ensures that immersive technologies are evaluated on their additional contribution rather than on novelty or aspiration. By comparing benefits, costs, risks, and time horizons against a non-metaverse baseline, this stage supports rational and defensible decision-making. The next stage consolidates these insights into a structured metaverse fit score.

6.7 CONSOLIDATION AND METAVERSE FIT SCORE

The final stage of the metaverse decision framework consolidates the outputs of the preceding assessments into a single, coherent decision view. This stage does not introduce new analysis; instead, it synthesises insights from business problem identification, readiness assessment, value chain gap analysis, and value quantification into a structured evaluation of overall suitability. The objective is to provide decision-makers with a clear, defensible conclusion regarding whether the metaverse is an appropriate solution, and if so, under what conditions.

6.7.1 Purpose of Consolidation

Complex decisions often fail not because of lack of analysis but because insights are fragmented across multiple assessments. Consolidation ensures that evidence is integrated and interpreted holistically.

In the context of the metaverse, consolidation is particularly important due to the diversity of factors involved. Technological feasibility, organisational readiness, value potential, and risk exposure must be considered together rather than in isolation. This stage transforms analytical outputs into actionable guidance.

6.7.2 Inputs to the Fit Assessment

The metaverse fit score draws on structured inputs from earlier stages of the framework. These inputs include the validated problem statement, readiness profile, prioritised value chain gaps, non-metaverse value baseline, and incremental value assessment.

Each input represents a different dimension of suitability. None is sufficient on its own to justify adoption, but together they provide a balanced view. The framework emphasises traceability, ensuring that each element of the fit score can be linked back to documented evidence.

6.7.3 Dimensions of the Metaverse Fit Score

The fit score is composed of multiple dimensions reflecting the breadth of considerations involved. Typical dimensions include problem relevance, organisational readiness, incremental value potential, risk exposure, and strategic alignment.

Each dimension is assessed independently to avoid conflating unrelated factors. This separation also highlights specific areas of strength and weakness.

The framework does not prescribe specific weighting schemes, allowing organisations to adjust emphasis based on context and priorities. Figure 6.7 presents a consolidated metaverse fit score, synthesising problem relevance, organisational readiness, value potential, and risk dimensions.

6.7.4 Scoring Approach and Interpretation

Scoring may be qualitative, quantitative, or hybrid, depending on organisational preference and data availability. The framework supports ordinal scoring to enable comparison without implying false precision.

Interpretation of scores should focus on patterns rather than absolute values. A high overall score may mask critical weaknesses in specific dimensions, while a moderate score may be acceptable if risks are manageable.

Decision-makers are encouraged to review underlying assumptions rather than relying solely on aggregate scores. Table 6.6 translates analytical results into clear go, defer, or reject decisions.

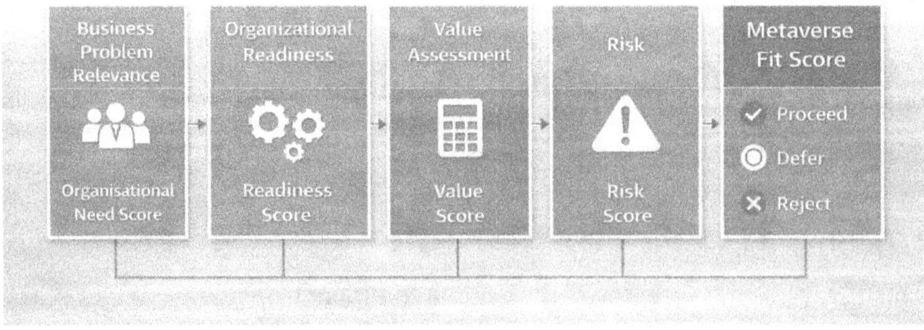

Figure 6.7 Consolidated Metaverse fit score synthesising problem relevance, readiness, value, and risk dimensions.

Table 6.6 Metaverse Fit Score Summary

Assessment Dimension	*Score (Low/ Medium/High)*	*Key Evidence*	*Risk Notes*
Problem relevance			
Organisational readiness			
Incremental value			
Risk and uncertainty			
Strategic alignment			
Decision Outcome:			
Proceed/Defer/Reject			

Note: This table presents a summary of metaverse fit score dimensions and decision outcomes.

6.7.5 Decision Outcomes

The metaverse fit score supports three primary decision outcomes. The first is to proceed, indicating that immersive technologies offer defensible incremental value and that the organisation is ready to implement them responsibly.

The second outcome is to defer, suggesting that potential value exists but that preparatory work is required. This may include improving readiness, addressing process gaps, or gathering additional evidence.

The third outcome is to reject, indicating that immersive technologies are not appropriate for the problem at hand. This outcome should be treated as a positive result of disciplined assessment rather than as failure.

6.7.6 Managing Stakeholder Expectations

Clear communication of the fit score and its implications is essential. Stakeholders may have invested expectations in immersive initiatives, and unfavourable outcomes may generate disappointment.

The framework encourages transparent explanation of reasoning and evidence. By linking conclusions to structured analysis, decision-makers can maintain credibility and trust. Managing expectations effectively supports organisational learning and future decision-making.

6.7.7 Role of the Fit Score in Ongoing Governance

The fit score should not be treated as a one-time artefact. As organisational conditions, technologies, or business priorities evolve, the assessment may need to be revisited.

In this sense, the fit score becomes part of ongoing governance rather than a static decision. Periodic reassessment enables organisations to adapt responsibly as circumstances change. This dynamic perspective aligns with the evolving nature of immersive technologies.

6.7.8 Limitations of the Fit Score

No scoring system can eliminate uncertainty. The framework acknowledges that judgement remains essential and that fit scores are only as reliable as the assumptions on which they are based.

Decision-makers should therefore treat the fit score as a structured aid rather than as an infallible verdict. Critical reflection and contextual awareness remain necessary. Recognising limitations enhances, rather than weakens, the credibility of the framework.

6.7.9 Section Summary

The consolidation and metaverse fit score stage integrates diverse analytical outputs into a clear decision view. By synthesising problem relevance, readiness, value, and risk, it supports informed and defensible conclusions regarding metaverse adoption. This stage completes the core decision framework and provides a bridge to subsequent chapters that explore implementation strategies and applied cases.

BIBLIOGRAPHY

Ball, M. (2022). *The Metaverse: And How It Will Revolutionise Everything*. Liveright Publishing.

Deloitte. (2022). *The Metaverse and the Future of Work*. Deloitte Insights.

Gartner. (2023). *Emerging Technologies: Frameworks for Evaluating Immersive Experiences*. Gartner Research.

McKinsey & Company. (2022). *Value Creation in the Metaverse*. McKinsey Digital.

Porter, M. E. (1985). *Competitive Advantage: Creating and Sustaining Superior Performance*. Free Press.

PwC. (2023). *Seeing Is Believing: How Virtual Reality and the Metaverse Are Transforming Business*. PwC Global.

WEF. (2023). *Defining and Building the Metaverse*. World Economic Forum.

Chapter 7

Metaverse Strategies

7.1 INTRODUCTION TO METAVERSE STRATEGY

Metaverse strategy is often misunderstood as a technology trend response or a set of innovation experiments. In enterprise contexts, however, strategy must be treated as a structured approach to decision-making, investment, and capability-building. The metaverse is not a single product or platform; it is a set of immersive and spatial computing capabilities that may be deployed in different ways, at different maturity levels, and for different organisational objectives. A coherent strategy is therefore required to define intent, scope, and execution pathways.

Early-stage metaverse activity across many organisations has been characterised by pilots and demonstrations. Such efforts can generate learning, but they often fail to translate into sustained value because they lack strategic anchoring. In the absence of strategy, initiatives tend to be technology-driven, fragmented, and evaluated using inconsistent criteria. In practice, the organisations that achieve durable outcomes treat immersive technologies as part of a broader transformation portfolio, governed with the same discipline applied to other strategic programmes.

This chapter focuses on how organisations should define and execute metaverse strategies in a way that is business-led, measurable, and operationally feasible. It builds directly on the decision framework in Chapter 6 by moving from assessment to action. Where Chapter 6 provides the method for determining fit and value, Chapter 7 explains how to translate those conclusions into strategy, operating model design, capability uplift, and governance.

7.1.1 Why Metaverse Strategy Matters

A strategy is necessary when decisions involve uncertainty, trade-offs, and long-term commitments. Metaverse initiatives meet all of these criteria. They often require cross-functional coordination, new capability development, changes to operating models, and adjustments to governance structures. Without a strategy, organisations are likely to experience predictable failure modes, including inconsistent prioritisation, duplication of effort, and limited reusability of assets.

Metaverse strategy matters for four primary reasons. First, immersive initiatives typically cut across business and technology boundaries. Training, collaboration, customer engagement, and design functions may all be involved. Strategy provides a unifying direction so that initiatives do not compete for ownership or diverge in incompatible ways.

Second, immersive technologies introduce a different set of adoption dynamics compared to conventional software deployments. User comfort, accessibility, behavioural norms, content moderation, and device management become material considerations. Strategy is required to ensure these factors are addressed systematically, rather than reactively.

Third, the metaverse introduces a high risk of misalignment due to external market hype. Organisations may face pressure to "do something" for reputational or competitive reasons. A strategy provides a disciplined mechanism to resist hype-driven decisions by anchoring adoption to value and readiness.

Fourth, immersive programmes often require longer investment horizons than stakeholders initially anticipate. A strategy defines sequencing and maturity pathways, helping organisations move from experimentation to scalable delivery without overcommitting prematurely. Figure 7.1 illustrates the metaverse strategy cascade, showing how strategic vision is translated into objectives, operating model choices, capability development, and measurable evaluation.

Table 7.1 links strategic intent to tangible value drivers, ensuring that metaverse initiatives are framed around business outcomes rather than immersive novelty.

7.1.2 Positioning the Metaverse within Enterprise Transformation

A metaverse strategy should not be separate from digital strategy, operational strategy, or transformation planning. It should be positioned as an enabling capability that supports targeted outcomes, rather than as a parallel agenda.

In practical terms, this means metaverse initiatives must align with one or more of the following:

- Workforce transformation and learning strategies
- Operational excellence and process redesign programmes
- Product and service innovation portfolios
- Customer experience strategies
- Risk management, safety, and compliance agendas

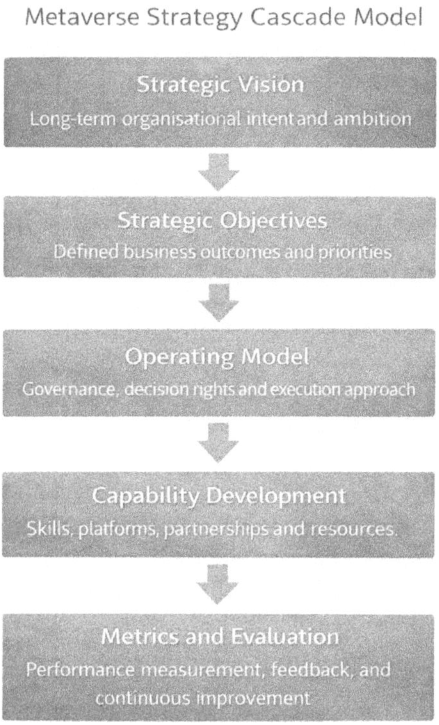

Metaverse Strategy Cascade Model

Strategic Vision
Long-term organisational intent and ambition

Strategic Objectives
Defined business outcomes and priorities

Operating Model
Governance, decision rights and execution approach

Capability Development
Skills, platforms, partnerships and resources

Metrics and Evaluation
Performance measurement, feedback, and continuous improvement

Figure 7.1 Metaverse strategy cascade model.

Note: Metaverse strategy cascade showing how strategic vision translates into objectives, operating model choices, capability development, and measurable evaluation.

Table 7.1 Strategic Objectives and Metaverse Value Drivers

Strategic Objective	*Primary Value Driver*	*Example Metaverse Applications*
Improve customer engagement	Experience immersion	Virtual showrooms, immersive brand experiences
Enhance workforce productivity	Training effectiveness	VR-based training and simulations
Reduce operational costs	Process optimisation	Digital twins for planning and optimisation
Accelerate innovation	Rapid prototyping	Virtual product design and testing
Strengthen collaboration	Spatial collaboration	Virtual workspaces and co-creation environments

Note: This table presents a mapping of strategic objectives to metaverse value drivers and representative enterprise use cases.

Where metaverse activity is disconnected from these broader agendas, it becomes vulnerable to budget reduction and organisational scepticism. Conversely, when integrated into transformation portfolios, it can be prioritised and governed alongside other initiatives, with coherent performance metrics and accountability.

7.1.3 From Pilots to Strategy: The Critical Transition

The transition from pilots to strategy is a critical inflection point. Many organisations can run a successful demonstration, but far fewer can scale immersive programmes sustainably. Scaling introduces complexity in device management, content maintenance, user support, integration with enterprise systems, and governance.

A strategy must therefore answer questions that pilots do not resolve, such as:

- Which use cases are strategically prioritised and why
- Which organisational units will adopt immersive solutions first
- What minimum capability baseline is required for expansion
- How value will be measured and reported consistently
- How risks such as privacy, safety, and conduct will be controlled

Without explicit answers to these questions, pilots often remain isolated and fail to produce repeatable patterns.

7.1.4 What a Metaverse Strategy Must Deliver

A metaverse strategy should deliver tangible outputs that enable execution. These outputs generally include:

- Strategic objectives linked to business value drivers
- A prioritised portfolio of use cases and an adoption roadmap
- An operating model that defines ownership and governance
- Capability uplift plans, including skills and sourcing strategy
- Risk and compliance frameworks appropriate for immersive environments
- Measurement frameworks for outcomes, adoption, and operational performance

These outputs ensure that immersive initiatives can progress beyond conceptual excitement and enter structured delivery.

7.1.5 Common Strategic Failure Patterns

Understanding common failure patterns improves strategy quality. The following patterns recur across organisations:

- Strategy defined as a technology roadmap rather than business outcomes
- Overly broad scope that attempts to cover many use cases without prioritisation
- Lack of ownership and unclear governance, leading to stalled decisions
- Underestimation of operational needs such as support, device lifecycle, and content maintenance
- Misinterpretation of engagement metrics as proof of business value
- Failure to address ethical, privacy, and behavioural considerations early

A strong strategy explicitly designs against these risks.

7.1.6 Link to Chapter 6 Decision Framework

This chapter assumes that an organisation has already applied the decision discipline introduced in Chapter 6. In particular, it assumes that:

- The business problem is clearly defined
- Baseline readiness and maturity are assessed
- Value chain gaps are identified
- Non-metaverse value and incremental metaverse value are quantified
- A metaverse fit conclusion is available

Chapter 7 then translates these outputs into practical strategic decisions: what to prioritise, how to organise delivery, how to build capability, and how to govern risk.

7.1.7 Section Summary

Metaverse strategy is essential for moving from experimentation to sustained value creation. It provides the structure required to prioritise use cases, design operating models, build capabilities, manage risk, and measure outcomes. Positioned correctly, metaverse strategy becomes part of broader enterprise transformation rather than a separate innovation agenda. The sections that follow build on this foundation by defining the strategic components and choices organisations must make to execute successfully.

7.2 DEFINING A METAVERSE STRATEGY

A metaverse strategy defines how immersive and spatial computing capabilities are intentionally deployed to support organisational objectives. It is not a technology catalogue, nor is it a collection of disconnected innovation initiatives. Instead, it represents a coherent set of decisions that align

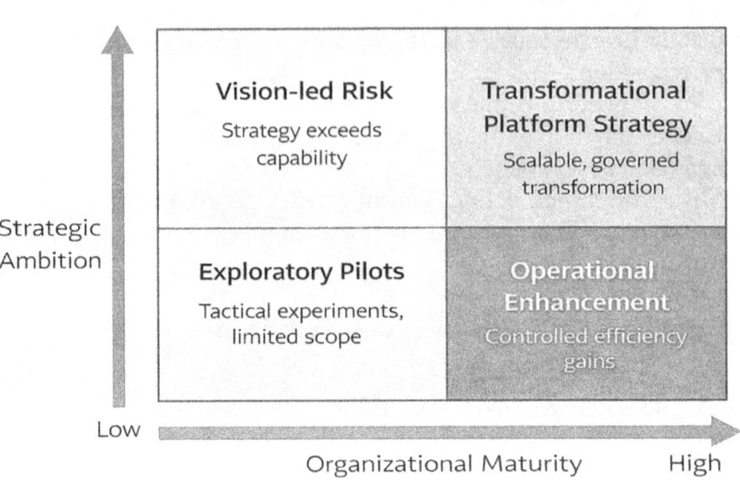

Figure 7.2 Strategy versus maturity matrix, illustrating the categorisation of Metaverse strategies based on strategic ambition and organisational maturity.

business intent, operating models, capability development, and governance mechanisms.

In practice, organisations often struggle at this stage because the metaverse does not map neatly onto existing strategic categories. It is neither purely a digital channel nor a traditional enterprise system. As a result, defining strategy requires deliberate clarification of scope, intent, and decision boundaries.

This section explains how organisations should define a metaverse strategy in a way that is disciplined, measurable, and resilient to hype-driven pressures. Figure 7.2 illustrates a strategy versus maturity matrix, showing how metaverse strategies can be categorised according to strategic ambition and organisational maturity.

Table 7.2 provides a structured comparison of operating models, supporting informed selection based on organisational maturity and governance requirements.

7.2.1 Distinguishing Strategy from Technology Roadmaps

A common early mistake is to equate metaverse strategy with a technology roadmap. Roadmaps typically focus on platforms, tools, and deployment timelines. While these elements are necessary for execution, they do not constitute strategy.

Table 7.2 Operating Model Characteristics and Trade-offs

Operating Model	*Key Characteristics*	*Advantages*	*Limitations*
Centralised	Single enterprise-led metaverse team	Strong governance, consistency	Slower innovation, less local flexibility
Decentralised	Business-unit led initiatives	Speed, tailored solutions	Fragmentation, duplication
Federated	Shared standards with local autonomy	Balance of control and agility	Requires strong coordination mechanisms

Note: This table presents a comparison of operating model characteristics and trade-offs for metaverse delivery.

Strategy answers different questions. It clarifies why immersive technologies are being adopted, what outcomes they are expected to influence, and which trade-offs the organisation is willing to accept. A roadmap may change frequently as technologies evolve, but strategy should remain stable over a defined planning horizon. Organisations that conflate strategy with tooling often find themselves locked into premature platform decisions that constrain future flexibility.

7.2.2 Strategic Scope and Boundary Setting

Defining scope is one of the most important aspects of metaverse strategy. Scope determines the functions, processes, or domains that are in focus and that are explicitly excluded.

Overly broad strategies attempt to address training, collaboration, customer engagement, and innovation simultaneously. Such breadth often leads to shallow execution and competing priorities. Conversely, overly narrow strategies may limit learning and reuse.

Effective strategies define an initial scope that is sufficiently focused to deliver measurable value while allowing for expansion if outcomes justify it. Explicit boundary setting also helps manage expectations among stakeholders and reduces the risk of scope creep.

7.2.3 Strategic Intent and Organisational Positioning

Strategic intent reflects what the organisation ultimately seeks to achieve through metaverse adoption. This intent may vary significantly across organisations and industries.

Some organisations pursue immersive technologies primarily to improve internal capability, such as accelerating skills development or enhancing safety training. Others view the metaverse as a means of differentiation, enabling new customer experiences or digital services. In certain contexts, strategic intent may be defensive, aimed at mitigating risk or responding to regulatory or operational constraints. Clarity of intent influences all subsequent strategic choices, including investment levels, capability priorities, and risk tolerance.

7.2.4 Alignment with Enterprise Strategy and Transformation Programmes

A metaverse strategy should be explicitly linked to existing enterprise strategies rather than positioned as a standalone initiative. This alignment ensures coherence across transformation efforts and reduces internal competition for resources.

In practice, alignment may involve linking immersive initiatives to workforce transformation programmes, operational excellence initiatives, product innovation portfolios, or customer experience strategies. Where such linkages are absent, metaverse initiatives often struggle to secure sustained executive support. Alignment also enables shared metrics and governance structures, simplifying oversight and accountability.

7.2.5 Strategic Trade-Offs and Prioritisation

Every strategy involves trade-offs. In the metaverse context, these trade-offs may relate to speed versus control, experimentation versus standardisation, or internal capability versus external dependency.

Explicitly acknowledging trade-offs strengthens strategic discipline. For example, prioritising rapid experimentation may require acceptance of higher short-term risk, while prioritising control may slow innovation.

Documenting these trade-offs helps decision-makers remain consistent over time and provides a reference point when pressures arise to deviate from strategy.

7.2.6 Time Horizon and Strategic Phasing

Metaverse strategies should define a realistic time horizon and be phased accordingly. Short-term objectives may focus on learning and validation, while longer-term objectives address scale and integration.

Phasing allows organisations to manage uncertainty and adjust direction based on evidence. It also supports staged investment, reducing exposure to early-stage risk. Without explicit phasing, strategies often oscillate between overcommitment and disengagement.

7.2.7 Indicators of a Well-Defined Metaverse Strategy

A well-defined metaverse strategy exhibits several characteristics. It is clearly articulated, aligned with business objectives, constrained in scope, and supported by defined governance and capability plans. It also includes measurable success criteria and acknowledges uncertainty.

Most importantly, it enables consistent decision-making. When new use cases or technologies emerge, the strategy provides a framework for evaluating relevance rather than requiring ad hoc judgement.

7.2.8 Section Summary

Defining a metaverse strategy requires more than selecting platforms or launching pilots. It demands clarity of intent, disciplined scope definition, alignment with enterprise priorities, and explicit trade-offs. When these elements are in place, immersive technologies can be evaluated and deployed as part of a coherent strategic agenda rather than as isolated experiments.

7.3 STRATEGIC OBJECTIVES AND VALUE ALIGNMENT

A metaverse strategy must be anchored in clearly articulated strategic objectives. Without explicit objectives, immersive initiatives risk drifting toward novelty-driven experimentation rather than value-driven execution. Strategic objectives provide the reference point against which prioritisation, investment, and performance can be evaluated.

In enterprise settings, strategic objectives should be expressed in terms that resonate with business leadership. Objectives framed around technology adoption or innovation signalling are insufficient. Instead, they must be linked to measurable improvements in performance, capability, resilience, or growth. This section explains how organisations should define, prioritise, and align strategic objectives to ensure that metaverse initiatives deliver tangible value.

7.3.1 Translating Business Strategy into Metaverse Objectives

Metaverse objectives should be derived directly from broader business strategy rather than developed independently. This translation process requires organisations to examine how immersive capabilities can support existing strategic priorities.

For example, an organisation pursuing operational excellence may identify objectives related to reducing error rates, improving process understanding, or enhancing workforce competence. An organisation focused on growth may prioritise objectives related to customer engagement, product innovation, or digital service differentiation.

The key principle is that metaverse objectives must be traceable back to enterprise-level goals. This traceability strengthens executive sponsorship and ensures alignment across functions.

7.3.2 Differentiating Primary and Secondary Objectives

Organisations often identify multiple objectives for metaverse adoption. However, not all objectives carry equal strategic weight. Failure to differentiate between primary and secondary objectives leads to diluted focus and conflicting priorities.

Primary objectives represent the core justification for investment. Secondary objectives may represent additional benefits but should not drive design decisions or success criteria. For instance, increased engagement may be a secondary benefit of immersive training, but improved competence or safety outcomes should remain the primary objective. Clear differentiation enables disciplined prioritisation and reduces ambiguity during implementation.

7.3.3 Value Drivers and Outcome Orientation

Strategic objectives must be linked to specific value drivers. Value drivers represent the mechanisms through which improvement translates into organisational benefit. Examples include productivity gains, risk reduction, cost avoidance, or revenue enablement.

Outcome orientation requires organisations to focus on what changes as a result of metaverse adoption, rather than on how frequently immersive tools are used. Usage metrics alone provide limited insight into value creation. By articulating objectives in outcome-oriented terms, organisations can design initiatives that target meaningful change rather than superficial adoption.

7.3.4 Aligning Objectives with Organisational Maturity

Strategic objectives must be realistic given the organisation's current maturity and readiness. Objectives that exceed organisational capability are unlikely to be achieved, regardless of technology potential.

For example, an organisation with limited digital maturity may struggle to pursue objectives related to advanced simulation or large-scale immersive collaboration. In such cases, objectives should focus on foundational improvements that build capability incrementally. Alignment between objectives and maturity supports achievable progress and reduces the risk of strategic overreach.

7.3.5 Managing Conflicting Objectives

Metaverse initiatives often involve multiple stakeholders with differing priorities. Training teams may focus on learning outcomes, while technology teams prioritise platform stability, and business leaders seek measurable returns.

A robust strategy explicitly addresses potential conflicts by establishing clear prioritisation rules. When trade-offs arise, decisions should be guided by the agreed primary objectives rather than by functional preferences. Transparent handling of conflicts supports sustained alignment and reduces friction during execution.

7.3.6 Linking Objectives to Measurement Frameworks

Strategic objectives must be accompanied by clear measurement frameworks. These frameworks define how progress and success will be assessed over time.

Measurement frameworks should balance quantitative and qualitative indicators. Quantitative measures support comparability and accountability, while qualitative insights provide context and interpretation. Early definition of measurement criteria reduces ambiguity and supports evidence-based decision-making throughout the lifecycle of metaverse initiatives.

7.3.7 Strategic Objective Review and Adjustment

Strategic objectives should not be static. As organisational context, technology maturity, and external conditions evolve, objectives may require refinement.

Regular review ensures continued relevance and alignment. However, frequent or reactive changes undermine strategic stability. Adjustments should therefore be deliberate and evidence-driven.

This balance between stability and adaptability is a hallmark of effective metaverse strategy. Figure 7.3 outlines a capability maturity ladder, showing how organisations progress from awareness and experimentation through formation, expansion, and optimisation.

Table 7.3 demonstrates that successful metaverse adoption requires coordinated development across technical, experiential, operational, and governance capabilities.

7.3.8 Section Summary

Strategic objectives provide the foundation for value-oriented metaverse strategies. By translating enterprise priorities into outcome-focused objectives, differentiating primary and secondary goals, and aligning ambition with maturity, organisations can ensure that immersive initiatives remain purposeful and measurable. The next section examines how these objectives are operationalised through operating model design.

Capability Maturity Ladder
for Metaverse Strategy Execution

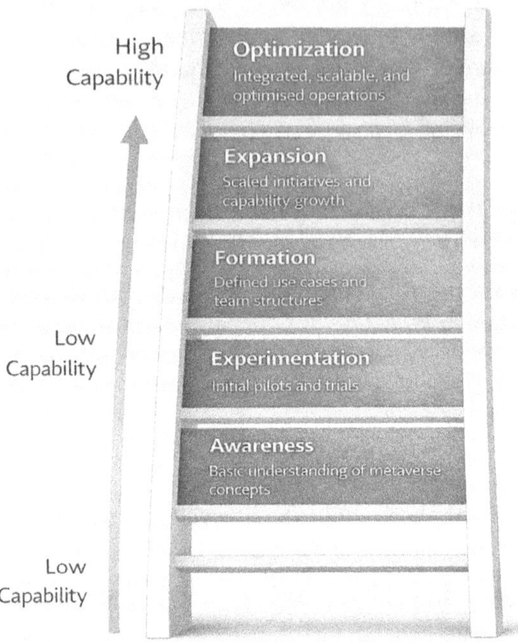

Figure 7.3 Capability maturity ladder for Metaverse strategy execution.

Note: Capability maturity ladder outlining how organisations progress from awareness and experimentation through formation, expansion, and optimisation.

Table 7.3 Metaverse Capability Domains

Capability Domain	*Description*	*Example Capabilities*
Technology	Platform and infrastructure	XR platforms, cloud, identity systems
Experience Design	User-centric design	3D UX, interaction design
Operations	Day-to-day running	Platform support, content moderation
Governance	Oversight and control	Risk management, compliance
Change Management	Adoption and skills	Training, organisational readiness

Note: This table presents the core capability domains required for sustainable metaverse adoption.

7.4 OPERATING MODEL DESIGN FOR THE METAVERSE

A metaverse strategy can only be executed effectively if it is supported by an appropriate operating model. The operating model defines how decisions are made, how work is organised, how resources are allocated, and how accountability is enforced. In the absence of a clear operating model, metaverse initiatives often stall, duplicate effort, or become fragmented across organisational boundaries. This section examines how organisations should design operating models that enable disciplined, scalable, and sustainable metaverse adoption.

7.4.1 Purpose of the Metaverse Operating Model

The primary purpose of an operating model is to translate strategic intent into repeatable execution. In the context of the metaverse, this involves coordinating multiple functions, including business units, technology teams, learning and development, legal, risk, and procurement.

Unlike traditional IT deployments, immersive initiatives often span experiential design, content creation, hardware management, and behavioural governance. The operating model must therefore accommodate a broader range of activities and stakeholders. A well-designed operating model reduces ambiguity, accelerates decision-making, and supports consistent delivery.

7.4.2 Centralised Operating Models

In a centralised operating model, ownership of metaverse initiatives resides within a single function or team, often aligned with digital innovation or enterprise technology. Centralisation offers several advantages. It promotes consistency in standards, architecture, and governance. It simplifies vendor management and enables reuse of assets across use cases. It also reduces risk by ensuring that policy and compliance considerations are addressed uniformly.

However, centralisation may limit responsiveness to business-specific needs. Business units may perceive immersive initiatives as detached from operational realities, reducing adoption and engagement. Centralised models are often most effective during early stages of adoption, when control and learning are prioritised.

7.4.3 Decentralised Operating Models

Decentralised operating models place ownership of metaverse initiatives within individual business units or functions. This approach maximises proximity to domain expertise and enables rapid experimentation.

Decentralisation supports contextual relevance and can accelerate value realisation in specific areas. However, it also introduces risks, including duplication of effort, inconsistent standards, and fragmented governance.

Without coordination mechanisms, decentralised models may lead to incompatible platforms, redundant investments, and increased operational risk. Decentralised models are most effective when organisational maturity is high and governance frameworks are well established.

7.4.4 Federated Operating Models

Federated operating models attempt to balance the strengths of centralised and decentralised approaches. In this model, a central function provides standards, shared services, and governance, while business units retain responsibility for use case definition and delivery.

Federated models support scalability and reuse while preserving domain relevance. They require clear delineation of responsibilities and effective coordination mechanisms. Successful federated models depend on strong leadership and well-defined interfaces between central and local teams.

7.4.5 Decision Rights and Accountability

Regardless of operating model, clarity of decision rights is essential. Ambiguity regarding who approves initiatives, allocates funding, or resolves conflicts is a common cause of delay and frustration.

Decision rights should be documented explicitly and communicated to all stakeholders. Accountability for outcomes must be clearly assigned, with performance measured against agreed objectives. Transparent decision structures support trust and reduce reliance on informal escalation.

7.4.6 Funding and Resource Allocation

Operating models must define how metaverse initiatives are funded and resourced. Funding mechanisms influence behaviour and prioritisation.

Central funding can promote strategic alignment but may reduce ownership at the business unit level. Local funding increases ownership but may limit scale and consistency. Hybrid funding models, combining central investment with local contributions, are often effective in balancing alignment and accountability.

7.4.7 Integration with Existing Operating Models

Metaverse operating models should integrate with existing organisational structures rather than creating parallel systems. Alignment with digital, learning, and innovation operating models reduces duplication and confusion.

Integration also simplifies governance and reporting, enabling immersive initiatives to be assessed alongside other transformation activities. Failure to integrate often results in organisational resistance and inefficiency.

7.4.8 Operating Model Evolution Over Time

Operating models should evolve as adoption matures. Early-stage models may emphasise control and learning, while later stages prioritise scalability and efficiency.

Periodic review of the operating model ensures continued alignment with strategic objectives and organisational capability. Evolution should be deliberate and evidence-based rather than reactive. Figure 7.4 compares centre-of-expertise structural models, showing how centralised, decentralised, and federated approaches organise metaverse capabilities differently.

Table 7.4 clarifies accountability across strategy, delivery, and governance roles, reducing duplication of effort and supporting consistent execution.

7.4.9 Section Summary

Operating model design is a critical enabler of metaverse strategy. By defining ownership, decision rights, funding mechanisms, and integration pathways, organisations can move from isolated experimentation to coordinated

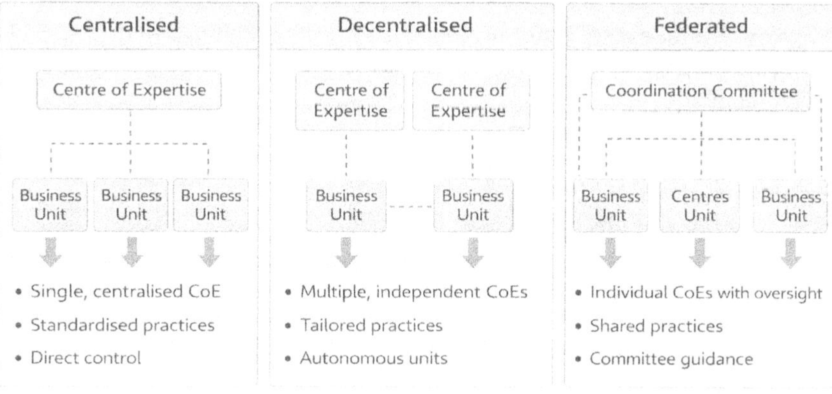

Figure 7.4 Centre of expertise structural models comparing centralised, decentralised, and federated approaches for organising Metaverse capabilities.

Table 7.4 Organisational Roles and Responsibilities

Role	*Primary Responsibility*	*Key Decisions*
Executive Sponsor	Strategic ownership	Investment approval
Metaverse Lead	Programme coordination	Roadmap prioritisation
Technology Lead	Platform architecture	Technology selection
Governance Lead	Risk and ethics	Policy enforcement
Business Owner	Use case delivery	Value realisation

Note: The table presents the key organisational roles and responsibilities supporting metaverse strategy execution.

execution. A well-designed operating model supports scalability, reduces risk, and reinforces strategic alignment.

7.5 CAPABILITY UPLIFT AND SKILLS DEVELOPMENT

A metaverse strategy is only as effective as the organisation's ability to execute it. Capability uplift and skills development therefore represent a critical pillar of successful metaverse adoption. Immersive initiatives introduce new technical, creative, and operational requirements that extend beyond traditional enterprise IT capabilities.

This section examines how organisations should identify required capabilities, assess gaps, and develop sustainable skills strategies that support long-term metaverse execution rather than short-term experimentation.

7.5.1 Understanding Metaverse Capability Requirements

Metaverse initiatives require a combination of capabilities that are rarely co-located within a single team. These capabilities span multiple domains, including platform engineering, experience design, content creation, facilitation, and operational support.

Technical capabilities include managing immersive platforms, integrating them with enterprise systems, ensuring performance and security, and supporting device lifecycles. Creative capabilities involve designing immersive experiences that are intuitive, purposeful, and aligned with learning or business objectives. Operational capabilities include facilitation, moderation, support, and ongoing content maintenance. Understanding the breadth of required capabilities is essential to avoid underestimating effort and complexity.

7.5.2 Assessing Existing Capability Maturity

Before investing in new skills, organisations must assess their current capability maturity. This assessment should consider not only formal skills but also informal experience, organisational capacity, and cultural readiness.

Capability maturity may vary significantly across functions. For example, learning and development teams may possess strong instructional design skills but limited exposure to immersive environments, while technology teams may understand platforms but lack experience in experiential design. A structured capability assessment enables targeted investment and reduces the risk of building redundant or misaligned skills.

7.5.3 Build, Buy, or Partner Decisions

Organisations must decide whether to develop capabilities internally, source them externally, or pursue partnerships. Each approach has implications for cost, speed, control, and sustainability.

Building internal capability supports long-term resilience and reduces dependency on vendors. However, it requires time, investment, and a commitment to continuous learning. Buying capability through vendors or contractors accelerates delivery but may limit knowledge transfer. Partnerships can provide access to specialised expertise while sharing risk. Most organisations adopt hybrid approaches, combining internal capability development with selective external support.

Table 7.5 supports capability sourcing decisions by balancing speed to market, control, cost, and long-term sustainability. It complements the capability uplift discussion by translating strategy into resourcing choices.

7.5.4 Capability Development Roadmaps

Capability uplift should be planned through phased roadmaps aligned with strategic priorities. Early phases may focus on foundational skills such as platform literacy, basic experience design, and facilitation. Later phases can introduce advanced capabilities such as simulation design, analytics, and optimisation.

Roadmaps should account for sequencing, dependencies, and resource constraints. Attempting to develop all capabilities simultaneously often leads to superficial skill acquisition and limited impact. Phased roadmaps also support progressive maturity and reduce organisational strain.

Table 7.5 Build, Buy, or Partner Decision Framework

Decision Factor	*Build*	*Buy*	*Partner*
Speed to delivery	Slow	Fast	Medium
Control	High	Low	Medium
Cost profile	High upfront	Subscription	Shared investment
Knowledge retention	Strong	Weak	Moderate
Long-term flexibility	High	Limited	Moderate

7.5.5 Workforce Enablement and Change Readiness

Skills development alone is insufficient if the broader workforce is not prepared to adopt immersive tools. Enablement initiatives should address awareness, confidence, and behavioural change.

This may include introductory sessions, guided onboarding, and ongoing support mechanisms. Clear communication regarding purpose and expectations reduces resistance and supports adoption. Enablement should be tailored to different user groups, recognising varying levels of comfort and experience.

7.5.6 Sustaining Capability Over Time

Metaverse capabilities are not static. Platforms evolve, use cases expand, and user expectations change. Sustaining capability therefore requires continuous learning and adaptation.

Organisations should establish mechanisms for knowledge sharing, skills refresh, and capability evaluation. Communities of practice and internal networks can support ongoing development and reduce reliance on external expertise. Sustained capability development is a hallmark of mature metaverse strategies.

7.5.7 Risks of Inadequate Capability Planning

Insufficient capability planning is a common cause of failure. Risks include overreliance on vendors, inconsistent experience quality, operational bottlenecks, and reduced credibility among stakeholders.

These risks often emerge after initial enthusiasm fades, making them difficult to address retrospectively. Proactive capability planning mitigates these issues and supports long-term value creation. Figure 7.5 illustrates the governance overlay model, showing how governance, risk, and ethics flow through strategy, operating model, and execution decisions.

7.5.8 Section Summary

Capability uplift and skills development are central to effective metaverse strategy execution. By understanding required capabilities, assessing maturity, and investing through phased and sustainable approaches, organisations can move beyond experimentation and build enduring competence. The next section explores how these capabilities are coordinated and governed through a metaverse Centre of Excellence.

7.6 ESTABLISHING ORGANISATIONAL STRUCTURES FOR METAVERSE STRATEGY EXECUTION

As metaverse initiatives move from isolated experimentation toward coordinated strategic programmes, organisations are required to introduce

Figure 7.5 Governance overlay model showing how governance, risk, and ethics flow through strategy, operating model, and execution decisions.

appropriate structural mechanisms to support execution. Without such structures, immersive initiatives tend to fragment across business units, evolve inconsistently, or fail to mature beyond pilot stages. Organisational structures provide continuity, governance, and knowledge retention, all of which are necessary for sustained value creation.

This section examines how organisations can establish structural arrangements that support metaverse strategy execution, with particular attention to coordination, accountability, and capability development. Rather than prescribing a single organisational model, the discussion focuses on principles and design considerations that can be adapted to different organisational contexts.

7.6.1 The Need for Coordinated Metaverse Structures

Metaverse initiatives typically cut across traditional organisational boundaries. They involve technology platforms, content creation, learning design, user experience, risk management, and behavioural governance. When these elements are managed independently, the organisation risks duplication of effort, inconsistent standards, and misalignment with strategic objectives.

Coordinated structures are required to ensure that immersive initiatives are guided by shared principles and informed by collective learning. Coordination also enables reuse of assets, transfer of knowledge, and accumulation of institutional capability over time. The need for coordination increases as the number of immersive use cases grows and as initiatives move closer to core business operations.

7.6.2 Structural Models for Metaverse Enablement

Organisations may adopt a range of structural models to support metaverse strategy execution. These models exist on a spectrum from informal coordination mechanisms to formalised centres of expertise.

At one end of the spectrum, coordination may be achieved through cross-functional working groups or steering committees. These arrangements are often suitable in early adoption stages, where the primary objective is learning rather than scale.

At the other end of the spectrum, organisations may establish dedicated functions or centres responsible for metaverse enablement. These structures provide greater continuity and authority but require careful design to avoid unnecessary bureaucracy. The appropriate model depends on organisational size, strategic ambition, and risk profile.

7.6.3 Role and Function of a Metaverse Centre of Expertise

Where formalised structures are adopted, a centre of expertise often plays a central role. Such a centre does not own all immersive initiatives but acts as a coordinating and enabling function. Its role is to support consistent execution while allowing business units to retain ownership of domain-specific use cases.

Typical functions of a centre of expertise include developing design principles, maintaining architectural guidance, supporting capability development, and advising on risk and compliance considerations. In some organisations, the centre also curates a portfolio view of immersive initiatives to support prioritisation and investment decisions. The effectiveness of this function depends less on formal authority and more on credibility, relevance, and trust.

7.6.4 Balancing Enablement and Control

One of the central challenges in designing metaverse-related structures is balancing enablement with control. Excessive control can slow innovation and discourage participation, while insufficient oversight increases risk and fragmentation.

Effective structures emphasise enablement by providing guidance, tools, and support while reserving control for areas where consistency and risk management are essential. This balance allows immersive initiatives to evolve organically while remaining aligned with organisational standards and values.

Clear articulation of what the structure enables and what it governs is critical to maintaining this balance. Figure 7.6 illustrates the risk, ethics, and value triangle, showing the balance required between risk mitigation, ethical use, and value creation in metaverse initiatives.

Table 7.6 links high-level risk areas to practical governance controls, supporting proactive management of risk in immersive environments.

7.6.5 Integration with Existing Organisational Functions

Metaverse-related structures should not operate in isolation. Integration with existing organisational functions, such as digital transformation offices, learning and development teams, and risk management functions, is essential.

Integration reduces duplication, leverages existing expertise, and embeds immersive initiatives within established governance mechanisms. It also

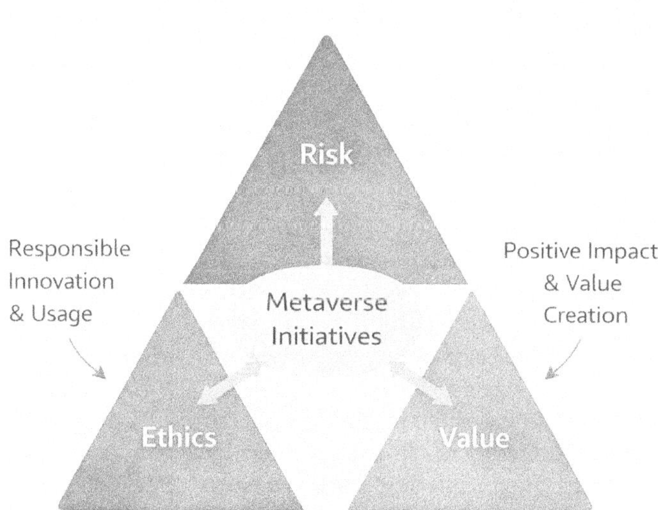

Figure 7.6 Risk, ethics, and value triangle, illustrating the balance required between risk mitigation, ethical use, and value creation in Metaverse initiatives.

Table 7.6 Governance Risk Categories and Controls

Risk Category	*Description*	*Representative Controls*
Data privacy and security	Sensitive immersive data	Access control, encryption
Ethical and behavioural risk	User conduct and wellbeing	Codes of conduct, moderation
Integrity and authenticity	Identity and trust	Identity verification, audit trails

Note: This table presents the governance risk categories and representative control mechanisms for metaverse initiatives.

signals that metaverse adoption is part of mainstream organisational activity rather than a peripheral innovation effort. Poor integration often leads to parallel processes and confusion regarding ownership and accountability.

7.6.6 Capability Development and Knowledge Retention

Structural arrangements play an important role in building and retaining organisational capability. Immersive initiatives generate valuable knowledge related to design, adoption, and impact. Without mechanisms to capture and disseminate this knowledge, organisations risk repeating mistakes and losing expertise when individuals move on.

Structures that support knowledge sharing, documentation, and mentoring contribute to institutional learning. Over time, this learning becomes a strategic asset that supports more effective and efficient metaverse adoption.

7.6.7 Governance and Ethical Oversight

Metaverse initiatives introduce governance and ethical considerations that extend beyond conventional digital systems. These include user behaviour, data privacy in immersive environments, and accessibility considerations.

Organisational structures should provide mechanisms for ethical oversight and policy alignment. This does not necessarily require new governance bodies, but it does require clarity regarding responsibility and escalation pathways.

Embedding ethical considerations into structural design reinforces trust and accountability. Figure 7.7 illustrates the value governance model, showing how strategic, financial, and social value are tracked through governance to support benefit realisation.

Table 7.7 illustrates how governance effectiveness can be measured through a combination of operational, risk, ethical, and value-based indicators.

Figure 7.7 Value governance model showing how strategic, financial, and social value are tracked through governance to ensure benefits realisation.

Table 7.7 Governance Metrics and Monitoring Indicators

Metric Category	*Example Indicator*	*Purpose*
Financial	Cost versus realised value	Investment justification
Operational	Platform uptime	Reliability
Risk	Incident frequency	Risk oversight
Ethical	Policy violations	Trust and safety
Adoption	Active users	Engagement tracking

Note: This table presents the governance metrics and monitoring indicators for tracking metaverse performance and compliance.

7.6.8 Evolution of Organisational Structures Over Time

Organisational structures supporting metaverse strategies should evolve as adoption matures. Early-stage structures may prioritise learning and coordination, while later-stage structures focus on optimisation, scalability, and integration.

Regular review of structural effectiveness helps prevent rigidity and ensures continued alignment with strategic objectives. Organisations that fail to adapt structures often find that early arrangements become constraints rather than enablers.

7.6.9 Section Summary

Establishing appropriate organisational structures is essential for translating metaverse strategy into sustained execution. By providing coordination, enabling capability development, and supporting governance, such structures reduce fragmentation and support long-term value creation. The design of these structures should be guided by organisational context, strategic ambition, and a clear balance between enablement and control.

7.7 GOVERNANCE, RISK, AND ETHICAL CONSIDERATIONS

Metaverse strategies introduce governance, risk, and ethical considerations that differ in both nature and scale from those associated with conventional digital systems. Immersive environments blur boundaries between physical and digital interaction, introduce new forms of data generation, and shape user behaviour in ways that are less predictable and less observable. As a result, governance frameworks must evolve to address these characteristics explicitly rather than relying solely on existing digital governance models. This section examines how organisations should approach governance, risk management, and ethical oversight to ensure that metaverse initiatives remain trustworthy, compliant, and aligned with organisational values.

7.7.1 Governance Challenges in Immersive Environments

Governance in immersive environments is complicated by the distributed and experiential nature of the metaverse. Decision-making authority may be fragmented across technology teams, business units, and external platform providers. In addition, responsibility for user behaviour, content moderation, and experiential design is often unclear.

Traditional governance models tend to focus on systems and data, whereas immersive environments require governance of experiences, interactions, and behavioural norms. Without explicit governance structures, organisations risk inconsistent policy application and unmanaged exposure. Effective governance frameworks define ownership, escalation pathways, and accountability across the full lifecycle of immersive initiatives.

7.7.2 Risk Categories Specific to Metaverse Adoption

Metaverse initiatives introduce a range of risk categories that extend beyond those typically associated with enterprise IT systems. These include operational risk related to platform stability and device management, reputational risk arising from inappropriate user behaviour, and legal risk associated with data collection and intellectual property.

There are also emerging risks related to psychological impact, accessibility, and exclusion. These risks are often less tangible but can have significant long-term consequences if left unaddressed.

Risk identification should be continuous rather than static, reflecting the evolving nature of immersive technologies and use cases. Figure 7.8 highlights the principal meta-risk areas in metaverse initiatives, showing the intersection of data security and privacy, ethical use and safety, and integrity and authenticity.

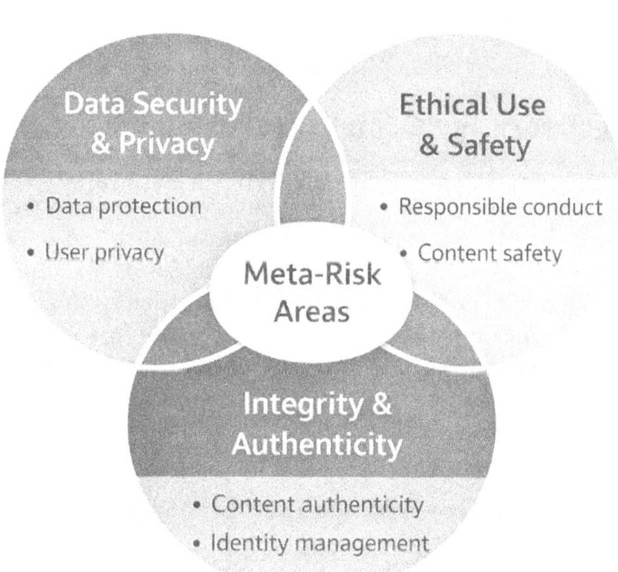

Figure 7.8 Meta-risk areas highlighting the intersection of data security and privacy, ethical use and safety, and integrity and authenticity

7.7.3 Data Privacy and Security Considerations

Immersive environments generate large volumes of data, including biometric, behavioural, and spatial data. This data is often more sensitive than traditional transactional data and may be subject to heightened regulatory scrutiny.

Organisations must ensure that data collection, storage, and usage practices comply with relevant privacy regulations and ethical standards. Transparency regarding data use is particularly important, as users may not fully understand what data is being captured within immersive environments. Security considerations include not only technical controls but also user authentication, access management, and protection against misuse or unauthorised recording.

7.7.4 Ethical Design and User Wellbeing

Ethical considerations play a central role in metaverse governance. Immersive experiences have the potential to influence behaviour, perception, and emotional response more strongly than conventional digital interfaces.

Ethical design principles should address issues such as consent, inclusivity, accessibility, and avoidance of manipulative design practices. Organisations must also consider the impact of prolonged immersion on wellbeing and establish guidelines for appropriate use. Embedding ethical considerations into design and governance processes reinforces trust and supports responsible innovation.

7.7.5 Regulatory and Compliance Alignment

Regulatory frameworks governing immersive technologies are still evolving. Organisations must therefore operate in conditions of regulatory uncertainty while maintaining compliance with existing laws and standards.

Governance frameworks should include mechanisms for monitoring regulatory developments and adapting policies accordingly. Engagement with legal and compliance functions is essential to ensure that immersive initiatives do not inadvertently breach existing obligations. Proactive alignment with regulatory expectations reduces future remediation effort and protects organisational reputation.

7.7.6 Integrating Governance into Strategic Decision-Making

Governance should not be treated as a downstream control function. Instead, it should be integrated into strategic decision-making from the outset.

Incorporating governance considerations into use case selection, platform choice, and operating model design ensures that risk and ethics are addressed proactively rather than reactively. This integration supports informed trade-offs and reduces the likelihood of later intervention. Effective integration requires collaboration between strategic, technical, and risk-focused stakeholders.

7.7.7 Measuring Governance Effectiveness

The effectiveness of governance frameworks should be assessed regularly. Metrics may include compliance adherence, incident frequency, user feedback, and audit outcomes.

Qualitative assessment is also important, particularly in relation to ethical considerations and user trust. Regular review enables continuous improvement and adaptation to emerging challenges.

Governance effectiveness should be viewed as an ongoing capability rather than a one-time achievement. Figure 7.9 illustrates the key governance levers in metaverse adoption, showing the practical mechanisms required for control across policy, roles and responsibilities, technology controls, ethical frameworks, and monitoring.

7.7.8 Section Summary

Governance, risk management, and ethical oversight are foundational to sustainable metaverse strategies. By addressing the unique characteristics of

Figure 7.9 Key governance levers in Metaverse adoption showing the practical levers required for control: policies, roles and responsibilities, technology controls, ethical framework, and monitoring and reporting.

immersive environments and integrating governance into strategic decision-making, organisations can mitigate risk while enabling responsible innovation. The final section of this chapter brings together the strategic, operational, and governance elements discussed to provide a consolidated perspective on metaverse strategy execution.

7.8 CHAPTER SUMMARY

This chapter has examined the strategic foundations required to move metaverse initiatives from conceptual interest to structured organisational execution. Rather than treating the metaverse as a standalone technology trend, the discussion has positioned it as a strategic capability that must be deliberately integrated into enterprise strategy, operating models, and governance frameworks.

This chapter began by defining what constitutes a metaverse strategy and emphasised the importance of clarity of intent, scope, and alignment with broader organisational objectives. Strategic objectives were shown to be most effective when they are outcome-oriented, prioritised, and grounded in organisational maturity rather than aspirational technology narratives.

The analysis then explored how strategy is translated into execution through operating model design. Centralised, decentralised, and federated models were examined as alternative approaches, each with distinct strengths and limitations. The discussion highlighted that no single operating model is universally optimal and that effectiveness depends on organisational context, risk appetite, and strategic ambition.

Capability uplift and skills development were identified as critical enablers of sustained metaverse adoption. This chapter demonstrated that immersive initiatives require a diverse set of technical, creative, and operational capabilities, and that these capabilities must be developed through phased, deliberate investment rather than ad hoc resourcing.

The role of organisational structures, including centres of expertise, was examined as a mechanism for coordination, knowledge retention, and governance. The discussion emphasised the importance of balancing enablement with control and ensuring that such structures evolve as adoption matures. Table 7.8 consolidates this chapter's governance mechanisms into a concise executive reference, reinforcing the strategic and operational lessons discussed.

Finally, this chapter addressed governance, risk, and ethical considerations, highlighting the unique challenges introduced by immersive environments. Effective governance was shown to require explicit attention to behavioural dynamics, data privacy, wellbeing, and regulatory uncertainty, with governance mechanisms integrated into strategic decision-making rather than applied retrospectively.

Table 7.8 Summary of Key Governance Levers

Governance Lever	*Description*	*Intended Outcome*
Policies	Rules and standards	Consistent behaviour
Roles and accountability	Clear ownership	Reduced ambiguity
Technical controls	Safeguards	Secure operations
Ethical framework	Values-based design	Responsible use
Monitoring and reporting	Ongoing oversight	Continuous improvement

Note: This table presents a summary of key governance levers supporting safe and scalable metaverse adoption.

Taken together, the elements discussed in this chapter provide a comprehensive framework for designing and executing metaverse strategies that are disciplined, scalable, and aligned with organisational values. The next chapter builds on this foundation by examining how these strategies are translated into measurable outcomes and assessed for long-term value creation.

BIBLIOGRAPHY

Deloitte. (2022). *The Metaverse and the Enterprise: Strategy, Use Cases, and Governance*. Deloitte Insights.

European Union Agency for Cybersecurity (ENISA). (2023). *Cybersecurity and Privacy Challenges of Extended Reality*. ENISA.

Gartner. (2023). *Emerging Technologies: Governance and Risk in Immersive Digital Environments*. Gartner Research.

ISO/IEC. (2015). *ISO/IEC 38500: Governance of Information Technology*. International Organization for Standardization.

McKinsey & Company. (2022). *Value Creation in the Metaverse: Beyond the Hype*. McKinsey Digital.

Organisation for Economic Co-operation and Development (OECD). (2015). *Digital Security Risk Management for Economic and Social Prosperity*. OECD Publishing.

PwC. (2023). *XR and the Future of Work: Strategy, Capability, and Risk*. PwC Research.

World Economic Forum. (2023). *Defining and Building the Metaverse: Ethics, Governance and Trust*. WEF.

Chapter 8

Metaverse Business Cases

8.1 PURPOSE OF A METAVERSE BUSINESS CASE

Metaverse initiatives often fail not because the technology is incapable but because the investment case supporting them is poorly constructed. Traditional IT business cases are typically designed around system replacement, cost efficiency, or incremental digital enhancement. Metaverse initiatives, by contrast, frequently involve new ways of working, behavioural change, and uncertain adoption patterns. As a result, they require a more disciplined and explicit business case approach.

A metaverse business case must therefore do more than justify technology spend. It must explain *why immersive approaches are appropriate for the problem being addressed*, what measurable change is expected, and how uncertainty will be managed. Without this clarity, metaverse initiatives risk being perceived as experimental, discretionary, or disconnected from core organisational priorities.

Another distinguishing feature of metaverse business cases is their reliance on *value mechanisms beyond direct revenue generation*. Many enterprise use cases focus on productivity improvement, risk reduction, safety enhancement, or capability uplift. These benefits are real, but they are often indirect and require careful framing to be credible to executive decision-makers.

This chapter positions the business case as a *decision-support instrument*, not a promotional document. Its purpose is to enable informed approval, prioritisation, and governance. A well-constructed metaverse business case should support three key decisions: whether to proceed, at what scale, and under what conditions.

Importantly, the absence of a compelling business case can be a valid outcome. In some situations, the most responsible decision is to delay adoption until organisational readiness, technology maturity, or regulatory clarity improves. Treating the business case as a gating mechanism, rather than a formality, helps organisations avoid premature or misaligned investment. Figure 8.1 illustrates the end-to-end lifecycle of a metaverse business case,

DOI: 10.1201/9781003405566-8

Figure 8.1 End-to-end lifecycle of a Metaverse business case, from problem definition through to investment decision.

Note: A structured view of the end-to-end steps used to develop, evaluate, and approve a metaverse business case.

showing how decision-making progresses from problem definition through to investment approval.

8.1.1 When a Metaverse Business Case Is Required

Not all metaverse-related activity requires a full business case. Exploratory research, small-scale experimentation, or vendor demonstrations may be appropriate without formal investment approval. However, a structured business case becomes essential when initiatives involve material cost, organisational impact, or reputational risk.

Triggers for requiring a formal metaverse business case typically include commitments to multi-year funding, changes to operational processes, large-scale workforce enablement, or exposure to sensitive data and regulated activities. In such cases, decision-makers require evidence that the proposed intervention is proportionate, necessary, and aligned with strategic priorities.

8.1.2 Characteristics of a Credible Metaverse Business Case

A credible metaverse business case shares several defining characteristics. First, it is *problem-led rather than technology-led*. The starting point is a clearly articulated business problem or constraint, not the availability of immersive tools.

Second, it distinguishes between *assumptions and evidence*. Where data is unavailable or uncertain, assumptions are stated explicitly and tested through sensitivity analysis rather than presented as facts.

Third, it balances ambition with restraint. Overly optimistic projections undermine credibility, particularly in emerging technology domains. Conservative estimates, clear risk articulation, and phased investment approaches are more likely to gain executive confidence.

Finally, a credible business case defines *decision points*, not just outcomes. It specifies what conditions must be met to proceed from pilot to scale, and what signals would trigger reassessment or termination.

8.1.2.1 Template 8.1 – Business Problem Definition

8.1.2.1.1 Purpose

To ensure the business case is anchored in a clearly defined, business-owned problem rather than a technology opportunity. As shown in Table 8.1, a robust metaverse business case begins with a clear definition of the business problem, affected processes, current pain points, supporting evidence, and ownership.

This template should be completed *before* any discussion of metaverse solutions. If the problem cannot be clearly articulated or owned by the business, the initiative should not proceed to solution design.

8.2 FRAMING THE BUSINESS PROBLEM

A metaverse business case must be grounded in a clearly framed business problem. Poorly framed problems lead to unfocused interventions, weak value articulation, and difficulty securing executive approval. Framing the problem correctly is therefore a critical step in determining whether a metaverse intervention is appropriate at all.

Effective problem framing requires organisations to move beyond high-level statements such as "improve collaboration" or "enhance training". These statements describe aspirations rather than problems. A well-framed problem identifies a specific constraint, inefficiency, or risk that materially affects organisational performance and cannot be addressed adequately through existing methods.

Problem framing also establishes the *boundary conditions* of the business case. Without clear boundaries, metaverse initiatives tend to expand in scope, incorporating additional features or use cases that dilute focus and complicate evaluation. By defining what is in scope and what is explicitly out of scope, organisations improve the clarity and credibility of the proposed investment.

Table 8.1 Business Problem Definition Template

Element	*Description*
Business problem statement	Clear description of the problem being addressed
Affected process or function	Business area(s) impacted
Current pain points	Inefficiencies, risks, or constraints
Evidence of the problem	Data, incidents, or stakeholder input
Consequences of inaction	Cost, risk, or missed opportunity
Business owner	Accountable executive or function

8.2.1 Outcome-Oriented Problem Definition

Outcome orientation is central to framing a credible business problem. Rather than focusing on activities or tools, the business case should define what must change as a result of intervention. Outcomes may include reduced incident rates, faster time to competence, improved decision accuracy, or lower rework costs.

Outcome-oriented framing helps distinguish between *usage* and *impact*. High usage of immersive tools does not necessarily imply value creation. Conversely, targeted use by a smaller group may deliver disproportionate benefits if it addresses a critical bottleneck or risk area.

When framing outcomes, it is important to identify who experiences the benefit and how it will be observed. Outcomes that cannot be observed or measured, even indirectly, are difficult to defend in an investment context. Figure 8.2 illustrates the relationship between baseline assessment and value realisation in metaverse business cases, showing why credible value ambition must be balanced with delivery feasibility and risk control.

8.2.2 Defining Scope and Constraints

Scope definition ensures that the business case remains tractable and decision-ready. This involves specifying the processes, roles, locations, and time horizons affected by the proposed intervention.

Constraints may include regulatory requirements, data protection obligations, technology dependencies, or organisational readiness factors.

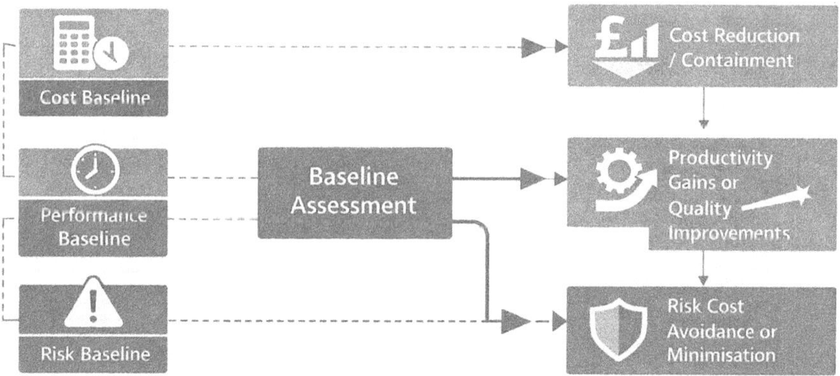

Figure 8.2 Relationship between baseline assessment and value realisation in Metaverse business cases.

Note: It highlights why strong business cases balance value ambition with delivery feasibility and realistic risk controls.

Explicitly acknowledging these constraints strengthens the business case by demonstrating realism and awareness of delivery conditions.

Clear scope definition also supports phased investment approaches. By limiting initial scope, organisations can test assumptions, gather evidence, and refine the intervention before committing to broader rollout.

8.2.3 Stakeholder Ownership and Accountability

Every metaverse business case must have a clearly identified business owner who is accountable for outcomes. Technology teams may support delivery, but ownership must sit with the function that experiences the problem and realises the benefit.

Stakeholder ownership influences both design and adoption. Business owners are better positioned to define success criteria, prioritise use cases, and enforce behavioural change. Without strong ownership, metaverse initiatives risk becoming disconnected pilots that struggle to transition into operational use.

8.2.3.1 Template 8.2 – Business Scope and Outcome Definition

8.2.3.1.1 Purpose

To formalise scope, outcomes, and ownership before designing a metaverse intervention. As shown in Table 8.2, a well-formed metaverse business case requires explicit definition of scope, outcomes, exclusions, ownership, and observable success indicators.

8.3 ESTABLISHING THE BASELINE (CURRENT STATE)

A credible metaverse business case cannot be constructed without a clear understanding of the current state. Establishing a baseline is essential for demonstrating value, as it provides the reference point against which any

Table 8.2 Business Scope and Outcome Definition Template

Element	*Description*
Defined business outcomes	Specific changes expected
In-scope processes	Processes affected by the intervention
Out-of-scope areas	Explicit exclusions
Key stakeholders	Functions and roles involved
Business owner	Accountable executive
Success indicators	How outcomes will be observed

improvement is assessed. Without a baseline, claims of benefit lack credibility and are difficult to validate during approval or post-implementation review.

Baseline analysis serves three purposes. First, it quantifies the scale of the problem being addressed. Second, it reveals where inefficiencies, risks, or delays are most concentrated. Third, it provides the data needed to calculate potential benefits and assess whether a metaverse intervention is proportionate to the problem.

Baseline definition should be pragmatic rather than exhaustive. The objective is not to model the organisation in full detail but to capture enough information to support informed decision-making. Figure 8.3 illustrates the spectrum of financial and non-financial value generated by metaverse interventions, helping decision-makers position initiatives within an appropriate investment band.

8.3.1 Cost Baseline

The cost baseline represents the direct and indirect costs associated with the current way of working. These costs may be visible, such as training expenditure or travel costs, or hidden, such as productivity loss, rework, or downtime.

When constructing a cost baseline, organisations should focus on costs that are materially affected by the proposed intervention. Attempting to account for every possible cost often introduces unnecessary complexity without improving decision quality. Examples of cost elements commonly included in metaverse business cases include instructor-led training costs, physical simulation expenses, travel and accommodation, incident remediation costs, and time lost due to process inefficiencies.

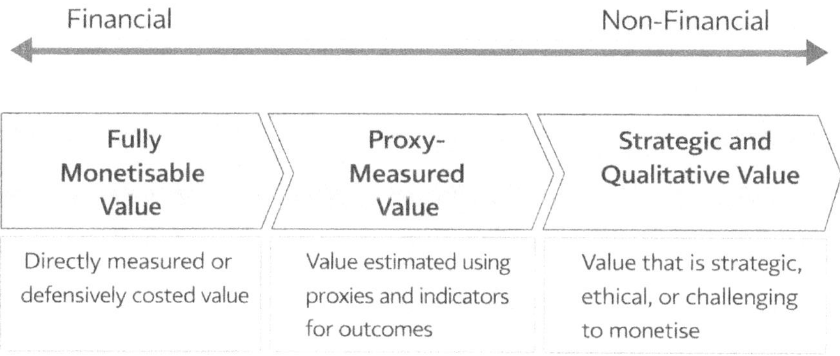

Figure 8.3 Spectrum of financial and non-financial value generated by Metaverse interventions.

Note: This spectrum helps decision-makers frame the proposed initiative in the right investment band, avoiding over-engineering or under-scoping.

8.3.2 Performance Baseline

The performance baseline captures how well current processes operate in terms of speed, quality, accuracy, or consistency. Performance indicators should be directly related to the outcomes defined earlier in the business case.

Performance baselines are particularly important when the metaverse intervention aims to improve skills, decision-making, or collaboration. In such cases, improvements may not be immediately visible in financial terms but can be observed through changes in error rates, time to competence, or cycle times. Where quantitative data is unavailable, qualitative assessments may be used initially, provided they are supported by stakeholder validation and are clearly identified as estimates.

8.3.3 Risk Baseline

The risk baseline identifies the level of operational, safety, compliance, or reputational risk associated with the current state. Many metaverse use cases derive value from reducing exposure to high-impact, low-frequency events that are difficult to rehearse or mitigate through traditional methods.

Examples include safety incidents, compliance breaches, or critical decision errors. Establishing a risk baseline involves assessing both the likelihood and impact of such events and understanding how existing controls perform.

Risk baselines should be articulated carefully. Overstating risk undermines credibility, while understating it weakens the rationale for intervention. Balanced, evidence-informed assessment is essential.

8.3.4 Data Limitations and Assumptions

In emerging technology contexts, baseline data may be incomplete or inconsistent. Rather than attempting to mask these limitations, credible business cases acknowledge them explicitly.

Assumptions used to fill data gaps should be documented, justified, and tested later through sensitivity analysis. Transparency at this stage strengthens trust and reduces resistance during approval.

8.3.4.1 Template 8.3 – Baseline Cost, Performance, and Risk Assessment

8.3.4.1.1 Purpose

To establish a structured current-state baseline against which metaverse-enabled improvements can be evaluated. As shown in Table 8.3, a credible metaverse business case depends on a baseline assessment of current costs, performance, risks, and data gaps, supported by clear evidence sources and documented assumptions.

Table 8.3 Baseline Assessment Template

Baseline Dimension	*Description*	*Evidence Source*	*Notes*
Current costs	Direct and indirect costs incurred	Financial records, estimates	Scope-limited
Current performance	Key performance indicators	Operational data	Time-bound
Current risks	Major risk exposures	Incident reports, assessments	Likelihood and impact
Data gaps	Missing or uncertain data	Stakeholder input	Assumptions documented

Completing this baseline assessment provides the foundation for credible value quantification in subsequent sections. It ensures that projected benefits are grounded in observable reality rather than aspirational targets.

8.4 DESIGNING THE METAVERSE INTERVENTION

Once the business problem has been clearly framed and the baseline established, the next step is to design the proposed metaverse intervention. This stage defines *what will change*, *how it will change*, and *what will remain unchanged* as a result of the intervention. Clear intervention design is essential to prevent scope creep and to ensure that the business case remains focused and credible.

A metaverse intervention should not be defined solely in terms of technology components. Instead, it should be described as a *change to processes, behaviours, and decision-making*, with immersive technology acting as an enabler rather than the objective. This distinction helps decision-makers understand how value will be realised and reduces the risk of investing in technology without operational impact.

8.4.1 Defining the Intervention Scope

Intervention scope describes the specific activities, roles, and contexts affected by the proposed solution. This includes identifying which processes will be redesigned, which user groups will participate, and where immersive environments will be applied.

Scope definition should be aligned with the earlier outcome-oriented problem framing. If the defined scope does not directly address the outcomes identified in Section 8.2, the intervention design should be revisited. Figure 8.4 makes the cost curve visible, ensuring early business cases plan for the full lifecycle rather than only initial build or pilot spend.

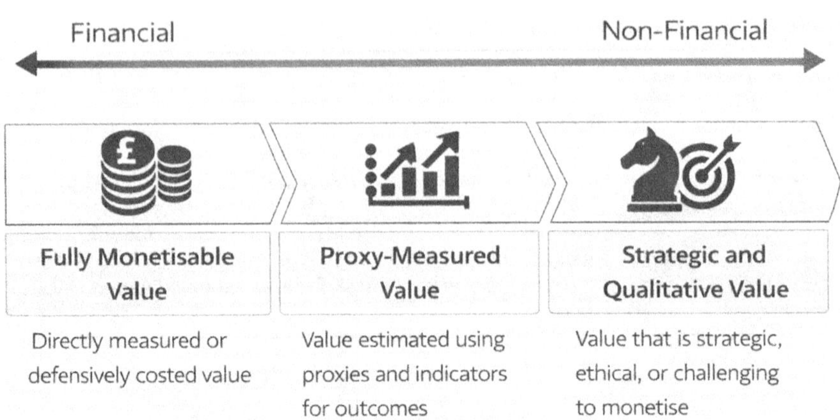

Figure 8.4 Spectrum of financial and non-financial value generated by metaverse interventions.

Importantly, scope definition should also clarify *what is explicitly excluded.* Exclusions help manage expectations and support phased delivery by preventing uncontrolled expansion of the initiative. Figure 8.4 helps position metaverse value across a spectrum from fully monetisable outcomes to proxy-measured and broader strategic or qualitative value.

8.4.2 Process and Behavioural Changes

Metaverse interventions typically introduce changes to how work is performed, learned, or coordinated. These changes may include new training methods, alternative collaboration practices, or revised decision workflows.

Documenting process and behavioural changes is critical for two reasons. First, it allows stakeholders to assess the feasibility of adoption. Second, it provides a basis for estimating value, as benefits arise from changed behaviour rather than from the presence of immersive tools. Where behavioural change is required, the business case should identify supporting measures, such as training, communication, or incentives.

8.4.3 Assumptions and Dependencies

All metaverse interventions rest on assumptions. These may relate to user adoption, technology performance, content availability, or organisational readiness. Dependencies may include vendor capabilities, data availability, or regulatory approvals.

Explicitly documenting assumptions and dependencies reduces risk by making uncertainty visible. It also supports later sensitivity analysis by identifying which variables have the greatest influence on outcomes.

Assumptions should be realistic and conservative. Where assumptions are optimistic, this should be acknowledged and justified.

8.4.4 What Does not Change

An often-overlooked aspect of intervention design is specifying what does not change. Not all processes or roles will be affected by the metaverse intervention, and some existing methods may continue in parallel.

Clarifying what remains unchanged helps stakeholders understand the scale of the initiative and prevents unrealistic expectations about transformation. It also supports accurate cost estimation by avoiding implicit assumptions of widespread change.

8.4.4.1 Template 8.4 – Metaverse Intervention Design

8.4.4.1.1 Purpose

To clearly define the proposed metaverse intervention, including scope, changes, assumptions, and dependencies. As shown in Table 8.4, a well-formed metaverse intervention design requires explicit definition of scope, target users, expected changes, assumptions, dependencies, and out-of-scope elements.

8.5 QUANTIFYING FINANCIAL VALUE

Quantifying financial value is one of the most scrutinised aspects of a metaverse business case. Decision-makers expect financial logic that is

Table 8.4 Metaverse Intervention Design Template

Element	*Description*
Intervention description	Summary of the proposed metaverse-enabled change
In-scope activities	Processes or tasks affected
Target user groups	Roles or populations involved
Process or behavioural changes	How work or learning will change
Assumptions	Key assumptions underpinning the design
Dependencies	External or internal dependencies
Out-of-scope elements	Explicit exclusions

conservative, transparent, and clearly linked to the baseline established earlier. Overstated or speculative financial benefits undermine credibility, particularly in emerging technology domains.

Financial value should be derived from *observable changes in cost, productivity, or risk exposure* resulting from the intervention. Where benefits are indirect, the causal link between the intervention and the financial outcome must be clearly articulated.

It is important to distinguish between *potential value* and *realised value.* Potential value represents the maximum achievable benefit under ideal conditions, whereas realised value reflects what can reasonably be expected given organisational readiness, adoption rates, and execution constraints. Business cases should be built around realised value, with potential value discussed separately as upside.

8.5.1 Cost Reduction and Avoidance

Cost reduction benefits arise when the metaverse intervention replaces or reduces existing expenditure. Common examples include reduced travel costs, lower reliance on physical training facilities, or reduced need for physical prototypes.

Cost avoidance refers to preventing future expenditure that would otherwise be incurred, such as avoiding the expansion of physical infrastructure or mitigating incident remediation costs. Although cost avoidance can be more difficult to validate, it is acceptable when supported by credible assumptions and historical trends. Both cost reduction and cost avoidance should be quantified over a defined time horizon and discounted appropriately where multi-year projections are used.

8.5.2 Productivity and Efficiency Gains

Productivity gains occur when tasks are completed faster, with fewer errors, or with less supervision. In metaverse use cases, productivity improvements often relate to faster onboarding, reduced time to competence, or improved collaboration efficiency.

When quantifying productivity benefits, organisations should avoid double counting. For example, time saved does not automatically translate into financial value unless it results in reduced labour costs or increased output. Productivity assumptions should be conservative and validated with business owners to ensure realism.

8.5.3 Risk Cost Avoidance

Some metaverse use cases deliver financial value primarily through risk reduction. Examples include reducing the likelihood of safety incidents, compliance breaches, or critical operational errors.

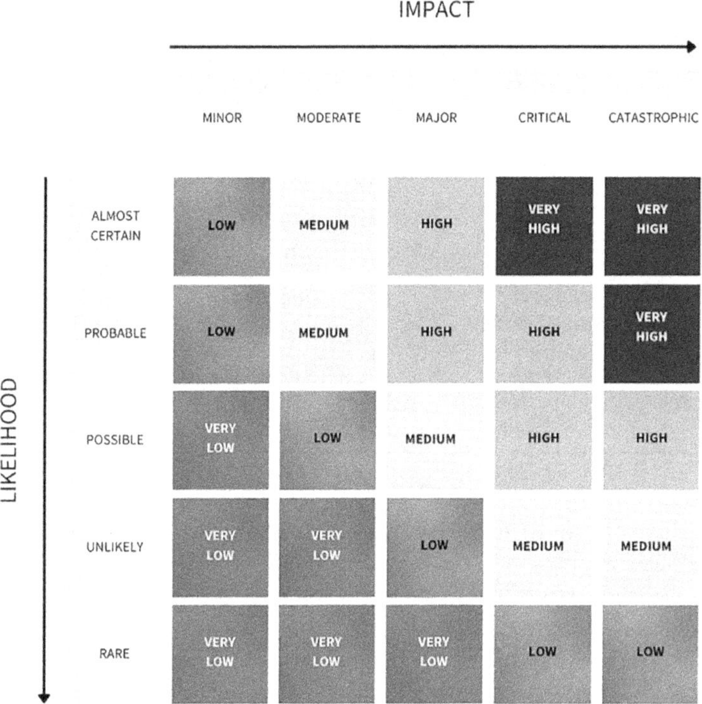

Figure 8.5 Risk assessment matrix for Metaverse initiative decisions.

Risk cost avoidance should be quantified by combining the estimated reduction in incident likelihood with the financial impact of incidents. Where precise quantification is not possible, ranges or scenario-based estimates may be used. Figure 8.5 illustrates a risk assessment matrix showing how likelihood and impact combine to shape whether a metaverse initiative should proceed, be constrained to a pilot, or be deferred.

8.5.4 Time Horizon and Phasing

Financial benefits rarely materialise immediately. Business cases should specify when benefits are expected to accrue and how they scale over time. Phased benefit realisation is particularly important for interventions that rely on behavioural change or capability development. Explicit phasing improves credibility and supports staged investment decisions.

8.5.4.1 Template 8.5 – Financial Benefits Quantification

8.5.4.1.1 Purpose

To quantify the financial benefits associated with the proposed metaverse intervention in a transparent and defensible manner. As shown in Table 8.5,

Table 8.5 Financial Benefits Quantification Template

Benefit Category	*Description*	*Baseline Value*	*Expected Change*	*Financial Impact*	*Time Horizon*
Cost reduction	Reduced existing expenditure	Current annual cost	Reduction amount	Annual savings	Year 1–3
Cost avoidance	Prevented future costs	Projected cost	Avoided cost	Avoided expenditure	Year 2–5
Productivity gain	Efficiency improvement	Current productivity	Improvement percentage	Financial equivalent	Year 1–3
Risk avoidance	Reduced incident cost	Historical incident cost	Reduced likelihood	Expected savings	Ongoing

financial benefits in a metaverse business case should be quantified by defining the baseline, expected change, resulting financial impact, and the likely time horizon for realisation.

Financial benefits quantified using this template should be reviewed and validated by the relevant business owners. Conservative assumptions and clear documentation strengthen the credibility of the business case and improve the likelihood of approval.

8.6 QUANTIFYING NON-FINANCIAL VALUE

Not all value generated by metaverse interventions can or should be expressed in direct financial terms. In many enterprise contexts, the most significant benefits relate to safety, quality, capability development, resilience, or strategic flexibility. These benefits are real and often decisive, but they require careful articulation to avoid appearing vague or promotional.

A credible metaverse business case distinguishes between *financial value*, which can be monetised, and *non-financial value*, which supports organisational objectives but may only be observable through proxy indicators. Treating non-financial value transparently strengthens the business case by acknowledging the limits of quantification while still providing decision-relevant insight.

8.6.1 Safety and Risk Reduction Outcomes

Safety improvements are a common non-financial benefit of immersive technologies, particularly in industries involving hazardous environments, complex equipment, or high-risk procedures. Metaverse-enabled simulations allow individuals to rehearse scenarios that would be unsafe or impractical to replicate in the real world.

While safety benefits may eventually translate into reduced incident costs, the primary value often lies in *risk exposure reduction* rather than immediate cost savings. Indicators such as reduced near-miss incidents, improved procedural compliance, or increased confidence in emergency response provide credible evidence of safety improvement.

8.6.2 Quality and Decision Accuracy

In some use cases, the metaverse improves the quality of outcomes rather than speed or cost. Examples include improved design decisions through immersive visualisation, better situational awareness in operational planning, or enhanced understanding of complex data through spatial representation.

Quality improvements may be measured through reduced rework, fewer design errors, or improved stakeholder alignment. Although these outcomes may eventually yield financial benefits, they should initially be framed as quality enhancements supported by observable indicators.

8.6.3 Capability Development and Time to Competence

Capability uplift is a critical non-financial value driver in training and learning use cases. Immersive learning environments can accelerate skill acquisition, improve retention, and increase learner confidence.

Time to competence is a particularly useful indicator, as it links capability development to operational readiness. Reductions in time to competence support workforce flexibility and resilience, even if they are not immediately monetised.

8.6.4 Strategic Optionality and Organisational Learning

Some metaverse investments create value by expanding organisational capability and optionality. Early experience with immersive technologies can improve organisational learning, inform future investments, and enhance the ability to respond to emerging opportunities or disruptions.

Strategic optionality should be articulated carefully. It does not justify speculative investment, but it can support measured experimentation where future relevance is plausible and aligned with strategy.

8.6.4.1 Template 8.6 – Non-Financial Value Mapping

8.6.4.1.1 Purpose

To document and assess non-financial benefits in a structured, decision-relevant manner. As shown in Table 8.6, non-financial value in a metaverse business case can be structured through proxy indicators and evidence

Table 8.6 Non-Financial Value Mapping Template

Value Dimension	*Description*	*Proxy Indicator*	*Evidence Source*	*Relevance*
Safety	Risk exposure reduction	Near-miss incidents	Safety reports	High
Quality	Outcome accuracy	Rework frequency	Operational data	Medium
Capability	Skill development	Time to competence	Training records	High
Resilience	Operational flexibility	Recovery time	Scenario testing	Medium
Strategic optionality	Future readiness	Leadership assessment	Strategic review	Low–Medium

sources across dimensions such as safety, quality, capability, resilience, and strategic optionality.

8.7 COST MODEL AND INVESTMENT PROFILE

A metaverse business case must present a clear and transparent cost model. While value discussions often attract the most attention, unclear or underestimated costs are a common reason for initiative rejection. Decision-makers require confidence that all material cost components have been identified and that the investment profile is appropriate for the level of uncertainty involved.

Metaverse cost models differ from traditional IT cost models in two important ways. First, they often combine *technology, content, capability, and governance costs* rather than focusing solely on platforms or infrastructure. Second, costs tend to evolve over time as initiatives move from pilot to scale, requiring explicit consideration of phasing and scalability.

8.7.1 One-Off and Recurring Costs

One-off costs include activities required to initiate the intervention, such as solution design, content creation, initial platform configuration, and user onboarding. These costs are typically incurred during pilot or early rollout phases.

Recurring costs include platform subscriptions, cloud services, content updates, support, moderation, governance activities, and ongoing training. These costs persist throughout the life of the initiative and must be assessed carefully to avoid long-term cost escalation. Distinguishing clearly between one-off and recurring costs improves cost transparency and supports accurate comparison with expected benefits.

8.7.2 Capital and Operating Expenditure

Depending on accounting treatment and organisational policy, metaverse investments may be classified as capital expenditure, operating expenditure, or a combination of both. Hardware purchases, bespoke content development, and long-lived platforms may be capitalised, while subscriptions, support, and governance activities are typically treated as operating expenditure. The business case should align cost classification with organisational finance standards and ensure that decision-makers understand the implications for budgeting and financial reporting.

8.7.3 Scaling Effects and Cost Sensitivity

Costs associated with metaverse initiatives often scale non-linearly. For example, adding users may increase platform costs marginally but significantly increase content, support, or governance effort.

Understanding how costs scale with adoption is essential for assessing the sustainability of the initiative. Business cases should identify cost drivers and test sensitivity to changes in scope or user numbers.

8.7.4 Vendor Dependency and Lock-in Considerations

Many metaverse solutions rely on external platforms or service providers. Vendor dependency introduces cost and strategic risk, particularly where switching costs are high or standards are immature. The cost model should explicitly identify vendor-dependent components and assess the financial implications of future changes in pricing, capability, or contractual terms.

8.7.4.1 Template 8.7 – Metaverse Cost Model

8.7.4.1.1 Purpose

To provide a comprehensive view of investment requirements and ongoing costs associated with the metaverse intervention. As shown in Table 8.7, metaverse cost modelling should account for both upfront and recurring expenditure across platforms, hardware, content, capability, and governance.

A well-structured cost model enables balanced evaluation of investment requirements against expected benefits and supports informed decision-making regarding scale, phasing, and affordability.

8.8 RISK, UNCERTAINTY, AND SENSITIVITY ANALYSIS

Metaverse business cases operate in an environment of elevated uncertainty. Technology maturity, adoption behaviour, regulatory expectations, and

Table 8.7 Metaverse Cost Model Template

Cost Category	*One-Off Cost*	*Recurring Cost*	*Cost Driver*	*Notes*
Platform and infrastructure	Initial setup	Subscription fees	User volume	Vendor dependent
Hardware	Device procurement	Replacement cycle	Usage intensity	Optional
Content development	Initial creation	Updates and maintenance	Scenario complexity	Skills intensive
Capability and training	Enablement	Refresh training	Adoption rate	Change-dependent
Governance and compliance	Framework design	Monitoring and reporting	Risk exposure	Mandatory

organisational readiness may all evolve during the life of the initiative. A credible business case therefore does not attempt to eliminate uncertainty but instead makes it visible and manageable.

Risk and sensitivity analysis enables decision-makers to understand *what could go wrong*, *how likely it is*, and *what the consequences would be*. It also supports disciplined decision-making by identifying which assumptions are most critical to the viability of the investment.

8.8.1 Key Risk Categories

Risks associated with metaverse initiatives typically fall into several broad categories. Adoption risk arises when users do not engage with the solution as expected or fail to change behaviour. Technology risk relates to platform stability, performance, interoperability, or vendor viability.

Regulatory and ethical risks may emerge as immersive technologies introduce new forms of data collection, behavioural monitoring, or user interaction. Finally, value realisation risk occurs when projected benefits fail to materialise due to incorrect assumptions or execution challenges. Identifying these risks explicitly strengthens the business case by demonstrating awareness and preparedness.

8.8.2 Assumption Sensitivity

Many elements of a metaverse business case depend on assumptions rather than hard data. Sensitivity analysis tests how changes in these assumptions affect overall outcomes.

Common variables tested include adoption rates, cost escalation, benefit realisation timing, and risk reduction effectiveness. Sensitivity analysis helps distinguish between *robust business cases*, which remain viable under a range of conditions, and *fragile cases*, which depend on optimistic assumptions.

8.8.3 Scenario-Based Assessment

In addition to testing individual assumptions, scenario-based assessment considers combinations of factors that may occur together. For example, slower adoption combined with higher operating costs may significantly alter the value profile of an initiative. Scenario analysis supports informed discussion at executive level and helps avoid binary decision-making based on a single forecast.

8.8.4 Risk Mitigation and Control Measures

Identified risks should be accompanied by mitigation strategies. Mitigation may include phased rollout, pilot testing, contractual safeguards, governance controls, or contingency planning. Effective mitigation does not eliminate risk entirely, but it reduces exposure to acceptable levels and provides confidence that risks are being actively managed.

8.8.4.1 Template 8.8 – Risk and Sensitivity Analysis

8.8.4.1.1 Purpose

To identify, assess, and test the impact of key risks and assumptions affecting the metaverse business case. As shown in Table 8.8, a robust metaverse business case should assess major risks and assumptions in terms of likelihood, impact, sensitivity, and planned mitigation.

By explicitly documenting risks and testing sensitivity, the business case moves beyond optimism toward disciplined investment decision-making. This analysis supports informed approval, prioritisation, and ongoing governance.

Table 8.8 Risk and Sensitivity Analysis Template

Risk or Assumption	*Description*	*Likelihood*	*Impact*	*Sensitivity*	*Mitigation Strategy*
Adoption rate	User uptake below expectation	Medium	High	High	Phased rollout, training
Technology maturity	Platform instability	Low–Medium	High	Medium	Vendor due diligence
Cost escalation	Higher recurring costs	Medium	Medium	Medium	Contractual controls
Regulatory change	New compliance requirements	Low	High	Low	Legal monitoring
Value realisation	Benefits delayed or reduced	Medium	High	High	Pilot validation

8.9 DECISION FRAMEWORK AND APPROVAL READINESS

A metaverse business case should culminate in a clear, decision-ready framework rather than an open-ended recommendation. Executive decision-makers require clarity on whether the initiative should proceed, at what scale, and under what conditions. Ambiguity at this stage undermines confidence and delays action.

Decision readiness is achieved when the business case presents a balanced view of value, cost, and risk, supported by transparent assumptions and clear governance mechanisms. The objective is not to eliminate uncertainty but to ensure that uncertainty is understood and managed. Figure 8.6 illustrates a phase-gate decision framework for metaverse initiatives, showing how structured gates and explicit outcomes support disciplined go/no-go decisions.

8.9.1 Go/No-Go Criteria

Clear go/no-go criteria help organisations avoid premature commitment or prolonged indecision. These criteria should be defined in advance and linked directly to the outcomes, assumptions, and risks identified earlier in the business case.

Typical criteria include minimum acceptable financial return, evidence of user adoption, regulatory acceptability, and alignment with strategic priorities. Where criteria are not met, the default decision should be to pause or stop rather than proceed optimistically.

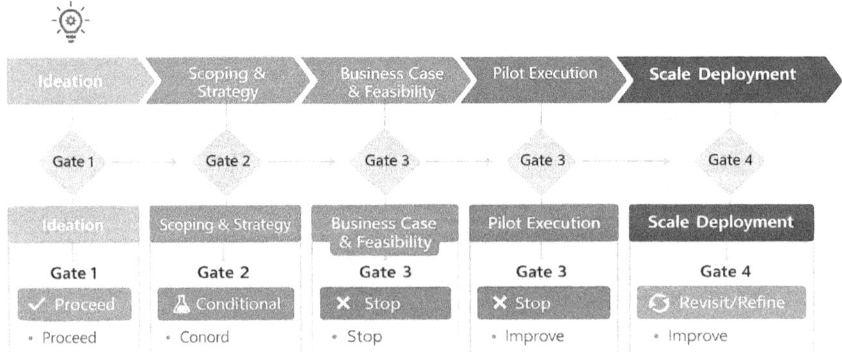

Figure 8.6 Phase-gate decision framework for Metaverse initiatives

Note: The framework operationalises the go/no-go logic by introducing structured gates and explicit outcomes, promoting disciplined investment decisions.

8.9.2 Pilot versus Scale Decisions

Many metaverse initiatives benefit from a phased approach, beginning with a pilot before committing to full-scale deployment. The business case should specify the conditions under which a pilot will transition to scale, including performance thresholds, adoption levels, and risk indicators.

Equally important is defining exit criteria. Clear exit conditions protect the organisation from sunk-cost bias and ensure that pilots do not continue indefinitely without delivering value.

8.9.3 Executive Confidence and Governance Readiness

Approval readiness depends not only on the numbers presented but also on confidence in execution capability and governance maturity. Decision-makers assess whether the organisation has the skills, structures, and controls necessary to deliver the proposed outcomes responsibly. Demonstrating governance readiness strengthens the case for approval, particularly in regulated or risk-sensitive environments.

8.9.3.1 Template 8.9 – Executive Decision Checklist

8.9.3.1.1 Purpose

To support executive decision-making by summarising readiness, risks, and conditions for approval. As shown in Table 8.9, executive metaverse decisions should be tested against strategic alignment, ownership, financial viability, risk management, governance readiness, and final approval logic.

Table 8.9 Executive Decision Checklist

Decision Dimension	*Key Question*	*Assessment*
Strategic alignment	Does the initiative support strategic objectives?	Yes/No
Business ownership	Is there a clear accountable owner?	Yes/No
Financial viability	Are benefits credible and conservative?	Yes/No
Risk management	Are key risks identified and mitigated?	Yes/No
Governance readiness	Are controls and oversight in place?	Yes/No
Approval decision	Proceed, pilot, or stop	Decision

8.10 CHAPTER SUMMARY

This chapter has demonstrated that credible metaverse investment decisions depend on disciplined business case construction rather than enthusiasm for immersive technology. By grounding initiatives in clearly framed problems, robust baselines, transparent value logic, and explicit risk management, organisations can make informed decisions about when and how to invest.

A metaverse business case should function as a decision-support tool, not a promotional artefact. It should enable organisations to proceed with confidence, pause when conditions are not favourable, or terminate initiatives that do not deliver value. This disciplined approach builds trust with stakeholders and supports sustainable adoption.

The frameworks and templates presented in this chapter provide a practical foundation for developing, assessing, and governing metaverse investments across a range of organisational contexts. Figure 8.7 illustrates a stage-gate metaverse project lifecycle, showing how controlled review checkpoints help protect value and reduce delivery risk.

8.11 COMPREHENSIVE METAVERSE BUSINESS CASE TEMPLATE

Note: Final reusable template suitable for publication, governance packs, or business case submissions.

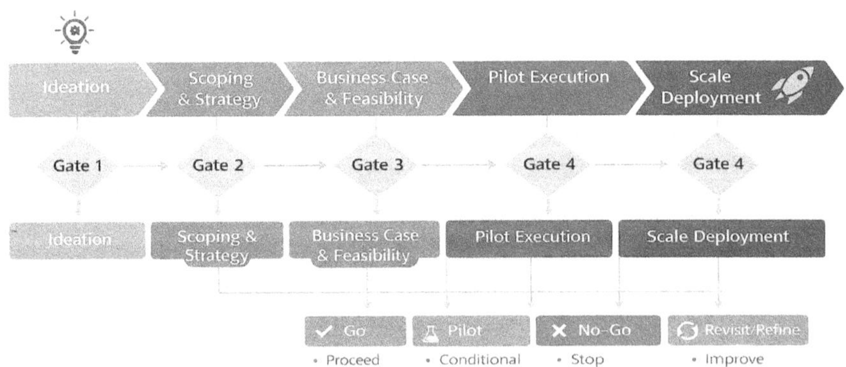

Figure 8.7 Stage-gate Metaverse project lifecycle.

Note: This figure reinforces that metaverse delivery should follow a controlled lifecycle, with review checkpoints that protect value and reduce risk.

8.11.1 Purpose

To consolidate all elements of the metaverse business case into a single, decision-ready document.

Figure 8.8 illustrates the stage-gate governance criteria for metaverse projects, showing how qualitative judgement can be translated into a more transparent and auditable investment decision.

As shown in Table 8.10, a complete metaverse business case should integrate problem definition, baseline assessment, value, cost, risk, governance, and implementation planning into a single structured document.

8.11.2 How to Use This Template

This template can be used as:

- An internal investment proposal
- A client-facing business case
- A governance artefact for approval committees
- A reusable consulting deliverable

By completing each section with conservative assumptions, explicit risks, and clear ownership, organisations can position metaverse initiatives as disciplined investments rather than speculative experiments.

Figure 8.8 Metaverse project stage-gate governance criteria.

Note: This figure provides a transparent basis for investment decisions by translating qualitative judgement into an auditable scoring outcome.

Table 8.10 Comprehensive Metaverse Business Case Template

Section	*Content*
Executive Summary	Problem statement, proposed intervention, investment request, decision required
Business Context	Current challenges, strategic relevance, urgency
Baseline Assessment	Cost, performance, and risk baselines
Proposed Intervention	Scope, changes, assumptions, dependencies
Financial Value Case	Cost reduction, productivity gains, risk avoidance
Non-Financial Value	Safety, quality, capability, strategic optionality
Cost Model	One-off and recurring costs, CAPEX/OPEX
Risk and Sensitivity	Key risks, scenarios, mitigation strategies
Governance and Controls	Oversight, ethics, compliance, monitoring
Implementation Roadmap	Pilot plan, scale criteria, exit conditions
Decision and Recommendation	Go/No-Go, confidence assessment

8.12 FICTITIOUS METAVERSE USE CASE: IOSPEED LIMITED

8.12.1 Immersive Data Observability and Incident Simulation Environment

A metaverse-enabled environment is designed to support real-time data observability, incident simulation, and operational response training.

8.12.2 Organisation

IOSpeed Limited (UK-based data, AI, and observability consultancy). Figure 8.9 illustrates the stage-gate governance criteria for metaverse projects, showing how strategic alignment, feasibility, risk, and projected value are assessed across successive decision gates.

8.12.3 Context

IOSpeed Limited supports financial services and regulated clients in improving data observability, operational resilience, and incident response maturity. A recurring challenge faced by clients is the *gap between theoretical incident playbooks and real-world execution under pressure*, particularly in complex, distributed data environments.

IOSpeed Limited Metaverse Initiatives Mapping to Strategic Objectives

	Revenue Growth	Customer Engagement	Operational Efficiency	Brand Innovation
	Increase Sales	Enhance Customer Journey	Streamline Processes	Boost Market Position
Virtual Showroom	✓	✓	✓	✓
Immersive Training Program	✓	✓	✓	✓
Enterprise Collaboration Hub	✓	✓	✓	✓
User Experience Gamification	✓	✓	✓	✓

High Alignment   Moderate Alignment   Morate Alignment   Low Alignment

Figure 8.9 Applied example mapping for IOSpeed Limited.

Note: This figure shows how the business case template can be applied in practice, translating a business problem into a measurable metaverse initiative.

Traditional training methods, such as tabletop exercises and documentation reviews, have limited effectiveness in preparing teams for high-stress, multi-system incidents.

8.13 SAMPLE METAVERSE BUSINESS CASE: IOSPEED LIMITED

This section applies the metaverse business case framework and templates presented in this chapter to the fictitious IOSpeed Limited use case introduced in Section 8.12.

8.13.1 Executive Summary

IOSpeed Limited proposes the development of a metaverse-enabled simulation environment to support immersive training for data observability incidents, including data pipeline failures, regulatory reporting disruptions, and cyber-related data integrity events.

The proposed solution would enable consultants and client teams to rehearse realistic incident scenarios in a controlled virtual environment, improving response capability and reducing operational risk.

Investment request: £185,000 (pilot phase, 18 months)
Decision required: Proceed with pilot (conditional Go)

8.13.2 Business Context and Problem Definition

This section outlines the business context and problem definition for the proposed use case. It identifies the operational environment, the current limitations or pain points, and the reasons why an immersive intervention is being considered. The aim is to ensure that the proposed solution is anchored in a clearly defined business need, expected outcomes, and measurable value.

8.13.2.1 Business Problem

Clients repeatedly demonstrate gaps in incident response capability despite having documented playbooks. Exercises fail to replicate the cognitive load, coordination challenges, and decision ambiguity present in real incidents.

8.13.2.2 Why Existing Approaches Are Insufficient

- Tabletop exercises lack realism
- Live-fire testing is risky and disruptive
- Knowledge transfer from exercises to real incidents is inconsistent

8.13.2.3 Business Owner

The business owner for this use case is the Director of Data Observability Practice at IOSpeed Limited. This role is accountable for defining the operational need, validating the business case, sponsoring the intervention, and ensuring that the proposed solution aligns with organisational priorities, risk controls, and expected outcomes.

8.13.3 Baseline Assessment

This section establishes the baseline against which the proposed metaverse intervention will be evaluated. It summarises the current cost exposure, operational performance, and risk conditions associated with the existing approach. Defining this baseline is essential for assessing whether the proposed intervention delivers measurable improvement.

8.13.3.1 Cost Baseline (Annual, Estimated)

The current cost baseline reflects the annual exposure associated with consultant-led incident rehearsals, client downtime during incidents, and rework or regulatory remediation support. These figures provide an indicative view of the recurring cost burden under the current operating model.

Cost Area	*Current Cost*
Consultant-led incident rehearsals	£120,000
Client downtime during incidents (attributable to poor response)	£250,000
Rework and regulatory remediation support	£90,000
Total Indicative Exposure	**£460,000**

8.13.3.2 Performance Baseline

The performance baseline summarises the current operational effectiveness of incident preparation and response. It highlights the limitations of the existing model in terms of speed, consistency, coordination, and learning effectiveness, providing a reference point for later comparison.

Indicator	*Current State*
Average incident resolution time	6–8 hours
Cross-team coordination effectiveness	Inconsistent
Playbook adherence	Partial

8.13.3.3 Risk Baseline

The risk baseline captures the principal operational, regulatory, and service risks associated with the current approach. It provides a structured view of the likelihood and impact of current weaknesses, forming the basis for later comparison with the proposed intervention.

- High dependency on senior individuals
- Inconsistent rehearsal quality
- Increased regulatory scrutiny on data resilience

8.13.4 Proposed Metaverse Intervention

IOSpeed Limited would design an immersive simulation environment replicating realistic client data landscapes, including data pipelines, dashboards, alerts, and escalation pathways. Participants would assume defined roles and respond to evolving incident scenarios under time pressure.

8.13.4.1 What Changes

- Training becomes experiential
- Teams practice real coordination, not hypothetical discussion
- Performance is observable and reviewable

8.13.4.2 What Does not Change

- Existing incident playbooks remain
- Production systems are untouched
- No replacement of core observability tooling

8.13.5 Financial Value Case (GBP)

This section summarises the expected financial value of the proposed intervention in GBP. It distinguishes direct cost reduction from broader productivity and risk-related benefits so that the business case reflects both measurable savings and operational value improvement.

8.13.5.1 Cost Reduction and Avoidance

The direct financial case is driven by reduced dependence on consultant-led rehearsals and lower remediation effort following incidents. These savings represent recurring annual benefits that can be estimated with reasonable confidence under the proposed model.

Benefit	*Annual Impact*
Reduced consultant-led rehearsals	£60,000
Reduced remediation effort	£45,000
Total Cost Reduction	**£105,000**

8.13.5.2 Productivity and Risk Avoidance

Additional value is expected through faster incident resolution, reduced escalation dependence, and improved operational response. Although some of these benefits are partly proxy-based, they provide a meaningful estimate of the productivity and risk-reduction value enabled by the intervention.

Benefit	*Estimated Value*
Faster incident resolution (20% reduction)	£70,000
Reduced reliance on senior escalation	£35,000
Total Productivity/Risk Value	**£105,000**

Note: Total Annual Financial Benefit (Conservative) £210,000

8.13.6 Non-Financial Value

In addition to direct financial benefits, the proposed intervention is expected to generate important non-financial value. These benefits include stronger capability under pressure, greater operational consistency, improved resilience, and enhanced client value. Although harder to monetise directly, they strengthen the overall case for investment and support longer-term organisational effectiveness.

Dimension	*Benefit*
Capability	Improved decision-making under pressure
Quality	Consistent execution of playbooks
Resilience	Reduced key-person dependency
Client value	Differentiated IOSpeed offering

8.13.7 Cost Model and Investment Profile (GBP)

This section sets out the expected investment profile for the proposed intervention in GBP. It distinguishes one-off implementation costs from recurring operating expenditure so that decision-makers can assess both the initial commitment and the ongoing cost implications of the model.

8.13.7.1 One-Off Costs

The one-off cost profile covers the initial expenditure required to establish the intervention, including design, environment setup, content development, and implementation support. These costs represent the upfront investment needed before operational value can begin to accrue.

Item	*Cost*
Scenario design and modelling	£45,000
Platform configuration	£30,000
Initial content development	£25,000
Total One-Off	**£100,000**

8.13.7.2 Recurring Costs (Annual)

Recurring costs reflect the ongoing expenditure needed to sustain the intervention once deployed. These include platform support, content maintenance, updates, administration, and any continuing operational or governance overhead.

Item	*Cost*
Platform subscription	£30,000
Content updates and maintenance	£25,000
Governance and facilitation	£15,000
Total Annual OPEX	**£70,000**

8.13.8. Risk and Sensitivity Analysis

This section summarises the principal risks and sensitivities associated with the proposed intervention. It identifies the most significant factors that could weaken adoption, increase cost, reduce value realisation, or limit scalability. Setting these risks out explicitly helps decision-makers judge whether the intervention remains acceptable under realistic operating conditions.

Risk	*Likelihood*	*Impact*	*Mitigation*
Low user adoption	Medium	High	Mandatory integration into engagements
Platform immaturity	Low	Medium	Vendor due diligence
Cost creep	Medium	Medium	Fixed-scope pilot
Client resistance	Low	Medium	Position as optional premium

8.13.8.1 Sensitivity Test

If adoption is *30% lower than expected*, annual benefit reduces to ~£145,000 – still exceeding annual operating cost.

8.13.9 Governance and Controls

- Clear scenario approval process
- No client production data used
- Ethical safeguards around behavioural monitoring
- Regular value review every 6 months

8.13.10 Implementation Roadmap

This section outlines the proposed implementation roadmap for the intervention, showing how delivery progresses through design, pilot, and scale decision points. The roadmap is structured to support phased investment, controlled learning, and clear governance at each stage.

Phase	*Duration*	*Decision Gate*
Design	3 months	Scope approval
Pilot delivery	9 months	Adoption and value review
Scale decision	Month 12	Go/No-Go

8.13.11 Decision and Recommendation

This section brings together the findings of the business case and translates them into an executive recommendation. It considers the balance of strategic fit, financial value, non-financial benefit, delivery feasibility, and risk in order to determine whether the intervention should proceed, be piloted, or be deferred.

8.13.11.1 Executive Assessment

The executive assessment provides a concise decision view of the proposed intervention. It summarises whether the use case is strategically justified, operationally feasible, financially credible, and governable within acceptable levels of risk.

Criterion	*Result*
Strategic alignment	Yes
Financial viability	Yes
Risk manageable	Yes
Governance readiness	Yes
Confidence level	Medium–High

8.13.11.2 Final Recommendation: Proceed with a Time-Bound Pilot (Go – Conditional)

The business case demonstrates a credible value proposition with conservative assumptions. Risks are manageable, and downside exposure is limited by phased investment. Full-scale rollout should be contingent on demonstrated adoption and measurable reduction in incident resolution time.

8.13.11.3 Fair Commentary (Explicitly Balanced)

This business case does not justify a large-scale platform investment at this stage. The value is *use case–specific*, not platform-driven. Over-expansion would introduce unnecessary risk. The recommended pilot allows IOSpeed Limited to test assumptions, refine delivery, and build evidence before scaling.

BIBLIOGRAPHY

Ballon, P. (2009). The platformisation of the European mobile industry. *Communications & Strategies*, 75, 15–33.

Brynjolfsson, E., & McAfee, A. (2014). *The Second Machine Age: Work, Progress, and Prosperity in a Time of Brilliant Technologies*. New York: W. W. Norton & Company.

Cooper, R. G. (2008). Perspective: The stage-gate® idea-to-launch process – update, what's new, and NexGen systems. *Journal of Product Innovation Management*, 25(3), 213–232.

Deloitte. (2022). *Value Creation in the Metaverse*. Deloitte Insights.

ISO. (2018). *ISO 31000: Risk Management – Guidelines*. International Organization for Standardization.

Kaplan, R. S., & Norton, D. P. (1996). *The Balanced Scorecard: Translating Strategy into Action*. Boston: Harvard Business School Press.

McKinsey & Company. (2023). *The Economic Potential of the Metaverse*. McKinsey Global Institute.

Porter, M. E. (1985). *Competitive Advantage: Creating and Sustaining Superior Performance*. New York: Free Press.

PwC. (2022). *Seeing Is Believing: How the Metaverse Can Transform Business*. PwC Report. PwC.

World Economic Forum. (2023). *Defining and Building the Metaverse: Governance, Value, and Trust*. WEF White Paper. WEF.

Chapter 9

Metaverse Case Study

Transforming Skills and Training in UK Further Education

9.1 SECTOR BACKGROUND AND SKILLS CONTEXT IN THE UK

The UK faces a persistent and widening skills gap across multiple sectors, particularly in construction, engineering, healthcare support roles, and digital services. Demographic change, technological acceleration, and shifting labour market expectations have combined to place significant strain on the Further Education (FE) and professional training ecosystem. Employers increasingly report shortages of job-ready candidates, while training providers struggle to modernise delivery models within constrained funding environments.

FE colleges and skills providers play a critical role in addressing these challenges. They serve a diverse learner population, including school leavers, adult learners, career switchers, and apprentices, often balancing academic instruction with practical, hands-on training. However, traditional training approaches rely heavily on physical workshops, specialist equipment, and in-person instruction. These models are costly to maintain, difficult to scale, and increasingly misaligned with the needs of a geographically distributed learner base.

Several structural pressures compound the issue. Capital investment in physical training infrastructure has not kept pace with demand, leading to outdated facilities and limited capacity. Health and safety requirements restrict access to realistic training environments for hazardous tasks, particularly in construction, engineering maintenance, and healthcare simulation. At the same time, the COVID-19 pandemic accelerated expectations for digital and remote learning, exposing the limitations of conventional e-learning platforms for practical skill acquisition.

Against this backdrop, immersive technologies began to attract interest within the education and skills sector. VR and AR tools offered the promise of simulated, repeatable, and safe training environments that could complement or partially replace physical instruction. The concept of a "metaverse" for education emerged not as a consumer-oriented virtual world but as a

DOI: 10.1201/9781003405566-9

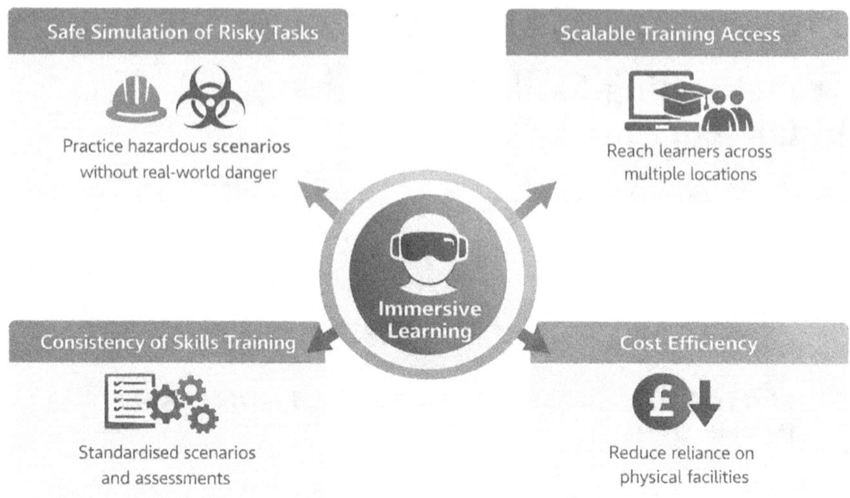

Figure 9.1 Strategic context and problem definition.

Note: This figure establishes the external and internal drivers that shaped the need for a new training approach.

collection of immersive, interconnected training environments designed to support skills development at scale.

This case study examines how a national UK Further & Professional Education consortium explored and implemented metaverse-enabled training as part of a broader transformation agenda. The focus is not on technology novelty but on how immersive platforms were used to address real operational constraints, improve learner outcomes, and support workforce development objectives. Figure 9.1 illustrates the strategic context and problem definition, showing the internal and external drivers that shaped the need for a new training approach.

Table 9.1 summarises the structural constraints facing the UK FE sector, establishing the operational context for exploring alternative training models.

9.2 ORGANISATIONAL CONTEXT AND STRATEGIC DRIVERS

The organisation at the centre of this case study is a fictional but realistic national consortium of UK FE colleges and accredited professional training providers. The consortium was established to coordinate curriculum development, share resources, and improve consistency of training outcomes

Table 9.1 Skills Challenges and Training Constraints in UK Further Education

Challenge Area	*Description*	*Impact on Training Delivery*
Skills shortages	Persistent gaps in construction, engineering, healthcare, and digital roles	Employers report job-ready skills deficits
Infrastructure limitations	Ageing workshops and limited specialist equipment	Restricted learner throughput
Safety constraints	Hazardous environments limit early-stage exposure	Reduced practical confidence
Geographic disparity	Uneven access between urban and rural providers	Inconsistent learner outcomes
Learner expectations	Demand for flexible, technology-enabled learning	Engagement challenges

across regions. Its membership included urban and rural FE colleges, specialist technical institutes, and adult education centres, collectively serving tens of thousands of learners each year.

The consortium operated within a complex governance and funding landscape. Core funding was provided through a mix of central government allocations, devolved authority grants, employer contributions, and apprenticeship levy funding. Accountability requirements were high, with performance measured against learner completion rates, employment outcomes, regulatory compliance, and value-for-money assessments.

Strategically, the consortium faced three interrelated challenges. First, it needed to expand training capacity without corresponding increases in physical estate costs. Second, it had to modernise learning delivery to remain relevant to employers adopting advanced technologies. Third, it was under pressure to demonstrate measurable improvements in learner readiness and employability.

Senior leadership recognised that incremental improvements to existing delivery models would be insufficient. Simply digitising classroom content or expanding video-based learning would not address the core limitation: the lack of scalable, high-quality practical training experiences. At the same time, large-scale capital investment in new workshops and laboratories was financially and politically unviable.

The strategic ambition therefore shifted towards blended and immersive learning models. The metaverse was not framed as a single platform or product but as an enabling layer that could support simulated training environments, instructor-led virtual sessions, and collaborative learning across institutions. Importantly, leadership positioned immersive training as a means to an end rather than an end in itself. The objective was to improve training quality, consistency, and accessibility while maintaining rigorous governance and cost control. Figure 9.2 illustrates the metaverse platform

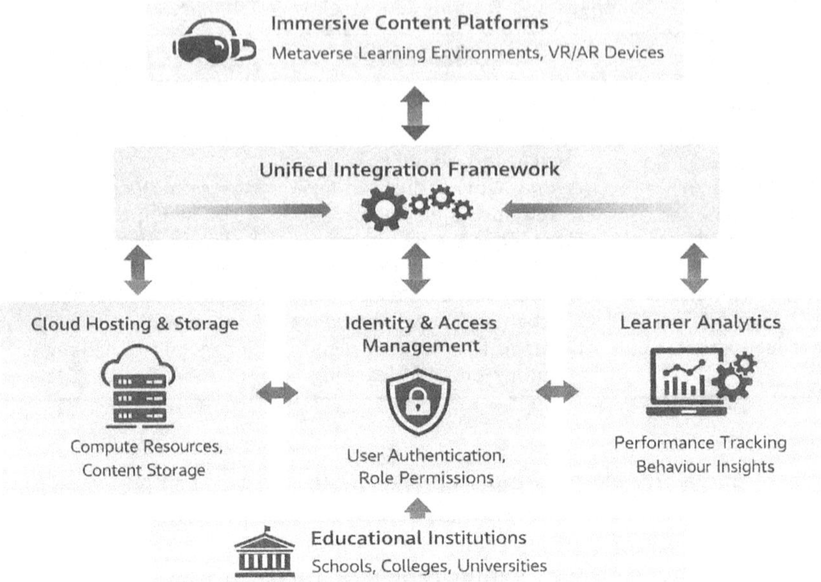

Figure 9.2 Metaverse platform and architecture design.

Note: This figure presents a visualisation of the metaverse platform and architecture design for immersive learning environments.

Table 9.2 Strategic Objectives and Design Principles

Strategic Objective	*Design Principle*	*Implication*
Expand training capacity	Virtual scalability	Reduce reliance on physical estate
Improve consistency	Shared immersive modules	Standardised learner experience
Enhance safety	Simulated environments	Risk-free skills rehearsal
Maintain governance	Central oversight with local delivery	Accountability preserved
Control cost	Modular architecture	Avoid vendor lock-in

and architecture design, showing the structural components required to support immersive learning environments.

Table 9.2 demonstrates how strategic intent directly informed the design principles underpinning the metaverse-enabled training initiative.

This strategic framing proved critical. By anchoring the initiative in workforce outcomes rather than technology experimentation, the consortium secured early support from regulators, funding bodies, and employer partners. The metaverse initiative was formally positioned as a strategic capability investment aligned with national skills priorities, rather than as an isolated digital innovation project.

9.3 PROBLEM DEFINITION AND BASELINE CHALLENGES

Before any technology decisions were made, the consortium undertook a structured assessment of its baseline challenges. This exercise revealed several systemic issues that constrained training effectiveness and scalability.

One of the most significant problems was uneven access to practical training environments. Learners in well-funded urban colleges often had access to modern equipment and specialist instructors, while those in smaller or rural institutions faced limited exposure to real-world scenarios. This inconsistency translated directly into variable learner outcomes and employer dissatisfaction.

A second challenge related to safety and risk. Many training programmes involved inherently hazardous activities, such as working at height, operating heavy machinery, or responding to emergency healthcare scenarios. These activities required strict supervision, limited learner throughput, and often excluded early-stage learners altogether. As a result, learners frequently reached workplace placements without sufficient practical preparation.

Cost pressures further constrained delivery. Physical training facilities required ongoing maintenance, insurance, and staffing, while utilisation rates were often low outside peak teaching periods. Scaling provision to meet fluctuating demand proved inefficient and expensive. Instructors also faced high workloads, limiting their ability to provide personalised feedback and assessment.

Finally, the consortium identified a growing misalignment between learner expectations and traditional training formats. Many learners, particularly younger cohorts and career switchers, expected interactive, technology-enabled learning experiences that mirrored modern workplace tools. Traditional classroom-based instruction struggled to maintain engagement, particularly for abstract or procedural content.

These baseline challenges established a clear problem statement: the consortium needed a way to deliver consistent, safe, scalable, and engaging practical training without unsustainable increases in cost or risk. This problem framing provided the foundation for exploring metaverse-enabled solutions in a disciplined and outcome-oriented manner. Figure 9.3 illustrates the UK metaverse initiative governance and operating model, showing how immersive simulation was embedded into the learning model to address the identified gaps.

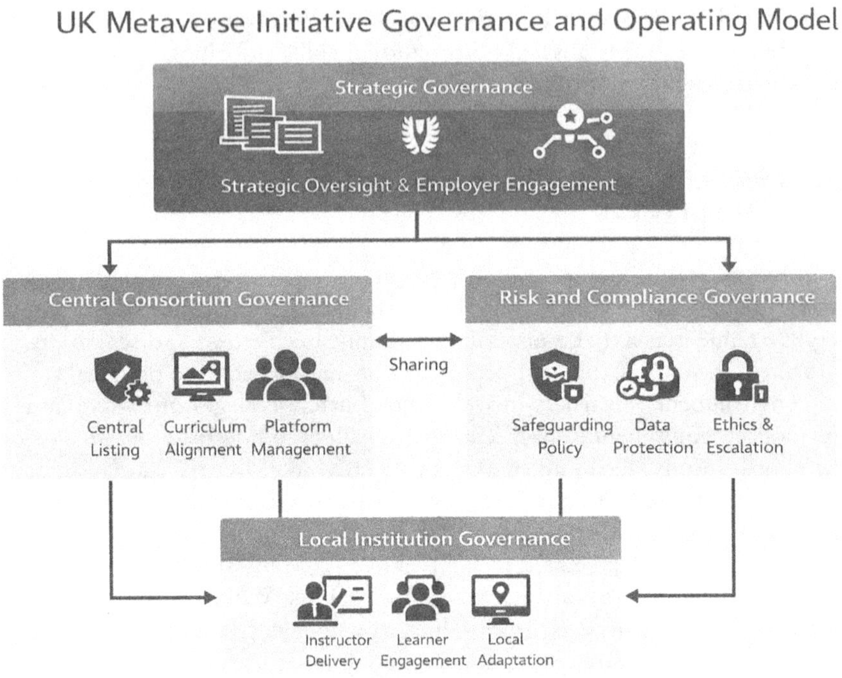

Figure 9.3 UK Metaverse initiative governance and operating model.

Note: This figure shows how immersive simulation was embedded into the learning model to address the identified gaps.

Table 9.3 Baseline versus Metaverse-Enabled Training Model

Dimension	*Baseline Model*	*Metaverse-Enabled Model*
Access to practice	Limited, scheduled	On-demand, repeatable
Safety	Restricted exposure	Risk-free simulation
Scalability	Capacity constrained	Multi-site concurrent access
Instructor load	High supervision burden	Focus on coaching
Learner confidence	Variable	Improved readiness

Table 9.3 highlights the systemic limitations of the baseline model and the specific capability improvements introduced through immersive training.

9.4 STRATEGIC RATIONALE FOR METAVERSE ADOPTION

With the baseline challenges clearly articulated, the consortium evaluated a range of potential interventions. These included expanding physical training facilities, increasing instructor headcount, outsourcing specialist training to third-party providers, and enhancing existing digital learning platforms. Each option addressed parts of the problem but failed to resolve the constraints in a holistic and sustainable way.

Physical expansion was quickly deprioritised due to cost, long lead times, and limited flexibility. Outsourcing introduced quality and consistency risks while also weakening institutional capability over time. Conventional digital learning platforms, although effective for theoretical content, lacked the experiential depth required for practical skills development.

The strategic rationale for adopting metaverse-enabled training emerged from this comparative assessment. Immersive environments offered the ability to simulate complex, hazardous, or resource-intensive scenarios in a controlled and repeatable manner. Learners could practise procedures, make mistakes, and receive feedback without exposure to real-world risk. From a capacity perspective, virtual environments could be accessed concurrently by learners across multiple institutions, reducing dependency on physical infrastructure.

Crucially, the consortium did not frame the metaverse as a replacement for hands-on training. Instead, it was positioned as an augmentation layer that would prepare learners more effectively before physical practice or workplace placement. This blended approach aligned with pedagogical best practice and reassured instructors concerned about over-reliance on technology.

From a strategic perspective, immersive training also supported consistency and standardisation. Shared virtual modules could be deployed across the consortium, ensuring that learners encountered the same core scenarios, assessments, and performance expectations regardless of location. This consistency was particularly attractive to employer partners seeking predictable skill levels from graduates.

The metaverse initiative also aligned with broader public sector objectives. It supported digital inclusion by enabling access to high-quality training without requiring travel or relocation. It contributed to sustainability goals by reducing the need for repeated physical setups and consumables. Finally, it positioned the consortium as an innovator in skills delivery, strengthening its case for future funding and partnerships.

By grounding the rationale in operational, educational, and strategic outcomes rather than technological novelty, the consortium established a defensible case for proceeding to solution design and platform evaluation. Figure 9.4 illustrates the metaverse-enabled learning delivery model, showing how strategic oversight, local delivery, safeguarding, and platform operations are coordinated.

9.5 PLATFORM AND ARCHITECTURE DESIGN DECISIONS

Once the strategic case for immersive training was established, the consortium turned its attention to platform and architecture design. This phase

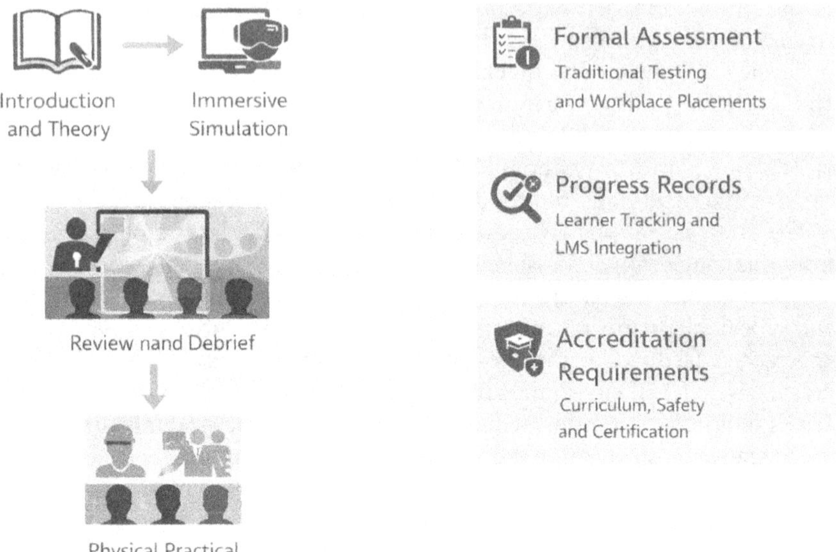

Figure 9.4 Metaverse-enabled learning delivery model.

Note: This figure clarifies how strategic oversight, local delivery, safeguarding, and platform operations are coordinated.

was guided by a clear principle: technology choices should serve educational outcomes and governance requirements, not constrain them.

Rather than procuring a single monolithic "metaverse platform", the consortium adopted a modular architecture approach. Core components included immersive content platforms, user access and identity management, learning management system integration, analytics and assessment tools, and secure hosting environments. This architecture allowed individual components to evolve independently while maintaining interoperability. Table 9.4 explains how architectural choices were aligned to educational outcomes, governance requirements, and long-term scalability.

Platform evaluation focused on several non-negotiable criteria. First, solutions had to support multi-user, instructor-led sessions as well as individual self-paced learning. Second, they needed to operate across commonly available hardware, including standard laptops and affordable VR headsets, to avoid excluding learners or institutions with limited budgets. Third, platforms had to integrate cleanly with existing learning management systems to ensure continuity of records, assessment, and reporting.

Table 9.4 Platform Architecture Components and Rationale

Component	*Function*	*Rationale*
Immersive simulation platform	Scenario-based training	Practical skill rehearsal
Identity and access management	Secure user control	Safeguarding and compliance
LMS integration	Assessment and records	Continuity with accreditation
Analytics layer	Performance insights	Evidence-based improvement
Cloud hosting	Scalability and resilience	Cost-effective growth

Data protection and safeguarding considerations played a central role in architecture decisions. Learner identity, session recordings, performance data, and behavioural analytics all required careful handling under UK data protection regulations. The consortium therefore prioritised platforms that supported role-based access controls, data minimisation, and clear audit trails. Hosting decisions favoured UK or UK-aligned cloud environments to simplify compliance and oversight.

Content creation and ownership were also addressed at the architectural level. Rather than relying exclusively on vendor-provided simulations, the consortium invested in internal capability to design and adapt training scenarios. This ensured alignment with curriculum requirements and reduced long-term dependency on external suppliers. Where third-party content was used, licensing arrangements were structured to support reuse and modification across institutions.

Finally, scalability and resilience were built into the design. The architecture supported incremental rollout, allowing pilot programmes to operate independently before being scaled across the consortium. This reduced risk and enabled iterative improvement based on instructor and learner feedback. By treating platform and architecture decisions as strategic enablers rather than technical afterthoughts, the consortium laid a foundation that balanced innovation with control, flexibility with standardisation, and experimentation with accountability.

Figure 9.5 presents the modular platform architecture adopted by the consortium, showing how immersive content, identity management, analytics, and learning systems were integrated to support scalability and governance.

9.6 OPERATING MODEL, GOVERNANCE, AND SAFEGUARDING

As the metaverse-enabled training initiative moved from concept to delivery, the consortium placed strong emphasis on establishing an operating model

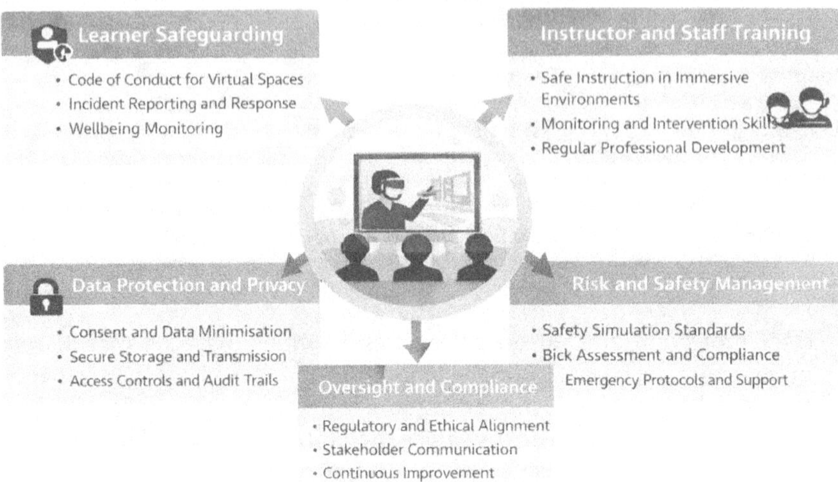

Figure 9.5 Governance and safeguarding in educational Metaverse environments.

that balanced innovation with accountability. Given the public-sector context and the diversity of participating institutions, governance arrangements needed to be robust, transparent, and adaptable.

The operating model was structured around a central coordinating function supported by distributed delivery teams within individual colleges and training centres. The central function was responsible for strategic oversight, platform governance, curriculum alignment, and vendor management. It also acted as the primary interface with regulators, funding bodies, and employer partners. This centralisation ensured consistency of standards and reduced duplication of effort across the consortium.

At the institutional level, local delivery teams retained responsibility for learner engagement, instructor facilitation, and contextual adaptation of immersive content. This decentralised execution model allowed training to reflect local labour market needs while remaining aligned with national frameworks. Clear role definitions were established to avoid ambiguity between central and local responsibilities.

Governance mechanisms were designed to operate across three layers. Strategic governance focused on alignment with skills priorities, funding objectives, and long-term capability development. Operational governance addressed delivery performance, platform reliability, and instructor readiness. Risk and compliance governance covered safeguarding, data protection, health and safety, and ethical use of immersive technologies.

Safeguarding was treated as a first-order design consideration rather than an afterthought. Immersive environments introduced new interaction patterns between learners and instructors, including voice communication, avatars, and shared virtual spaces. Policies were therefore updated to cover acceptable behaviour, session monitoring, escalation procedures, and incident reporting within virtual environments. Instructors received additional training to manage learner conduct and wellbeing in immersive settings.

Data governance arrangements ensured that learner performance data, session recordings, and analytics were collected and used responsibly. Access controls limited who could view or export sensitive information, and retention policies were aligned with regulatory requirements. Importantly, learners were informed clearly about how their data would be used, reinforcing trust and transparency.

By embedding governance and safeguarding into the operating model from the outset, the consortium created a stable foundation for experimentation and scale. This approach reduced resistance from stakeholders and provided assurance that innovation would not compromise learner safety or institutional integrity. Figure 9.6 illustrates the value realisation pathway for

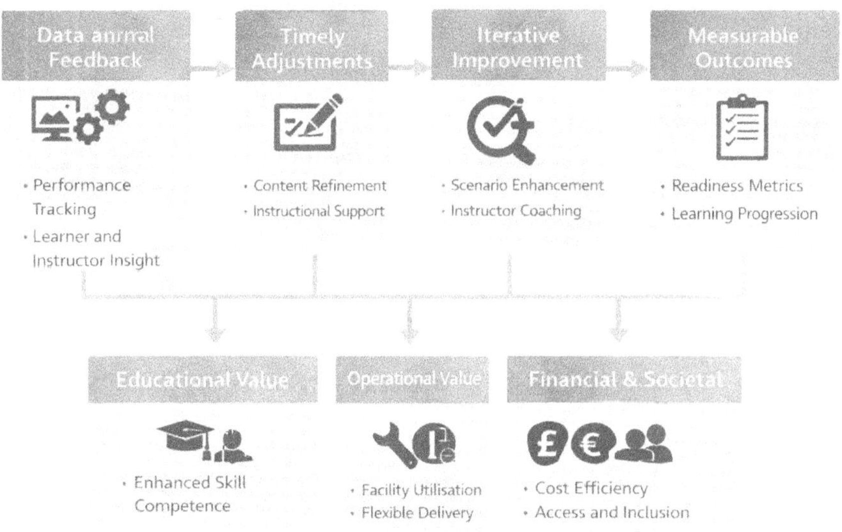

Figure 9.6 Value realisation pathway for immersive training.

Note: This figure illustrates the multi-layer governance model covering strategic oversight, operational delivery, and safeguarding controls across immersive learning environments.

Table 9.5 Governance, Safeguarding, and Accountability

Governance Layer	*Responsibility*	*Owner*
Strategic	Skills alignment and funding	Consortium board
Operational	Delivery performance	Central programme team
Safeguarding	Learner wellbeing	Designated safeguarding leads
Data governance	Privacy and compliance	Data protection officers
Platform control	Access and configuration	Technical governance team

immersive training, showing how benefits emerge through the coordinated interaction of delivery, governance, and safeguarding controls.

Table 9.5 clarifies accountability across governance layers, ensuring that immersive innovation operates within established safeguarding and compliance frameworks.

9.7 LEARNING EXPERIENCE DESIGN AND DELIVERY MODEL

The success of the metaverse initiative ultimately depended on the quality of the learning experience delivered to learners. Recognising this, the consortium invested significant effort in redesigning curricula and instructional approaches to take advantage of immersive capabilities rather than simply replicating traditional lessons in a virtual environment.

Learning experience design followed a blended model. Immersive sessions were used to introduce learners to complex environments, procedures, and scenarios before they encountered them in the physical world. For example, construction trainees could practise site navigation and hazard identification in a simulated environment, while healthcare learners could rehearse patient interactions and emergency responses without real-world risk.

Each immersive module was structured around clear learning objectives and assessment criteria. Scenarios were designed to be repeatable, allowing learners to practise until competence was demonstrated. Immediate feedback was integrated into the experience, enabling learners to understand the consequences of their actions and reflect on alternative approaches.

Instructors played a critical role in facilitating immersive learning. Rather than acting solely as content deliverers, they functioned as guides, observers, and coaches. Instructor-led sessions allowed for real-time intervention, discussion, and debriefing, reinforcing learning outcomes and linking virtual experience to practical application.

Accessibility considerations informed delivery design. Not all learners had access to advanced VR hardware, so modules were designed to function across multiple device types. Where immersive hardware was required, institutions provided shared facilities and scheduling mechanisms to ensure equitable access.

Assessment and progression were integrated with existing learning management systems. Performance data from immersive sessions informed learner evaluation but did not replace traditional assessment methods. This hybrid approach ensured that immersive learning complemented rather than disrupted established accreditation processes.

By focusing on pedagogy rather than technology, the consortium ensured that the metaverse enhanced learning effectiveness. The delivery model demonstrated that immersive environments could support deep learning when designed intentionally and supported by skilled instructors.

9.8 VALUE REALISATION, MEASUREMENT, AND OUTCOMES

From the outset, the consortium recognised that demonstrating value would be critical to sustaining investment and stakeholder support. Value realisation was therefore treated as an ongoing management activity rather than a post-implementation exercise. Measures were defined early, tracked consistently, and reviewed at regular governance checkpoints.

Value was assessed across multiple dimensions. Educational outcomes formed the primary focus, with metrics such as learner engagement, completion rates, assessment performance, and readiness for workplace placement. Early pilots indicated that learners who completed immersive modules entered physical training sessions with greater confidence and procedural understanding. Instructors reported reduced time spent on basic orientation, allowing more focus on higher-value coaching and assessment.

Operational value was also significant. The use of virtual environments reduced pressure on physical facilities, particularly for high-demand courses. Institutions were able to increase learner throughput without proportionate increases in estate or equipment costs. Scheduling flexibility improved, as immersive sessions could be delivered outside traditional workshop hours and across institutional boundaries.

Financial value was measured through cost avoidance rather than direct revenue generation. Savings were realised through reduced equipment wear, lower consumable usage, and decreased reliance on external training providers. While upfront investment in platforms and content development was material, these costs were amortised across multiple cohorts and institutions, improving the overall cost-effectiveness of provision.

Non-financial benefits were captured through qualitative feedback from learners, instructors, and employer partners. Learners consistently highlighted the ability to practise repeatedly without fear of failure, while employers reported improved baseline competence among trainees entering

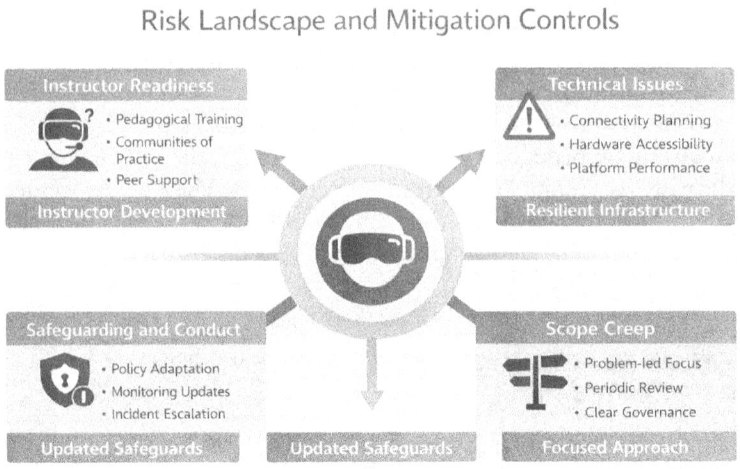

Figure 9.7 Risk landscape and mitigation controls.

Note: This figure summarises the multidimensional value framework used to track educational, operational, financial, and stakeholder outcomes throughout the implementation lifecycle.

Table 9.6 Value Realisation and Outcome Metrics

Value Dimension	*Metric*	*Observed Outcome*
Educational	Learner preparedness	Improved baseline competence
Operational	Facility utilisation	Reduced congestion
Financial	Cost avoidance	Lower equipment wear
Stakeholder	Employer feedback	Improved satisfaction
Reputational	Funding confidence	Increased credibility

placements. These outcomes strengthened the consortium's reputation and supported continued engagement with funding bodies.

By framing value realisation in holistic terms, the consortium avoided over-reliance on simplistic usage metrics. Instead, it demonstrated how immersive training contributed meaningfully to educational quality, operational efficiency, and stakeholder confidence. Figure 9.7 illustrates the risk landscape and mitigation controls, showing the principal risk areas and the measures required to manage them across the implementation lifecycle.

Table 9.6 links immersive training adoption to tangible educational, operational, and stakeholder outcomes.

9.9 CHALLENGES, RISKS, AND COURSE CORRECTIONS

Despite positive outcomes, the implementation of metaverse-enabled training was not without challenges. Several issues emerged during pilot phases that required adjustment and, in some cases, rethinking of initial assumptions.

One early challenge related to instructor readiness. While many instructors embraced immersive tools, others were hesitant or lacked confidence in facilitating virtual sessions. This highlighted the importance of targeted professional development and peer support. The consortium responded by establishing instructor communities of practice and providing hands-on training focused on pedagogy rather than technology operation alone.

Technical reliability also posed risks. Connectivity issues, device availability, and platform performance varied across institutions, particularly in rural areas. To mitigate this, delivery plans were adjusted to include offline alternatives and flexible scheduling. Technical requirements were refined to prioritise stability over advanced graphical features.

Governance complexity increased as the initiative scaled. Balancing local autonomy with central control required ongoing negotiation, particularly around content adaptation and data usage. Clear escalation routes and periodic governance reviews helped maintain alignment without stifling innovation.

Safeguarding considerations evolved as immersive environments became more widely used. Unexpected learner behaviours and new interaction patterns prompted updates to policies and monitoring approaches. The consortium treated these incidents as learning opportunities, strengthening safeguards rather than retreating from innovation.

Perhaps the most important course correction involved scope management. Initial enthusiasm led some stakeholders to propose immersive solutions for problems better addressed through simpler interventions. Reinforcing the principle of problem-led adoption helped refocus efforts on areas where immersive training delivered genuine value.

These challenges underscored that metaverse adoption is not a linear process. Success depended on adaptability, continuous learning, and willingness to refine approaches based on evidence rather than assumptions.

9.10 OUTCOMES, IMPACT, AND BENEFITS REALISED

By the end of the initial multi-year implementation period, the consortium was able to demonstrate tangible outcomes and broader impact across educational, organisational, and stakeholder dimensions. While the initiative did not eliminate the need for physical training environments, it materially reshaped how and when those environments were used.

Educational outcomes showed consistent improvement across participating institutions. Learners who completed immersive modules prior to physical workshops demonstrated higher baseline competence, reduced error rates, and greater confidence when undertaking practical tasks. Instructors reported that learners progressed more quickly through foundational concepts, allowing classroom and workshop time to be used more effectively for advanced instruction and assessment.

Completion rates improved modestly but consistently, particularly in programmes with historically high attrition. Learner feedback indicated that immersive training reduced anxiety associated with unfamiliar or hazardous environments, contributing to increased persistence and engagement. For adult learners and career switchers, the ability to practise skills repeatedly without embarrassment or risk proved especially valuable.

From an organisational perspective, the consortium achieved improved utilisation of training resources. Physical facilities experienced less congestion during peak periods, and equipment downtime decreased as some training activities were shifted to virtual environments. This translated into operational flexibility and reduced pressure to invest in additional physical infrastructure.

Employer partners reported improved satisfaction with trainee preparedness. While immersive training did not replace workplace learning, it shortened the time required for trainees to reach productive competence. This strengthened employer relationships and reinforced the consortium's role as a trusted skills partner.

At a strategic level, the initiative enhanced the consortium's credibility with funding bodies and regulators. Demonstrable outcomes supported continued investment and enabled the consortium to influence broader policy discussions around digital skills delivery. The metaverse programme became a reference point for innovation grounded in measurable public value rather than technology experimentation.

9.11 TRANSFERABLE LESSONS FOR PRACTITIONERS

This case study offers several transferable lessons for organisations considering metaverse-enabled training or similar immersive initiatives. The first and most important lesson is the necessity of problem-led adoption. Immersive technologies delivered value only when applied to clearly defined challenges that could not be addressed effectively through simpler means.

Second, governance and operating models matter as much as technology. Establishing clear accountability, safeguarding arrangements, and data governance frameworks enabled experimentation without undermining trust. Organisations that treat governance as an enabler rather than a constraint are better positioned to scale innovation responsibly.

Third, capability development must extend beyond technical skills. Instructor confidence, pedagogical adaptation, and cultural readiness proved critical to success. Investment in people and practices was as important as investment in platforms and content.

Fourth, value measurement should be holistic and continuous. Focusing solely on usage metrics or cost savings risks undervaluing broader educational and societal benefits. Combining quantitative indicators with qualitative insight provides a more accurate picture of impact.

Finally, metaverse initiatives should be approached as evolving programmes rather than one-off projects. Iterative delivery, feedback-driven refinement, and willingness to course-correct enabled the consortium to adapt to emerging challenges and opportunities.

For practitioners, the central message is clear. The metaverse is neither a panacea nor a passing fad. When applied thoughtfully, governed carefully, and aligned with real-world needs, immersive technologies can play a meaningful role in transforming skills development and professional training.

BIBLIOGRAPHY

Ball, C. (2022). *The Metaverse: And How It Will Revolutionize Everything.* New York: Liveright Publishing.

Deloitte. (2023). *The Metaverse and the Future of Learning.* Deloitte Insights.

Department for Education (DfE). (2023). *Keeping Children Safe in Education.* London: UK Government.

European Commission. (2022). *Ethics Guidelines for Trustworthy AI.* Publications Office of the European Union.

Kavanagh, S., Luxton-Reilly, A., Wuensche, B., & Plimmer, B. (2017). A systematic review of virtual reality in education. *Themes in Science and Technology Education*, 10(2), 85–119.

Meta. (2023). *Responsible Innovation Principles for Immersive Technologies.* Meta Platforms Inc.

OECD. (2021). *Digital Education Outlook 2021: Pushing the Frontiers with AI, Blockchain and VR.* Paris: OECD Publishing.

Slater, M., & Sanchez-Vives, M. V. (2016). Enhancing our lives with immersive virtual reality. *Frontiers in Robotics and AI*, 3, 74.

UK Information Commissioner's Office (ICO). (2023). *Guide to the UK GDPR.* Wilmslow: ICO.

World Economic Forum. (2023). *Defining and Building the Metaverse: A Governance Framework.* Geneva: WEF.

Chapter 10

Conclusion and Future Outlook

10.1 REFRAMING THE CENTRAL QUESTION: HOAX OR MISAPPLIED CAPABILITY?

This book began with a deliberately provocative question: *Is the metaverse a hoax?*

By the end of the preceding chapters, the answer is necessarily nuanced.

The metaverse is *not a hoax in the sense of being technically unworkable or entirely without value*. Nor is it a universally applicable solution that justifies the scale of investment, hype, and expectation that surrounded it during peak adoption cycles. Instead, the evidence presented across sectors, operating models, and case studies points to a more precise conclusion:

The metaverse is a *real but conditional capability* whose success depends almost entirely on *where*, *why*, and *how* it is applied. Where organisations treated the metaverse as a destination, a brand exercise, or a speculative growth narrative, outcomes were consistently weak. Where it was deployed as an enabling layer to solve clearly defined problems, measurable value emerged. The difference was never the technology itself but the discipline of application.

This reframing is critical. It moves the discussion away from binary judgements of success or failure and towards a more mature understanding of enterprise technology adoption. Figure 10.1 illustrates the maturation of the metaverse from hype and experimentation towards governed programmes and embedded capability.

10.2 WHAT THE EVIDENCE ACROSS CHAPTERS ACTUALLY SHOWS

When viewed collectively, Chapters 1–9 reveal a set of consistent patterns that cut across industries and organisational types.

First, *problem-led adoption consistently outperformed technology-led experimentation*. Whether in financial services, industrial training, or

DOI: 10.1201/9781003405566-10

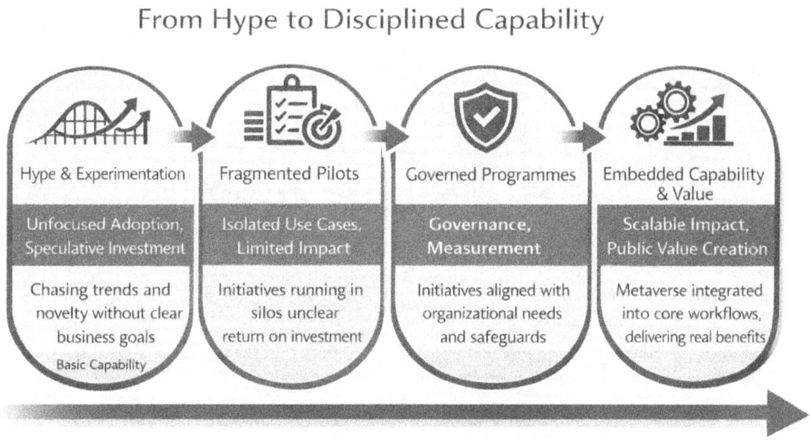

Figure 10.1 The maturation of the Metaverse from hype to disciplined capability.

Note: This figure illustrates the transition from fragmented experimentation towards a structured, governance-led approach, reinforcing this chapter's central conclusion that sustainable metaverse adoption depends on discipline rather than novelty.

public-sector education, initiatives grounded in operational constraints and outcome metrics delivered clearer benefits than those driven by innovation mandates or executive curiosity.

Second, *governance proved to be a stronger predictor of success than technical sophistication.* Organisations that invested early in operating models, data protection, safeguarding, and accountability structures were able to scale cautiously and sustainably. Those that deferred governance in favour of speed or novelty often stalled or reversed course.

Third, *value was realised primarily through cost avoidance, risk reduction, and capability uplift*, rather than direct revenue generation. This finding challenges many early investment cases, which were often framed around speculative growth rather than measurable operational improvement.

Finally, *human capability and organisational readiness mattered more than platform choice.* Instructor confidence, change management, cultural acceptance, and skills development were decisive factors in determining whether immersive initiatives became embedded or abandoned. Figure 10.2 illustrates metaverse adoption maturity across education, enterprise, public sector, and regulated environments, showing how capability and governance evolve across organisational contexts.

Taken together, these patterns suggest that the metaverse behaves less like a disruptive frontier technology and more like an advanced infrastructure layer: powerful when integrated thoughtfully, ineffective when bolted on.

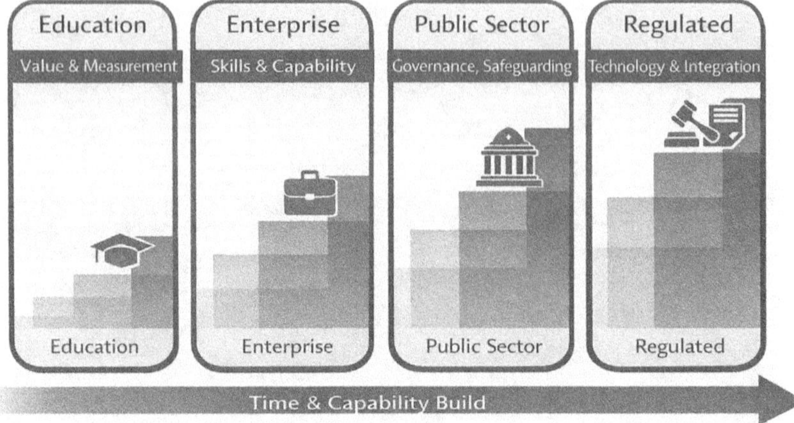

Figure 10.2 Metaverse adoption maturity across education, enterprise, public sector, and regulated environments.

Note: This figure positions metaverse adoption as a maturity journey, showing how value measurement, skills capability, governance, and technology integration evolve across different organisational contexts.

10.3 WHY THE METAVERSE FAILED AS A NARRATIVE BUT SURVIVED AS A TOOL

A key insight from this research is that the *metaverse failed primarily at the level of narrative*, not capability.

The dominant public narrative framed the metaverse as:

- A successor to the internet
- A universal social and commercial environment
- A new digital economy detached from existing systems

These claims were neither necessary nor helpful for enterprise adoption. They inflated expectations, distorted investment priorities, and encouraged organisations to pursue visibility over viability.

In contrast, the metaverse survived where it was reframed as:

- A *set of immersive interaction techniques*
- An *extension of existing digital ecosystems*
- A *means of improving learning, simulation, and collaboration*

Figure 10.3 illustrates a future outlook for the metaverse, showing how immersive technologies, artificial intelligence, data, and regulation are expected to converge across near-, mid-, and long-term horizons.

This distinction explains why consumer-facing "metaverse worlds" struggled while enterprise use cases in training, simulation, and design quietly

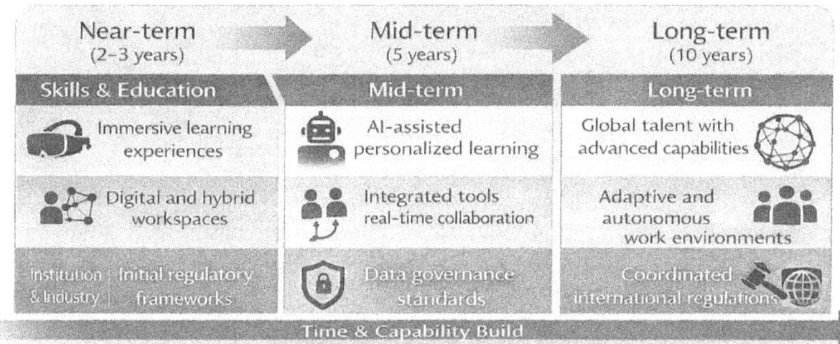

Figure 10.3 Future outlook showing the convergence of immersive technologies, artificial intelligence, data, and regulation across near-, mid- and long-term horizons.

Note:This perspective frames the future of the metaverse as a convergence of immersive experience, artificial intelligence, data governance, and regulation, highlighting how institutional readiness must evolve over time.

progressed. The latter did not require mass adoption or cultural transformation. They required precision.

10.4 IMPLICATIONS FOR ENTERPRISE LEADERS AND POLICYMAKERS

For enterprise leaders, the primary implication is restraint paired with clarity.

The metaverse should not be approached as a standalone strategic pillar. It should be treated as a *conditional capability* evaluated alongside other digital tools – subject to the same scrutiny applied to cloud platforms, analytics systems, or automation initiatives.

Leaders should ask the following:

- What specific constraint are we trying to remove?
- Why is immersive interaction superior to existing alternatives?
- What governance obligations does this introduce?
- How will success be measured beyond usage?

The future development of the metaverse is likely to be shaped less by grand consumer-facing virtual worlds and more by targeted integration into enterprise workflows, spatial computing environments, digital twins, training systems, and operational simulation. Figure 10.4 provides a structured view of these future directions.

For policymakers and public-sector sponsors, the lesson is equally pragmatic. Immersive technologies can support public value objectives – particularly in education, skills, and safety-critical training – but only when funding models reward outcomes rather than experimentation.

Figure 10.4 Decision framework for evaluating when and where immersive technologies deliver organisational value.

Note: This figure consolidates the practical decision principles emerging from this book and provides leaders with a structured lens for determining when and where immersive technologies deliver genuine organisational value.

Policy frameworks that incentivise novelty without accountability risk repeating the cycle of hype and retreat. Those that embed immersive tools within broader capability-building programmes are more likely to generate durable impact.

10.5 THE FUTURE OUTLOOK: QUIET INTEGRATION, NOT GRAND REINVENTION

Looking forward, the most likely future of the metaverse is *not a dramatic resurgence* but a gradual normalisation.

Immersive capabilities are already being absorbed into:

- Training and simulation platforms
- Design and engineering workflows
- Remote collaboration tools
- Digital twin and modelling environments

In many cases, the term "metaverse" will disappear altogether, replaced by more specific language describing function rather than vision. This is not a failure; it is a sign of maturation.

The future trajectory suggests:

- Fewer standalone "metaverse programmes"
- More embedded immersive components within existing systems
- Greater emphasis on interoperability, standards, and governance
- Reduced tolerance for speculative business cases

Figure 10.5 illustrates organisational readiness and maturity progression, showing the capabilities required to support sustained metaverse adoption.

In this sense, the metaverse's ultimate success may depend on its ability to become unremarkable.

10.6 FINAL REFLECTION: WHAT THIS BOOK ULTIMATELY ARGUES

This book does not argue for or against the metaverse: It argues for *discipline*.

- Discipline in defining problems
- Discipline in selecting tools
- Discipline in governance, measurement, and expectation-setting

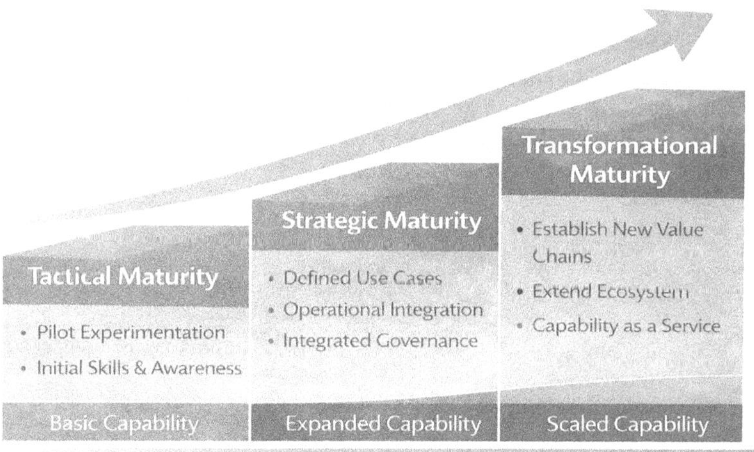

Figure 10.5 Organisational readiness and maturity progression.

Note: This figure summarises the organisational capabilities required for sustained metaverse adoption, reinforcing the conclusion that success depends on alignment between strategy, people, governance, and technology.

When applied with such discipline, immersive technologies can deliver real, sometimes significant value. When applied without it, they become expensive distractions. The metaverse is therefore neither a hoax nor a revolution. It is a *test of organisational maturity*. Those who pass that test will use it quietly, effectively, and without fanfare. Those who do not will continue to ask whether it ever worked at all.

BIBLIOGRAPHY

Ball, M. (2022). *The Metaverse: And How It Will Revolutionize Everything*. New York: Liveright.

Deloitte. (2023). *Immersive Technologies and the Future of Work*. London: Deloitte Insights.

European Commission. (2022). *Ethics Guidelines for Trustworthy AI*. Brussels: European Union.

Gartner. (2023). *Emerging Technologies: Metaverse and Immersive Experiences*. Stamford, CT: Gartner Research.

HM Government. (2023). *Pro-Innovation Regulation of Technologies Review: Immersive and Digital Technologies*. London: UK Government.

ISO/IEC. (2022). *ISO/IEC 27001: Information Security Management Systems*. Geneva: International Organization for Standardization.

McKinsey & Company. (2022). *Value Creation in the Metaverse*. London: McKinsey Digital.

OECD. (2021). *AI, Data Governance and Digital Transformation*. Paris: Organisation for Economic Co-operation and Development.

PwC. (2023). *Seeing Is Believing: How Virtual Reality and Augmented Reality Are Transforming Business*. London: PwC.

World Economic Forum. (2023). *Defining and Building the Metaverse: Governance, Safety, and Inclusion*. Geneva: WEF.

Index

A

B

D

E

I

L

M

S

For Product Safety Concerns and Information please contact our EU representative GPSR@taylorandfrancis.com
Taylor & Francis Verlag GmbH, Kaufingerstraße 24, 80331 München, Germany

www.ingramcontent.com/pod-product-compliance
Lightning Source LLC
LaVergne TN
LVHW010549110826
845149LV00003B/609

* 9 7 8 1 0 3 2 5 2 1 8 3 1 *